To Carol With Love

To
Carol
With
Love

Cecil Bewes

Christian Focus Publications

ISBN 1-85792-112-7

Published by
Christian Focus Publications Ltd
Geanies House, Fearn, Ross-shire,
IV20 1TW, Scotland, Great Britain.

FOREWORD

There exists in the possession of the Bewes family a photograph, taken in the early 1920s by the author of these daily studies. Cecil Bewes, himself a student at Cambridge University, was assisting in the leadership of a Christian beach mission at Southwold, on the east coast of England. It was held under the auspices of the Children's Special Service Mission.

The photograph features a number of boys who formed the group that Cecil had been given to lead. Behind them was Clarence Foster who, in later life, was to emerge as Secretary of the famed Keswick Convention in the north of England. On the right was Quintin Carr, who rose to prominence in the developing work of the Scripture Union. On the left was Herbert Taylor, who would become renowned as the founder of the Pathfinder youth movement in Britain.

Between those two in the very centre of the photograph appears a smiling Donald MacLean who evidently, in that seaside mission, was to have at least a brush with the Christian message before going on to study at Cambridge. It was in Cambridge that MacLean came into contact with Burgess, and others, in the Spy of the Century scandal that rocked governments on both sides of the Atlantic.

It is fascinating to be able to trace the destinies of individuals who have been faced at some point by the Bible's message. There is nothing automatic about its effect on our lives; yet it is obvious that a voluntary and thorough exposure to it can only bring salvation and integration into the lives of its readers - as illustrated in Clarence Foster, Quintin Carr and Herbert Taylor.

And what of Donald MacLean? Thankfully it is not up to us

to pronounce on him; that is God's business, not ours. We can only be wistful when we think of what might have been, if the Scriptures had been more central to his mindset. According to the reports, he died as a disillusioned alcoholic in a lonely Moscow flat. Surely that need not have been!

These daily notes were written by Cecil Bewes towards the end of his life, when he was in his eighties. He had never intended them for a wide public. They were actually written for one of his grandchildren, Carol Bewes, at a time of prolonged illness. Later, however, when Carol herself was recovered, and active in Christian service, the idea was born that these notes could be shared with others. If Cecil Bewes could be used by God to touch the lives of young at both ends of the twentieth century, then why not, after his own homecall to heaven? He died in January 1993, in great peace, while 2 Timothy 4:13-18 was being read to him. Cecil Bewes, said the Rev Roger Huddleston at the funeral on February 1st, was a man with 'a twinkle in his eye, a rose in his buttonhole and Christ in his heart'.

The Bible was fundamental to his life. There was the Crusaders Union (he founded the group in Exeter) and the Inter-Varsity Fellowship (IVF - now UCCF) - Cecil was a leading member of the Christian Union at Cambridge University. He later married Sylvia De Berry, who was the first-ever IVF Treasurer; she kept the entire national funds in a biscuit tin under her bed! On top of these activities - and the celebrated Southwold CSSM - came overseas missionary leadership in Kenya, involving the establishing of numerous churches and a share in the translation of the Bible into Kikuyu. Kabete, Kabare, Weithaga and Nairobi - here was front-line work where mud roads, droughts, locust plagues and the challenge of the witch doctors were part of everyday life.

On returning to the UK, many years later, Cecil Bewes co-ordinated the mission work of CMS across the African continent. At times he had to use his skills as a diplomat and international envoy - not least at the time of the Mau Mau emergency in Kenya. He was to re-visit Kenya on behalf of the British government as part of the process that paved the way for the peaceful transfer of political power from European to African hands. His book *Kikuyu Conflict* was widely read in the 1950s.

Prayer ... and the life of the Bible can open your horizons to the ends of the earth! It doesn't take much to start the process rolling. In the case of the Bewes family, it was a single sermon by American evangelist D L Moody in 1882, that injected a specifically Christian element into a line that has stretched over several generations, up to the time of Carol Bewes, and even beyond. It was Carol's great-grandfather, Tommy Bewes, who responded to the preaching of D L Moody on that Tuesday September night, later to become the first in a family of preachers.

It's a catching thing, with the Bible; you dig into its truths, and the likelihood is that, without anyone telling you, you begin to enthuse and encourage others with your discoveries. As Augustine of old put it, One loving spirit sets another on fire. Cecil Bewes never seemed to lose an opportunity. When I was about twelve there was a boy at my school in Kenya called Christopher. One day he simply wasn't around; we were all told that he was ill and had been taken to hospital. Weeks passed; it seemed that he was really quite ill. We told our parents about Christopher.

Then we were asked, 'Would you like it if some little Bible notes were done for Christopher, for every day - and sent to him? You don't have to write them - but they can be sent with your love.' Of course we agreed, and Dad began writing the notes. One a day! So you see, what you have here in your hands isn't a one-off phenomenon. It's been something of a way of life with the author. He had been proving the power of the Bible in Cambridge, in Kenya, in Tonbridge where he was vicar for twelve years, at the Keswick Convention where he led the prayer meetings for sixteen years - and where he maintained contact with Clarence Foster. Up to his very last day on earth he was still taking in - and passing on - the truths of the Scriptures, which are able to make you wise to salvation, through faith which is in Christ Jesus.

I'm glad Carol held on to her daily notes. They come to you now, not only from her, but from the rest of us too.

RICHARD BEWES
Rector
All Souls
Langham Place
London

To
Carol
With
Love

January 1

Lead me, O LORD, *in Thy righteousness... make Thy way straight before me* (Psalm 5:8).

Most of us like to plan out what we're going to do - who we're going to be - what job we shall undertake - what country we'll live in, and what sort of a home we want to make.

And sometimes things happen so that we wonder if it's any good making plans, because it doesn't look as if they'll work out. What is important is that we *begin* the right way. How? By asking *God* to lead us. If we're Christians, we'll know that God *never* makes a mistake with His servants. Sometimes He lets things happen to us that we don't like, but later they turn out for our good, though we can't see it at the time.

So today - *NEW YEAR'S DAY* - make a note that you are now deliberately asking God to lead you. Put yourself into His Hands. And having done so, reckon that from now on you're under *His* control, His direction. Whatever happens to you today, whatever you feel like, God has taken over. *Trust Him.*

The second thing you may ask is that He will 'straighten out' His way before you. You can't see far ahead. Don't ask for that. But ask for *THE NEXT STEP*. And whatever that step may be, God is in it with you. You're not alone.

PRAYER

Thank you, Lord, for the promise of the Lord Jesus: 'I am with you always, even unto the end of the world.' AMEN.

All Scripture is inspired by God and profitable
for teaching, for reproof, for correction,
and for training in righteousness (2 Timothy 3:16).

When we read the Bible, we're not just reading some old book
written hundreds of years ago by people who are dead and
gone, we are reading *THE WORD OF LIFE*, sent to us by God
Himself, to show us how to live in this twentieth century, and
how to find our way through all the pitfalls and temptations of
life in the world today, and to make a glorious success of Life.

Notice four things the Bible has to teach us:

1. *TEACHING*. It's not just a story book, though it
includes that. It takes us through the life and behaviour of
hundreds of people, good and bad, and shows us what life is
meant to be under God's guidance.

2. *REPROOF*. None of us is perfect. We sin, we make
mistakes, we go wrong, and God has to remind us and rebuke
us, and we find this hard to take. But rebuke by itself is not
enough.

3. *CORRECTION*. Where our life has gone wrong, it
needs to be put right again, and so - continually - the Bible
leads us back into God's way for us. It's like the weaving of
a rug or carpet. If the weaver makes a mistake, he has to undo
the work right back to the mistake, and start again. So, keep
short accounts with God. Put things right with Him *every* day.

4. *TRAINING*. Training in righteousness. This is not something you can bring to a finish. It goes on all your life long - even
if you live to be 100! We need to be taught afresh every day.

PRAYER
Open Thou mine eyes that I may learn wondrous things out
of Thy Law. AMEN.

The Lord stood by Paul and said, 'Take courage, for as you *have* testified about Me at Jerusalem, so you must bear witness also at Rome' (Acts 23:11).

'Jerusalem ... Rome' - what was the difference?

Jerusalem was where most Christians were; in Rome there were very few. In Jerusalem, Paul was *free*. Rome was to be his *prison*. But Rome was, ultimately, his biggest triumph. From Rome, Paul wrote his Prison Epistles: Ephesians, Philippians, Colossians, 2 Timothy and Philemon. In Rome he made contact with servants of the Emperor Nero's household, and won them for Christ. It was probably from Rome that Matthew, Mark and Luke wrote their Gospels. It was in Rome that the martyrs were burned.

A Christian begins by witnessing at home. Then in circles where friends live. But later God leads to more difficult spots, where there may be few - if any - Christians. The secret of Paul's success was however to be in these words: *The LORD stood by Paul.* And the same Lord stands by you, where you are now (in hospital), and bids you too to *TAKE COURAGE.*

The letters you write from hospital bear fruit. (Your one to me I found *very* encouraging, a lovely letter). The people you mix with in a hospital will also be under the influence of a child of God - and that doesn't count for nothing. The friends you make there may be won for Christ.

God be with you, dear Carol.

> Dare to be a Daniel,
> Dare to stand alone,
> Dare to have a purpose firm.
> And dare to make it known.

Moses said to God, 'Who am I that *I* should go to Pharaoh?'
... God said, 'But I will be with you' (Exodus 3:11-12).

The two 'I's' in this conversation between Moses and God are interesting. Moses knew that he was a 'nobody' - nothing special about him. Why should God pick on a 'nobody' to rebuke the greatest ruler in the then known world? God knew that Moses was nothing special - what made the difference was that God promised to be with him, and no Pharaoh could really stand up to God.

The other verse that I think goes with this one was a word spoken to Moses' successor, Joshua. It is in Joshua 1:5: 'As I *was* with Moses, so I *will be* with you.' What God was, He will be. And you and I as His servants can claim the same promise for ourselves. We're very ordinary people, not brilliantly clever, not extra-saintlike, not even persuasive preachers or teachers. But when God takes hold of us and makes us into His servants, however humble, that makes all the difference. Nobody knows what God can do with a humble person who is obedient to Him.

> Trust and obey,
> For there's no other way
> To be happy in Jesus,
> But to trust and obey.

PRAYER

Lord, I can do nothing worth while in just my own strength. But You can work Your work through me if I obey You. Make me obedient to You today. For Jesus' sake. AMEN.

'Simon, son of John, do you love Me?' Peter said to Jesus,
'Yes, Lord, You know that I love You' (John 21:16).

You'll remember that marvellous story of the breakfast on the seashore, after the Resurrection of Jesus. Peter hadn't seen Jesus since the Sunday after Easter. But he had a troubled conscience. He could never forget that night before the Crucifixion. In the trial before Caiaphas the High Priest, Peter had been challenged by a servant-girl to admit that he was a follower of Jesus. And Peter got scared, and three times over he denied that he even knew Jesus. He had wept when he remembered it.

But now, after breakfast, Jesus took Peter aside for a little talk, and three times over He asked if Peter loved Him. And that morning, he came right back to his Master in penitence and sorrow and love.

Every one of us constantly needs God's forgiveness when by deed or thought we have denied Him. But John reminds us in 1 John 1:9: 'If we confess our sins, God is faithful and just and will forgive our sins, and cleanse us from *all* unrighteousness.'

However feeble and faithless we are, Jesus doesn't let go of us, does He?

PRAYER
Create in me a clean heart, O God, and renew a right spirit within me. AMEN.

That which was from the beginning, which we have *heard*,
which we have *seen* with our eyes, which we have looked
upon and *touched* with our hands (1 John 1:1).

John was writing, of course, about Jesus. And he begins by
telling us who Jesus really is:

1. *He was from the beginning.* He took part with His
Father in the creation of the world - right back before there was
a world at all - Jesus was there. He made the world for
Himself. And He put Man in it so that He might make friends
with His world. Man was made in God's image, like God to
look at. Ultimately in Jesus, God became Man.

2. *We have heard Him.* I wonder, don't you, what His
Voice sounded like? John knew, he had heard Him, listened
to His stories and teaching, heard Him as He healed people.

3. *We have seen Him.* What a marvellous thing, to have
actually seen Jesus. How many people could say that today?
Do you remember when Thomas went on his knees to Jesus
and cried out, 'My Lord, and my God'? And Jesus replied,
'Thomas, you only believe because you have seen Me; but
blessed are those who have not seen, and yet have believed.'
And that means me, and you, doesn't it? We are blessed.
We've never seen Him, but we believe Him.

4. *We've touched Him.* That's tremendous, too, to have
actually *touched* Jesus! How do you touch? With a hand.
When He touched people, or they touched Him, often they
were healed. Fingers are very expressive. When we shake
hands, we express love to people. A touch can bring JOY.

May His JOY be yours this day!

Before they call I will answer, while they are yet speaking
I will hear (Isaiah 65:24).

This day is all about Prayer. And what a lot all of us have to learn about Prayer.

But here Isaiah tells us a *fact* - that when a Christian prays, God hears, yes, even before the prayer has been made, it has reached Him.

If I write you a letter, it will take 3 or 4 days before you get it. We used to be able to send telegrams, and they could reach you in an hour. I can pick up the phone, and that takes just a second. But a word to God is instantaneous.

When you pray, you know God hears. And if you are praying according to His will, He answers. But He doesn't always answer 'Yes'. Nor does He always answer at once. Sometimes He may say, 'Wait'. Sometimes He may answer 'No', because what we are asking is not according to His Will. The important thing is that He does hear, and He does answer. And He cares for every single one of us.

Many people are praying to God for you at this time, and we know God is answering. He certainly hears us, He certainly cares, and I personally believe He is going to heal you.

We may have to be patient a bit, and so may you! Keep in touch with Him daily - and so will we. Incidentally, you might like to pray today specially for Uncle Richard and his family. In 5 days from now he will become Rector of All Souls, Langham Place. And he will need all God's strength and wisdom and love if he is to be able to do God's will in that great Church.

January 8
God created man in His own image
(Genesis 1:27).

What is God like? So many people ask that question, and don't know the answer. But ask, What is man like?, and the answer is - He is like God. And as you begin to look at men and women today, can we picture God as *like* the people we see? Not often, I think. But sometimes we can see people whom we know, and we think, 'God is like that man'. Anyway, that's what we are meant to be like - like God - made in God's image.

Why did He do it? I think perhaps He was lonely - up in Heaven with nobody but Himself and the angels! So He had the marvellous thought of making a home for beings like Himself. He made the world, placed trees, birds, animals, fish, reptiles in His world - and then He put people into it to care for His world as His wardens. You get the sample of what God was after in the story of the garden of Eden. And Adam and Eve spoilt the picture by sin, and they were driven out of God's garden. But God still had a hankering for human fellowship, so He finally sent His dear Son to be a human being, and to paint the original picture over again - Man without sin, to redeem sinful man. Jesus is the Saviour. What is God like? Philip asked Jesus that question, and Jesus answered, 'Have *I* been all this time with you, Philip, and you don't recognise Me? Whoever has seen Me, has seen the Father - has seen God.'

So in Him we have both our pattern, and our Saviour.

PRAYER
Thank You, God, for giving us Your dear Son. Help us to be more like the pattern, like Jesus. AMEN.

He Himself bore our sins in His body on the tree
(1 Peter 2:24).

Lots of people wonder how the death of the Lord Jesus on
Calvary in AD 33 can have any connection with the sins that
you and I and other people commit 1960 years *after* His
death? Whilst His death might have been for the people who
are alive at that time, how does it affect us nearly 2000 years
later?

Well - I think perhaps we have to remember that the
Person we are concerned with is God Himself, who created
the world and the universe, and He is concerned for the whole
of His creation - past, present and future. If His death doesn't
affect us today, then neither does His offer of Eternal Salvation apply to us.

Secondly, we have to reckon that Time, as we know it, is
a man-made thing. It is *we* who reckon in terms of seconds,
minutes, hours, days, weeks, months, years and centuries.
Time with God is different. Peter says in 2 Peter 3:8: One day
is with the Lord as a thousand years, and a thousand years as
one day. So we could say (fancifully by human terms) that
'Jesus died two days ago, so His death covers me.' In other
words, His death and His Salvation are timeless. Both deal
with all mankind from Creation until the end of the Age.
Thank God they do!

PRAYER
Thank You, Lord Jesus, for forgiving all my sins. Help me
to live daily as a true disciple of Yours. AMEN.

January 10

Your ears shall hear a word behind you, saying, 'This is the
Way, walk in it', when you turn to the right, or when you
turn to the left (Isaiah 30:21).

Conscience is a natural gift of God to every person who is born
into the world. It is a knowledge of the difference between
right and wrong, the little inner voice that whispers gently in
your mind when the temptation comes to do or say something
that you know to be wrong. Is it possible to kill your conscience? Yes, I think it is, if you continually go on doing what
you want to do, *even* if you know it is wrong.

Sometimes, of course, when you are faced with, say, two
alternatives of what you might do, it is difficult to decide what
is right, and conscience alone is not a sufficient guide. In that
case you have to use other helps. The Bible is usually a clear
guide - but sometimes even there you can't be sure. A
Christian friend can sometimes advise. But when all these fail
to give clear guidance, probably the best thing to do is to take
the line that your own heart guides, and ask God to make you
uncomfortable if your decision is wrong! I believe then you
can trust God not to let you go astray.

PRAYER.

Keep me, O God, walking in Your way today. Through
Jesus Christ, our Lord. AMEN.

Cast all your anxieties on Him, for He cares about you
(1 Peter 5:7).

Is it wrong to be anxious? No - I don't think so, but it is quite possible to let your anxieties overwhelm you. And if you're a Christian, you know that nothing happens to you without God knowing, understanding and caring.

Very often, our anxiety stems from a general feeling of insecurity. We're not sure what is going to happen to us, so we begin to worry. Will we lose our home, our health, our job? Many people today must be asking that kind of question, especially the last one. Is it possible for a *Christian* to lose his job? Yes, certainly, like anybody else. But a Christian knows he can take the situation to God.

For instance, if a Christian becomes a missionary, it means, probably, leaving a settled job here and going over-seas. That overseas door may close later, and he or she has to lose a home. And no job may be on offer. It may well mean taking an unusual job, moving to a strange place, even being out of a job of any kind for a time. But God who called them overseas knows, cares and understands, and there is a place in God's purposes for everyone, somewhere.

Take it to Him, and keep your eyes open! That takes the anxiety off your shoulders, and puts it where it rightly belongs, into His loving Hands.

And the Peace of God ... will keep your hearts and your minds in *Christ Jesus* (Philippians 4:7).

January 12
I have called you friends
(John 15:15).

A person who has no friends is indeed in trouble. Everybody needs to have at least one friend - most of us have several - and some are very special friends. When you have good news, often the first thing you think of is to share it with your friend. If things go wrong and you are in trouble, again you think at once of talking to your friend about it.

Have you ever thought that Jesus Himself had need of friends? When He was in the Garden of Gethsemane and the officers came to arrest Him, we read that 'all His disciples forsook Him and fled'. Just when He most needed them, they were no longer there. How sad!

But if you have made Him your friend, He has promised, 'I will never leave you nor forsake you' (Hebrews 13:5). And that's marvellous - to know that, whatever circumstances you find yourself in, *He* is there too, even if nobody else is - He cares.

I find it wonderful that Jesus wants *me* to be a friend of His - what an honour! I'm nobody special, why should He want me? But, yes, it's *ME* He wants. And that news I can share with my other friends too, because He also loves them.

We love Him, because He first loved us.

Speak truth to one another; render in your gates judgments that are true and make for peace; do not devise evil in your hearts against one another, and love no false oath, for all these things I hate, says the LORD (Zechariah 8:16,17).

This verse has to do with our relationships with other people, both Christian and non-Christian. If we slip up in our conduct with them, we cannot bring glory to our Master, Christ. People watch our behaviour when they know we are professing Christians, and if they find us not living up to our profession, it brings both us and the Lord Jesus into disrepute.

Are we glad when our enemies come to grief or disaster? We should not be, we should get alongside them in sympathy if we can, because we want to win them, and make them into friends instead of enemies.

The President of Kenya, Daniel Arap Moi, was once asked what should be done with those who had plotted his death. He said, 'Warn them, and let them go. I don't want to make enemies, only friends.' He was taking the Christian line here.

It is lovely to be known as a peace-maker. Gossip ought to be *out* for a Christian, and if people give us their confidence, we should be able to keep a secret. Of course, if people have done wrong, they should be urged to confess and put it right, but we should not betray them.

PRAYER
Help me, Lord, to be true, and loving in all my relationships, and especially towards those who dislike or oppose me. Remind me that I am to be an example of a true Christian in all my dealings. For Your Name's sake, AMEN.

Happy is the man who listens to Me, watching daily at My
gates, waiting beside My doors (Proverbs 8:34).
He is like a tree planted by streams of water, that yields its
fruit in its season, and its leaf does not wither. In all that he
does, he prospers (Psalm 1:3).

This is a lovely description of the person who is day by day
drawing strength from a personal meeting with God. The tree
that is planted close to a river puts its roots down the bank, and
it never dries up because its roots are in contact with fresh,
running water. The countryside all round may be dusty and
parched, but the tree flourishes.

So with the Christian. We have hidden resources that the
world knows nothing about. When people might expect us to
be sad and miserable because we are ill or bereaved, we
continue to be cheerful and bright because we are in daily
touch with the Lord Jesus. You may remember Paul had a
disability which three times he asked God to take away. And
God didn't - but He reminded Paul, 'My strength is made
perfect in weakness.' So Paul was able to say, 'I will therefore
rather glory in my infirmity, so that God's power may shine out
through me.' People think that it was partial blindness in Paul,
perhaps a cataract. Anyway, it was something that wasn't
going to heal up. But it didn't stop Paul from witnessing.

So we can pray:

> Keep me shining, Lord,
> Keep me shining, Lord,
> In all I say and do;
> That the world may see,
> Christ lives in me,
> And learn to love Him too.

The heavens proclaim the Glory of God, and the firmament
shows His handiwork (Psalm 19:1).

When you look at the world around you, ask yourself again
and again, Who made it? Scientists spend a lot of time trying
to find out and *explain* why the world is as it is. And they can't.
As far as we know (and we don't know everything) there is no
other planet which has people on it, or even animal or bird life.
Astronauts have been to the moon, sputniks have circled other
planets, but so far, no report of *life*, as we know it, on any of
them.

Why? Why did God make this world at all? And why did
He make it differently from all the others? If He hadn't put a
sun in our universe, could we have lived? And does evolution
explain it all? There had to be a *beginning* somewhere. And
the Bible tells us: In the beginning - GOD (Genesis 1:1).

Look at the feathers of a butterfly under a microscope. No
'Man' could have made such an exquisite, delicate beauty as
that! Look at the eyes of a bluebottle fly, and marvel at the
extent of them. Look at the markings on a giraffe, or your own
finger-prints - each is *unique*. No two are identical. And why
did God make *you*?

It was to do what David says the heavens do, proclaim
God's Glory. And we can only do *this* when we know God as
our Creator, and Jesus as our Saviour. So, let's praise Him
today.

No temptation has overtaken you that is not common to
man. But God is faithful, who will not let you be tempted
beyond your strength, but with the temptation will also
provide the way of escape, that you may be able to bear it
(1 Corinthians 10:13).

What a blessing this particular verse has brought to millions
of people! Temptation to do wrong comes to all of us. And it's
easy to give way - and if we are Christians, we feel bad about
it afterwards. Sometimes temptation is very strong, and we
find our non-Christian friends not bothering about it, just
doing wrong and taking pleasure in it. Why don't we just copy
them?

We can't - because we know God has said, *You shall not*.
And it would grieve Him. But does God really understand
how strong *my* temptations are? Yes, He does. For the very
same kind of temptations came to Jesus too. What then can we
do about ours?

Remember:

1. It isn't wrong to be *tempted* - Jesus was.

2. Sometimes we should *run away* from the temptation.

3. Sometimes we should *face it out* - in God's strength.

4. Sometimes we should immediately do something *else*.

5. Sometimes we should *pray* about it.

6. Sometimes we shouldn't even *think* about it.

7. And always remember 'Whose we are, and Whom we
serve' (Acts 27:23).

PROVERB
You can't stop a bird landing on your head,
but it need not make its nest there.

A word *fitly spoken* is like Apples of Gold
in Pictures of Silver (Proverbs 25:11).

What a lovely description of what the human voice can do! It can cause a war; it can make a peace. It can stir up hatred in someone else. It can make love. There used to be an annual calendar printed called 'Apples of Gold Calendar'. I wonder if it still is. It contained godly messages given by well known preachers, one for each day of the year.

Now the human voice is like a beautiful musical instrument. It can give out excruciating discord or marvellous sweet melody, all determined by the character and temperament and skill and love of the speaker. And where the speaker is a person truly possessed by Christ, that voice will be used to bring joy and peace, and comfort and friendship, to those who hear.

A gossiping tongue can easily destroy friendship and plant hatred and resentment in its place. We should be very careful what we say of, or do, to other people. We can hurt more by word of mouth than even by physical cruelty. Do we know of someone who appears to have no friends? Can we do something to change that situation?

Set a guard over my mouth, O LORD, keep watch over the door of my lips (Psalm 141:3).

We were ready to share with you not only
the Gospel of God, but also our own selves
(1 Thessalonians 2:8).

Every servant of Jesus needs to remember that as we try to pass on the Good News of His Salvation, people will only receive it if they find that we want them for *themselves*, not just for their Salvation. Some people will reject what we try to tell them about the Gospel. But even if they do, we still want to try and make friends with them, and never to *force* the Gospel on them. Often they will be more ready to accept, when they find we are just *sharing* ourselves with them. Entering into their interests, their hobbies, and understanding their standards, even if we can't share them.

I have sometimes found that bringing a friend into our house, and sharing what we normally do at home, such as family prayers, grace at meals, and our kind of recreations and games, has much more effect than a direct preaching of the Gospel to them. If our home setting is attractive to us, others may find it enjoyable too.

Serve the LORD with gladness (Psalm 100:2).

What tremendous claims Jesus Christ made for Himself: If He was wrong in any of these, He is a liar. But if He was *not* wrong, how dare anyone reject Him?

Think of some of them: The Way, the Truth, the Life, the Bread of Life, the Light, the Resurrection, the Good Shepherd, the Door. In other words, He is in Himself all that man needs from the cradle to the grave, and beyond. To get into life at all, you must go in by the *Door*. When you're inside, you have to find the *Way* along. And you have to see the Way, so there must be *Light* on the road. If you slip, you have to be rescued, so like a sheep, you need a *Shepherd*. And when you come to the end of the road, is that all? No - after death, He is the *Resurrection* too.

Complete and utter safety and joy is offered to me all along the road I travel. That doesn't mean there'll be no suffering or sadness, but He is there with me at every step. So I can trust Him completely, knowing He'll never let me down.

Commit each new day to Him as you enter it.

He who hears My Word, and believes on Him who sent
Me, has Eternal Life; he will not come into judgement, but
has passed from death to Life (John 5:24).

This verse really covers the whole of what it means to become
a Christian. Since it was spoken by Jesus Himself, we can
accept it as true. And it's worth while studying the tenses of
the verbs in it.

'The one who hears and believes *has* Eternal Life.' That
is the present tense. So this is not something we look forward
to when we die. It is here and now. We don't have to wait for
it - God has given us Eternal Life *now*.

'He *will not* be condemned.' This is the future tense. So
our *future* is safe, in God's hands. Yes, even though we are
sinners - when Christ has forgiven us - we are freed from our
sins, for ever.

'He *has* passed out of death into Life.' That is a *past tense*.
So, if I'm a born-again Christian, I am alive now, and forever
more. Yes, my body may die, but not *me* - I won't.

So, in Christ, the whole of life is covered: Past, Present
and Future.

As soon as anyone becomes a Christian, Jesus is with him
or her for ever. And He has promised, 'I will never leave you
nor forsake you' (Hebrews 13:5).

So, that is the difference. You are embarked upon a wholly
new way of Life, and your present and your future are assured.

Kept by the Power of God (1 Peter 1:5).

January 21
To obey is better than sacrifice
(1 Samuel 15:22).

This comes from an Old Testament story. King Saul, the first
King of Israel, had been warned that when God commits a
person to a task for Him, He expects total obedience. Saul's
task was to destroy all the Amalekites, and their flocks. But
after the battle, Saul kept back the best of the flock, and so did
his people. He didn't obey God - and he lost his kingdom over
his disobedience. He said he would sacrifice these animals to
God - but that was not what God asked. So the prophet Samuel
said to Saul, 'God expects obedience, and sacrifice is not a
substitute which you can offer.'

How easily we can be tempted just to disobey a tiny bit,
so that we get what we think is a bit of advantage for ourselves.
What do we reckon is the most important thing in our lives?
What comes first? Money? Friends? Popularity? A home? A
marriage partner? Comfort? 'Seek *first* His kingdom and His
righteousness, and all these things shall be added to you as
well' (Matthew 6:33). What were 'those things'? Food, drink,
clothing - all the necessities of life. We can always commit
both our needs and our desires to our Heavenly Father - and
He will see that we do not lack. He will give us 'more than we
can either desire or deserve' - but we must also *obey*.

> Trust and obey,
> For there's no other way
> To be happy in Jesus,
> But to trust and obey.

(See January 4)

The Law of the Spirit of Life in Christ Jesus has set me
free from the Law of sin and death (Romans 8:2).

This chapter of Romans is one of the very great chapters of the
Bible. In it Paul sets forth the conditions governing Salvation.
Here in this second verse Paul tells us that the 'natural' law of
sin followed by death is a law from which we can be rescued
and also be set free from condemnation.

But the only place where any sinner is set free is 'in Christ
Jesus'. And when we enter into Christ, we come under a new
Law - the 'Law of the Spirit of Life'. So, for the Christian, life
is guided, directed, and mastered by the Holy Spirit of God.

And from that point on, we begin to *grow*. People sometimes think that once you become a Christian, everything will
be easy - no more temptation - no more sin. But that isn't true.
No - what happens is that we now see sin in its true perspective, something that grieves God, the thing which brought
Jesus to the Cross. Temptation may become even stronger
than before, but we now have a new Master who is living with
us, and within us, and He gives us strength not only to fight the
battle - but to *win*.

The battle will go on all through life, but now we know we
are on the winning side. There will be suffering. But, says
Paul, 'the suffering will be far outweighed by the *glory*'
(Romans 8:18). So -

> Fight the Good Fight with all thy might,
> Christ is thy strength, and Christ thy right.
> Lay hold on Life, and it shall be
> Thy joy and crown eternally.

As Moses lifted up the serpent in the wilderness, so must
the Son of Man be lifted up, that whoever believes in Him
may have Eternal Life. For God so loved the world that He
gave His only Son, that whoever believes in Him should
not perish but have Eternal Life (John 3:14-16).

This last verse (16) is, I suppose, the best-known verse in the
whole Bible. It's the foundation-stone on which the Christian
life and faith is built - and it's Jesus Himself who spoke it.

But why did He couple it with the bit about the serpent?
Didn't He remember that when the Creation first began, it was
the serpent who brought about Man's sin and downfall? How
could He liken Himself to a serpent? In Genesis 3:15 God told
the serpent, 'I will put enmity between you and mankind ... he
will bruise your head, and you will bruise his heel.'

Come back to the story of the serpent in the wilderness.
Remember, the Children of Israel had been disobedient to
God, and serpents had been killing them. They begged for
relief, and God told Moses to put 'a brass serpent on a pole in
the middle of the camp, and every man who looked to the brass
serpent would be healed'.

When Jesus went to the Cross, He took the sins of all
mankind on Himself: '*He* became sin for us, who knew no sin,
that *we* might be made the righteousness of God in Him' (2
Corinthians 5:21). That brass serpent - symbolic of sin cleansed,
was a foretaste in symbol of the Saviour who was to come. So
now we can say with David, 'Thou hast delivered my *soul*
from death, my *eyes* from tears, my *feet* from stumbling; I
walk before the Lord in the land of the living' (Psalm
116:8,9).

I have not come to call the righteous,
but sinners to repentance (Luke 5:32).

Jesus was constantly faced with many self-righteous people, particularly the Pharisees, who prided themselves on keeping the whole Law of God. Hence His story of the Pharisee and the Publican. Whose prayer was acceptable? The Pharisee 'prayed with himself' - just swanking about how good he was. The Publican stood afar off, beat his breast, and cried for mercy because of his sins. He was truly sorry.

Do we need to be sorry *all* the time? In one sense yes, because we are sinful people, and seldom does a single day pass without our sinning in thought, word or deed. But there is this difference - as Christians, we know our sins are already forgiven; we know God hears us. The non-Christian can only really pray one prayer which includes confessing his sin, asking for God's mercy, and determining to receive Jesus; and then going on to live for Him.

Repentance means 'turning around' and going in the opposite direction. In other words, right about turn, away from the sin. And as we do so, God's joy comes flooding in. So repentance and joy go together. The relationship with our Heavenly Father is restored.

PRAYER
Lord, have mercy upon us,
and incline our hearts to keep Thy Law. AMEN.

January 25
He had set me apart before I was born ...
and was pleased to reveal His Son to me
(Galatians 1:15,16).

When you remember what Paul was like before his conversion on the Damascus road, you wonder how he could say that
God had chosen him before he was born! Yet Paul was very
certain of this, for he writes in Ephesians 1:4: 'God chose us
in Christ *before* the foundation of the world'! And that's quite
a long time back.

Now, if that was true for Paul, it is also true for you and me.
Before the world was made, God knew that one day, thousands of years ahead, a girl to be called Carol Bewes was
going to be born, and He chose her beforehand to be a
Christian, and a servant of Jesus Christ!

And all through the centuries, He has been preparing for
you. And now, you've come, and you have been chosen too.

I think knowing that God has chosen you should give you
great encouragement in pressing forward for Christ all your
life.

PRAYER
Thank You, God, for revealing Your Son to me. Help me
to serve *Him* faithfully always. AMEN.

To all who received Him, who believed in His Name,
He gave power to become children of God;
who were born, not of blood, nor of the will of the flesh,
nor of the will of man, but of God
(John 1:12.13).

Becoming a Christian is a matter of birth, not just a matter of personal choice. The action is first of all, *God's* action. God has to call you first, and it is when you feel His pull on your life that you can begin to respond. John is very clear about this, and in this verse he points out what the New Birth is *not*.

1. He says it is not 'being born into a chosen family'. Your family may be a Christian family, but that doesn't make you a Christian. They may influence you, but they cannot force you against your will, and you cannot *drift* into becoming one.

2. 'Not by the will of the flesh.' You can't just say, 'I think I'd like to try being a Christian.' *You* don't choose - God does.

3. 'Not by the will of man.' Your father can't say, 'I'm going to have all my family turned into Christians.' He can try, but the ultimate choice doesn't rest with him.

4. To be re-born, spiritually, comes solely from God Himself. John says, 'You may receive Him, then God can make you into one of His children - and He wants to do so.'

The world into which Jesus was born, the world that was His own, didn't recognise Him. And when He came, the people who were His own, the Jews, didn't receive Him. But he started a new Creation, and those who did receive Him, He gave the right to become children of God. And when that happens, we can 'behold His Glory'.

We say, He's Wonderful.

One thing I do, forgetting what lies behind, and straining
forward to what lies ahead, I press on toward the goal for
the prize of the upward call of God in Christ Jesus
(Philippians 3:13,14).

Paul is here thinking of the great chariot races of Rome. The
charioteer stands on a tiny platform over sturdy wheels and
axle. His knees are pressed against a curved rail, his thighs
flexed. He bends forward from the waist, stretching out hands
and head over the horses backs - eyes fixed only on the goal
ahead - forgetting the roaring crowds, the racing rivals, past
mistakes. What was the prize for Paul? JESUS HIMSELF.

God called him. Jesus started him off. He must not dwell
on his past failures, but set his sights straight towards Jesus.
He can forget the past - that has been forgiven. He can trust for
the present, because Jesus is entirely with him. His job in life?
To be his very best for Christ all his days. To that purpose he
needs to be fit in body, mind and spirit. He must keep himself
fit. Paul says he's not yet reached perfection. But that's what
he aims at - and he won't reach it until finally he stands at the
end of the race, face to face with his beloved Master. Then he
will hear Him say, 'Well done, good and faithful servant, enter
into the Joy of your Lord.'

What was true for Paul, is also true for us.

I press towards the mark.

January 28
Whatever your task, work heartily,
as serving the Lord and not men (Colossians 3:23).

This particular word is written to Christian *slaves* (look back to verse 22). It must have been a great temptation to these new Christians to hope that, now they've become Christians, they could escape the slavery which bound them, and be set free - by Christ. But no - Paul exemplified this in his letter to Philemon, in sending back a runaway slave (Onesimus) to his master. When his master would give him a job to do, he had to remember that he was really serving Christ, yes, even in slavery.

When your parents ask you to do something, or your teacher sets you a task - no grumbling! You do it *as unto Christ*, and you won't want to offer Him anything shoddy or slipshod. And, incidentally, it will in fact bring glory to your Master, Christ, for your work will be the very best you can give - and that will please *men* as well as God. And if they know you are a Christian, they'll reckon your faith making you trustworthy.

A Moslem trader in Kenya wanted a trustworthy accountant in his shop, and asked me to find one. I sent him a young Christian man, and he told me that from then on nothing was stolen. But later the Christian was sacked because he wouldn't work on Sunday! He was putting God first. I explained to the trader, and he took the Christian back. His business flourished!

Whatever your task, do it heartily!

The kingdom of God does not consist in talk, but in power
(1 Corinthians 4:20).

Jesus taught a lot about the Kingdom of God, because the real
thing was so very different from what the people of His day
thought. And Paul says in his letter to the Christians in Corinth
that God's Kingdom is not just good advice - but it is very
powerful. And today's church has to learn that over and over
again. Good advice given from the pulpit isn't enough - there
must be God's power behind the advice, so that people will
feel compelled to respond, not to the preacher, but to God
Himself.

And what is true of the preacher is also just as important
for the Christian in the pew. We may be quite eloquent in our
speaking to people about the Christian faith, but none of our
advice will get anywhere, unless they see that our lives are
being lived close to our Master, and that we are - in ourselves
- like Him.

Some of the Corinthian Christians had been swanking
about how good they were, and Paul had heard about it. And
in the two previous verses he says, 'When I come, I'll see - not
just what you *say* - but what *power* you have.'

You and I can have no power except what comes from
Christ Himself. It is 'Christ in you that is the hope of Glory'
(Colossians 1:27).

Now the serpent was more subtle than any other wild
creature that the Lord God had made (Genesis 3:1).

In Scripture, the serpent is often a symbol of Satan. And
Satan's chief effort is pressed against the Christians, because
although he can't steal them back from Christ, he can destroy
their Christian witness, he can make them powerless. Get
hold of a copy of C S Lewis's *The Screwtape Letters* and read
it through very carefully, because Lewis describes most
vividly how Satan goes about his task - sometimes by frightening people, but much more often by soothing them into
losing touch with their Master.

He tried that with Adam and Eve, when he said to them,
'Has God *really* said you would die if you took the forbidden
fruit? He just *couldn't* be so harsh to you!' Planting the seed
of doubt.

Read how he even tempted Jesus, three times in very
subtle ways. 'You're all-powerful, and You're hungry. Why
not use Your power to provide Yourself with a bit of bread?
You want all the world to be Yours? Right, I'll give it You -
if You just bow down once to me. God said in Scripture that
He would stop You from dashing Your foot against a stone.
Right, then just throw Yourself off the pinnacle of the temple,
and everyone will know You *must* be God. That's what You
want, isn't it?'

Peter was *frightened* into denying Christ.

Ultimately, Satan is doomed. But at present he can harm
us a lot. We need constantly to hide in Christ, the only safe
place.

Put off the *old nature* which belongs to your former manner of life, and is corrupt through deceitful lusts, and be renewed in the spirit of your minds, and put on the *new nature*, created after the likeness of God in true righteousness and holiness (Ephesians 4:22-24).

'Put off ... Put on.' In material life, I think this is rather like the caterpillar and the butterfly. The caterpillar has a crawling existence, he creeps about slowly, and then he turns into a Chrysalis (like death), but out of death comes a totally new and shining creature that can fly up into the air - a thing of beauty. Do you ever think, 'Does that butterfly ever remember his early existence as a caterpillar?'

It's a little bit like that when a person becomes a Christian. Before conversion, they reckon it's up to them to decide how to live and behave, and they do just what they like, and it often lands them in trouble.

But then, when they come to Christ, they come under 'entirely new management'. Their sins are forgiven, they have a new incentive for living. They have a new power to help them, and they have a 'Friend that sticketh closer than a brother'.

And people notice the difference. They are nicer to live with - they don't live just for self. They are concerned for other people.

Another thing. 'Put on the New' - it has to be put on fresh every day. And that's one reason why it's good to begin the day WITH GOD.

February 1

We know that in everything, God works for good with those who love Him (Romans 8:28).

For me, as for many other people, this is a favourite verse, and especially when the situation personally doesn't seem too good. When Paul wrote these words, he mentioned, in verses 35-39, some of the hardships he himself had had to endure: trouble, hardship, persecution, famine, even lack of clothing, danger of execution. And he is saying that, as God's servant, he is totally under God's protection. He is facing death every day - yet he knows that no harm can touch him without God knowing exactly what He is about.

Personal sickness, fear for one's loved ones, opposition from people who dislike what we stand for, pressure of exams, misunderstandings with friends - all sorts of things can cause us depression.

Anxiety tends to drive us sometimes almost to despair but, Paul says, this is needless. It just shows we aren't really trusting our Heavenly Father. I can remember in my own early days the great grief and anxiety I had when Grannie and I broke off our engagement to be married, so that God's work could continue without our being separated. There was fear that we might never get married at all - and it was then, I think, that we both claimed this verse for ourselves! And just over a year later, we were husband and wife!

If there is a worry, claim this verse, and hang onto it - remembering that God never breaks His promises.

Abraham believed God ...
and he was called the friend of God (James 2:23).

This verse really follows on from yesterday's choice. Here
was a man who had been called by God to leave his home in
Ur of the Chaldees, and go out into the unknown world, to be
a wanderer until God showed him where he was to live. And
then at a later stage, when he was getting so old that it didn't
look as if he and his wife would ever have a son, miraculously
God gave them Isaac. This precious boy meant everything to
them both. Then the day came when God spoke to Abraham
again and asked if he was willing to give up this precious son
- and let him *die*. How could God's promise to make Abraham
the Father of many nations be fulfilled, if he was to sacrifice
his only son?

But Abraham obeyed, and took Isaac up onto the moun-
tain ready to give him back to God. And as God saw his faith,
He showed him the better way - the ram for the sacrifice, and
Isaac was saved.

And the result? Abraham was called *the friend of God*.
What a lovely title to be given! But it was because 'he knew
that God could keep His promises'. And that is always true,
isn't it. Think of the many promises that have been given to
God's people all down the ages, and are still being given today
- and not one has been broken. Has God given one to you too?
He will certainly keep it, and bring it to pass.

I am the Alpha and the Omega, says the Lord God, Who is,
and Who was, and Who is to come, the ALMIGHTY
(Revelation 1:8).

This brings us back to the beginnings of everything, the start
of the world and all that is in it, from that day to this, and away
on into all Eternity. God is always there.

Notice the tenses of the verbs used in that short sentence.
'Is', 'Was' and 'Will be'. Past, Present and Future. The Bible
begins with the words: 'In the beginning God' (Genesis 1:1).

I can't remember, are you studying Greek? If so, you will
know that in Greek, Alpha is the first letter of the alphabet, and
Omega is the last. Our A to Z. The very word Alphabet comes
from the recital of the Greek Alphabet, which begins 'Alpha,
Beta, Gamma, Delta.'

All the words that can be written in any language in the
world, millions and millions of them, are only possible
because God gave us speech and spelling!

Think of the thousands of languages into which the Bible
has been translated. Pray specially today for the Bible Society
and its translating of God's Word so that people of every
tongue can have it in their own language. I have in front of me
at this moment a letter from the Bible Society, asking for help
to get the Bible into Uganda.

Pray for Uganda today, and for this Word to reach them.

The gospel which has come to you, as indeed in the whole world, is bearing fruit and growing (Colossians 1:5,6).

When Paul wrote these words, probably only a few thousand people had ever heard about Jesus, let alone accepted Him as their Saviour. But there was Paul, in faith, saying that it had now come to all the world!

The stories of how the Word of God has been preserved and passed on and translated into thousands of languages, could fill many books. How many other actual books written in AD 1, or before, are still here to be read today? Very few indeed.

In Israel there is a copy of Isaiah, written before Jesus was born, carefully scrolled up round a great metal column, inside a fortified tower which can be sunk into the ground in an instant in case of air attacks from an enemy. If it could be sold, it would fetch millions and millions of pounds - it is *so* precious. It was preserved in a cave in a hillside, lost for centuries, and it only came to light this century, found by a shepherd boy.

Paul's letters were carried by hand out of Rome, and delivered to the tiny band of Christians in each town to which he wrote. He himself was a prisoner, shortly to be executed because he was a Christian. However did the letters get to their destinations? And who kept them from later decay or destruction, so that we have them today? We'll know all the stories one day.

The Bible is still the most popular book in the world. It ought to be very precious to us too.

The best book to read is the Bible.

Grow up in every way into Him (Ephesians 4:15).

If we don't eat, we will not grow. Some people think that once a person becomes a Christian, he can just relax and all will be well - there is no need to do anything more about it. But the Christian life is really just like the physical life - a baby that doesn't drink milk will eventually just shrivel up and die. And spiritually, a Christian who doesn't feed regularly on God's Word, who doesn't pray day by day, who doesn't seek to model his or her life on that of Jesus, soon becomes a useless person - as far as the gospel is concerned.

For a Christian, growing up goes on all through life - we will never reach a point where we can say, 'There now, I've got there.' No, there's always lots more to learn if we're ever going to be mature Christians. It is very easy for us to get lazy and slip away from God. Then we gradually lose the joy of Christ - till we come back to Him again.

We should expect to find something new in our Bible study every time we open God's Word - even in very familiar passages - because the written Word is introducing us to the Living Word, the Lord Jesus Himself, who said, 'Behold, I make all things *new*' (Revelation 21:5).

Levi made Him a great feast in his house; and there was a
large company of tax collectors and others sitting at the
table with them (Luke 5:29).

This is, of course, one of the very exciting stories of the New
Testament. Levi was also called Matthew, and later in life he
wrote the first of our four Gospels. But at this time, he was one
of the rather disreputable people who collected taxes for the
Roman Empire, and usually extracted much more than they
should, keeping the change for themselves. So they were a
hated people.

Matthew was a rich man. When Jesus passed along the
seashore where Matthew was collecting, He said to him,
'Follow Me.' Literally, 'Come and travel with Me; take My
road, be My friend, be My companion.' And the record says,
Matthew 'forsook all, rose up, and followed Him'. What
happened to the money? I don't know. Matthew left it immediately. It was a sudden Call, and a sudden Response. He
became the King's recorder, and wrote the Gospel of the
Kingdom.

But he began with a celebration - he had broken with the
Roman Empire, but not with his friends. The feast was for
Jesus, but Matthew's friends must hear what has happened.
The Pharisees criticised this: 'He eateth with publicans and
sinners.'

Thank God that Jesus did. That's what He came for: 'I
come ... to call sinners to repentance,' He said. Whatever did
Matthew's friends think? Did any become disciples? History
doesn't tell us, but at least they heard the gospel. May it
always be so with us too.

The wisdom from above is first pure, then peaceable,
gentle, open to reason, full of mercy and good fruits,
without uncertainty or insincerity (James 3:17).

What is wisdom? I turned it up in my dictionary, which says,
'Soundness of judgement, in matters relating to life and
conduct.' It puts that first, before 'learning or knowledge'.
People may be very clever, but at the same time be very
unwise in their behaviour or judgment. And James is writing
here about the true wisdom which, he says, 'is from above'.
In Colossians 2:2,3, Paul says that '*all* the treasures of
wisdom are hid in Christ'.

So if we want real wisdom, that is where we have to go to
get it. It's a lovely quality to have. Remember away back in
the Old Testament, when Solomon became the third king of
Israel, God asked him what gift he would like to receive, and
Solomon asked for wisdom. God gave him not only wisdom,
but a great deal more besides. What a pity that he departed
from this real wisdom as he grew older!

The intellects God has given us must be used to find out
how God wants us to live. What matters is not whether we
know a lot or only have a little knowledge - but *how* we
exercise the brains we have! They are quite sufficient for us,
if they are put at Christ's disposal.

Let the Word of Christ dwell in you richly ... in all wisdom
(Colossians 3:16).

He is able to save to the uttermost those who come unto
God by Him, seeing He ever liveth
to make intercession for them (Hebrews 7:25).

I like the phrase 'save to the uttermost', because it really means that there is nothing God cannot do for those who fully trust Him. The RSV has 'for all time' instead of 'uttermost' (AV), and it is not nearly so expressive.

I think when you are praying for yourself, or for other people in need, it's good to make use of this phrase in our prayers - we don't want the job half-done, we want to see a complete healing. And God *can*.

In Daniel 3:17 we find the story of the young men about to be thrown into the burning fiery furnace unless they worshipped King Nebuchadnezzar. It didn't look as if there was any escape for them. Yet when they were challenged by the king, they replied: 'Our God *is able* to deliver us ... but if not, be it known unto thee, O king, that we will not serve your gods, or worship the golden image you have set up.' So - it was a case of 'God can', but if He decides against it, 'we stick to our guns!'

It does mean, of course, that we must do as God tells us - not just decide for ourselves how we want to live. We are under His orders and, like any other soldiers, we have to obey our Captain.

God did not give us a spirit of timidity, but a spirit of
power, and love and self-control (2 Timothy 1:7).

These marvellous qualities God has given to every one of His
servants; yet very often these qualities clash with what we
normally find in ourselves. Let's look at them.

1. *NO TIMIDITY*. Often we are afraid of what other people
may think of us. We look to see how our friends behave and
live, and try to copy them. If we don't conform, we fear we
may be laughed at; and we don't like that. But we need to
remember that, as Christians, we are citizens of two countries
- our earthly one, but also our Heavenly one. And the Heavenly takes precedence. So - no *fear*.

2. *POWER*. Whose power? Not mine - *His*. In the Old
Testament there's a story of a young man serving with his
master, a prophet. The prophet was in danger of his life,
enemies on all sides. The young man was scared, and the
prophet asked God to open the servant's eyes - and He did.
And the young man suddenly saw they were surrounded by
hundreds of angels! 'They that are with us are more than they
that are with them!' (2 Kings 6:16). Read that story!

3. *LOVE*. Our world today is desperately in need of Love.
People are lonely, sad, in despair. A little bit of love shown to
them does wonders, makes them feel that somebody cares.
We who live in Christian homes know what real love is like
- many others never experience it. But it's God's *gift*.

4. *SELF-CONTROL*. And that's important, too. It makes
each of us a well-balanced person. Not going off the handle
when people try to rile us.

We are His representatives - not our own.

The sheep follow Him, for they know His Voice ... They
do not know the Voice of strangers (John 10:4,5).

We thought about the *human* voice on January 17, but this is
a different Voice - the Voice of the Lord Jesus. And John is
describing it like the voice of a shepherd calling his flock. I
don't think in England we quite understand what he means;
but if we lived in Israel, we would understand.

When I was there in 1966, I stood at a country hillside
well, where a shepherd boy was watering his flock. He had a
reed pipe which he blew very tunefully and, when they had
drunk, he called them to follow him up the hill. He knew each
of them by name - Mrs. Jig-jog, Old Crumple-horn, Miss
Black-nose, and so on. If any strayed away, he shouted at
them and, if they didn't respond, he threw a pebble near them.
In England, we have a dog to chase them up. That boy had no
dog - but 'they knew his voice'.

Do we know the Voice of Jesus? If we are His sheep, I
think we must do. We may not obey - but we know, and we
hear. And if we want to be safe, we shall respond to Him. 'His
voice was like the sound of many waters' (Revelation 1:15).

> Speak, Lord, in the stillness
> Whilst I wait on Thee;
> Hushed my heart to listen
> In expectancy.
>
> Fill me with the knowledge
> Of Thy glorious will;
> All thine own good pleasure
> In Thy child fulfil.

February 11

The Law of the Spirit of Life in Christ Jesus has set me
free from the law of sin and death (Romans 8:2).

This great chapter begins with the words *no condemnation*.
And it links the subject with what Paul wrote in Romans 7.
But it goes further back, to what Isaiah had said 700 years
earlier, 'There is no peace, says my God, to the wicked'
(Isaiah 57:21). The only place in which the sinner can find
himself or herself set free from condemnation is 'in Christ
Jesus'. If you turn back to Romans 5:9, you can read, 'Being
now justified by His Blood, we shall be saved from the wrath
of God through Him.'

The other day there was a terrible accident, in which a man
and three policemen were all drowned in a storm at the
seaside. Lifebelts were thrown to them, but the ropes were not
long enough to reach them; so they drowned.

In the storms of life, we have a lifebelt thrown to us by
Jesus, and no distance is too great for the rope to reach us,
however far off from Him we are. If we turn to Him, we are
safe for all time. At the end of this great chapter, Paul says,
'Who shall separate us from the Love of God?' After looking
at every possibility, he says, 'Neither death, nor life, nor
angels, nor powers, nor height, nor depth, nor any other
creature can separate us from the Love of God which is in
Christ Jesus our Lord.' Hallelujah for that!

Praise God from Whom all blessings *flow*.

After this, many of His disciples drew back
and went no more with Him (John 6:66).

Whatever could have caused some of the disciples to turn away from Jesus? You'll need to look up the chapter in John to see. The people had just had the feeding of the 5,000, close to Capernaum. The very next day, large crowds came to hear Jesus again, and He talked to them about the Bread of Life. He told them, 'I am the Bread of Life' (verse 48). They took it literally, but He meant it spiritually, and that they couldn't understand.

How easily can people be put off from Christ! They often start well, but then something happens and they drift away again. Jesus even wondered if the twelve disciples would leave Him. But Peter spoke up and said, 'Lord, to whom shall we go? For You have the words of Eternal Life, and we believe and are sure that You are the Christ, the Son of the Living God' (verse 69).

Thank God for the very down-to-earth Peter! It's a good thing to be simple in our belief in Jesus, and not to worry about things we don't understand. He won't let us go astray if we really trust Him.

This is the confidence that we have in Him, that if we ask
anything *according to His Will*, He hears us. And if we
know that He hears us in whatever we ask, we know that we
have obtained the requests made of Him (1 John 5:14,15).

All about Prayer! What a lot we have to learn about this
subject. Have you read Uncle Richard's book, *Talking about
Prayer*? If not, you should. I imagine your Dad has a copy of
it. It's only 20 chapters, each about 2 pages long, and very
readable.

I quote from page 14 of his book:

> I know You are there, Lord, because I have
> Your word for it. I know You are listening,
> because You say that You are. I know You
> have a plan for this world because of Christ -
> and by my prayer life I choose deliberately to
> involve myself in Your plan for our world.

And I specially like Richard's chapter called 'Little and
often'. You see, you can pray anywhere, any time. You can
send up what is sometimes called an 'Arrow Prayer', shoot a
quickie up to God, because you need an immediate answer,
and sometimes you will get just that. But all our praying, to be
effective, needs to be 'according to His Will'. We don't
always know His Will and when that is so, we need to add, 'If
it is according to Your Will'.

God be with you as you learn.

So the woman ... went away into the city, and said to the
people, 'Come, see a man who told me all that ever I did.
Can this be the Christ?' (John 4:28,29).

What is an ambassador? He is a man sent by his king to
represent his king's interests in a foreign land. And that, of
course, is exactly what a Christian is meant to be - Christ's
ambassador to a world that doesn't know Him.

This woman at the well was a Samaritan. Jesus, weary and
thirsty, was sitting there at midday. Grannie and I went to that
very well - it's deep, but has lovely water at the bottom. Jesus
asked the Samaritan woman for a drink. She was surprised.
'Jews don't talk to Samaritans,' she said. 'Also, you are a
man, I'm a woman.'

Then Jesus spoke about the Living Water, and asked her
to fetch her husband. She hadn't got one, but was living with
a man who was not her husband. Jesus knew this - and she was
surprised.

Finally she ran to the town to tell all the people she knew,
that this must be the coming Messiah. They came running up
to see, and many believed on Jesus that day. They said to her,
'It wasn't just because you said it, but we have seen Him for
our very selves, and we know He is the Christ.'

What a lovely testimony to her faith, and to her witness to
them.

We don't all have to be preachers, but we do all have to be
witnesses. And we can only witness to what we *know*.

I am not ashamed of the gospel: for it is the power of God
for salvation to every one that believeth (Romans 1:16).

All the way through this letter of Paul to the Christians at
Rome, we find him glorying in the gospel, and counting it a
high honour to be allowed to proclaim it. I think the important
thing he is here proclaiming is that it is not only the truth, but
that it is the strongest *power* in the world, the power of God
for salvation to all who put their trust in God's mercy through
Christ.

It's absolutely fascinating to see how this works out,
especially among those who have been almost totally under
the bondage of some great sin, like drink or drugs. Specialists
spend their time and wisdom in trying to get people out of such
slavery, and often with little or only temporary success. But
when Jesus takes a hand with people, He can and does lift
them right out of their sins into the glorious freedom of His
gospel.

Paul can think of no greater honour than to be allowed the
privilege of passing on the Good News to any who will listen
to him. He did it in the middle of a shipwreck; he did it in
prison, when he was suffering from a beating; he did it in the
market-place, arguing with Stoics and Epicureans (people
who had a philosophy that couldn't stand up when confronted
with the gospel).

That privilege is also yours and mine. It can be done in
hundreds of different ways, according to the gifts that God has
given to us. We need to see how best we can pass it on to our
own age-group and to others. We don't have to be clever to do
so - only to be obedient.

Call upon Me and come and pray to Me, and I will hear
you. You will seek Me and find Me; when you seek Me
with all your heart, I will be found by you, says the LORD
(Jeremiah 29:12-14).

Most Christians find that there are times when it is very
difficult to remember that God is with them; times when they
seem to be very much alone; times when they want to follow
Jesus, but somehow He seems to be far away, and their
prayers are dead and cold. If that is ever your experience, and
I'm sure it will be sometimes, take courage from this verse.

The verse is part of a letter that the prophet Jeremiah wrote
to the Jews who had been carried away into exile. They felt
very far away from God, for they were far from home and were
despairing that perhaps they'd never get back again. They
could pray happily on their own soil but not in a strange land.
Their prophets, who were with them, said, 'Don't worry;
you'll soon be home again. Just a matter of a few weeks and
your troubles will be over.'

But Jeremiah says to the exiles, 'Don't listen to them. It's
all lies. It'll take 70 years for you to get back. So what should
you do? Serve God faithfully where you are. He put you there,
and your presence should help that land to prosper. Seek the
peace and prosperity of that land. And meanwhile keep very
close to God. He's always close to you.'

That was the message, and it's a good one. Wherever you
are, and in whatever circumstances, God's got His Hand on
you. Put your hand into His - it's a Strong One.

By this we know that we abide in Him and He in us,
because He has given us of His own Spirit (1 John 4:13).

These days there is a great emphasis in Christian circles upon
the work of the Holy Spirit. And it's good that this should be
so, because it's so easy to think about God as Jesus, and to
forget that He is a three-fold God - Father, Son and Holy Spirit.
Why does the Holy Spirit have to be there?

Well, for one thing, Jesus came to earth to show us what
God was like, and to redeem us from sin. But He was not
always to remain on the earth in human form. And when He
told the disciples that He was soon going back to His Father
in Heaven, they were dismayed. How would they get on
without Him?

And Jesus said, 'Don't worry. I'm not going to leave you
with no strength. When I go, I'm going to send you another
Comforter (or Champion, Strengthener) - and I'll still be with
you, even though you can't see Me.' And He went on to say,
'When He comes, His work will be never to magnify Himself,
but to magnify Me' (John 16:14).

I think the sign that a person really has begun to learn what
it means to be a Christian is when they begin to magnify Jesus
so much in their way of life and in their speech. That is a sign
that the Holy Spirit of God is at work in them. 'He who
believes in the Son of God has the testimony in himself' (1
John 5:10).

The wages of sin is death,
but the gift of God is Eternal Life (Romans 6:23).

'Wages' or a 'Gift' - which would you rather have? Well, what's the difference?

Wages are what you have rightly earned by the work that you have performed. You work so many hours a day for so many days a week and, at the end, you collect your rightful wages. You have earned it - you deserve it.

A Gift is something you certainly haven't earned, something that the Giver can give you if he wants to, out of sheer love for you. You don't deserve it, and He doesn't have to give it to you if he doesn't want to.

And so Paul says, the wages you have *earned* are the wages due to a sinner, and your earnings are *death*. You deserve it, you have worked for it, and it's your due. And you don't want it when the time comes. But, thank God, there is an alternative. In place of taking wages, you can come to God, and ask His forgiveness for your sins, and He has promised to give His forgiveness. What He gives you, and gives at once, is His free *Gift* of *Eternal Life*.

Those two alternatives are offered to you and me, and to everyone else in the whole world. Half the world doesn't even yet know it, and it's the job of those who do know to pass on the good news to those who don't. You can't deal with the whole world, but you can deal with one other person.

Those that turn many to righteousness
shall shine as the stars for ever and ever (Daniel 12:3).

For as the heavens are high above the earth, so great is His
steadfast love towards those who fear Him; as far as the
east is from the west, so far does He remove our transgressions from us (Psalm 103:11-12).

Some Christians are always in fear that, somehow, their sins
will one day catch up on them, and God will condemn them
in the end. There are plenty of Scripture verses that contradict
that fear, and this is one of them. God has promised that if we
truly repent and turn away from our sins, we are already
forgiven by the Lord Jesus, who bore the penalty for our sins
when He died for us on Calvary.

What is the distance from East to West? I suppose some
10,000 miles - might be more. In other words, when your sins
are forgiven, you'll never see them again. They're gone for
ever.

The prophet Micah says, 'Thou wilt cast all our sins into
the depths of the sea' (Micah 7:19). From East to West, and
down to the bottom of the deepest sea - how much further can
you go? Read Hebrews 7:25: 'He is able to save to the
uttermost them that come unto God by Him.' As someone has
put it, 'From the guttermost to the uttermost!'

Where does the chorus come from which says:

> Gone, gone, gone, gone,
> All my sins are gone?

Anyway it's true - in Christ. Hallelujah for that!

Be thou faithful unto death,
and I will give thee the crown of Life
(Revelation 2:10).

It is a fruitless exercise to try and compare your own gifts and usefulness to God with that of some other person. We think, 'If only I could be like so-and-so, I could be much more useful in God's service; if only I could be a preacher like Billy Graham, a nurse like Florence Nightingale, a violinist like Kreisler, what couldn't I do for God?' The answer is that God has given to *every* Christian certain gifts, and it is His business to choose what gifts He wants to give. Our job is to make certain that the gifts we have received are being properly used, and that we are being faithful to our Calling.

God never called us to be successful - He called us to be faithful. If we are Christians, we are 'called and chosen and faithful'. God calls us and chooses us; our response is to be faithful.

Faithfulness to God also means being faithful to our friends, and to other people too. It's a great thing when people know they can trust you.

February 21

Thanks be to God who in Christ always leads us in triumph, and through us spreads the fragrance of the knowledge of Him everywhere. For we are the aroma of Christ (2 Corinthians 2:14,15).

What a lovely thought for Christians - we bring a 'whiff' of the fragrance of Jesus with us wherever we go! We are here, not to attract people to ourselves, but to draw them towards Jesus. When they see us, they should be thinking, 'How attractive Jesus Christ is!' - not 'How attractive *we* are!'

Attractive people, and there are some, need to exercise great care, because they are naturally tempted to be popular, to draw friends to themselves, to want to be always in the centre of the crowd, with people flocking round *them*. Even great preachers can do that; but when they disappear, there is nothing left, because they have only been drawing people to themselves. But God is always there, Jesus Christ is 'the same, yesterday, today and forever' (Hebrews 13:8). When you and I have gone to glory, Jesus will still be here and people we led to Him will still find Him, although we are gone.

Note that we are also described as 'salt' and 'light'. Salt keeps things fresh and clean. Light shows people the way to live.

There is one God, and there is one mediator between God and men, the man Christ Jesus, who gave Himself as a ransom for all (1 Timothy 2:5,6).

When God made the world, He made Man last of all. He was more concerned about Man than about any of the rest of His Creation - because 'He made Man in His own Image. In the Image of God created He him' (Genesis 1:27). Man fell - and God was sad; so sad that He determined to rescue Man, and resume His relationship with him. But the only way He could do it was by Himself becoming Man. Fancy the Creator becoming one of His own Creation!

The Second Adam, God-made-Man, became our Redeemer. Paul reminds us that it is only through that Second Adam, the Lord Jesus, that we can come back to God. He is the only One who can stand between us and God, and we cannot reach God in any other way, except through Him.

The other day, a man lost his dog in a rough sea, and he plunged into the sea to save his dog. But he failed - he was himself drowned. He gave his life for his dog, but sadly, both were lost. Jesus gave His life to save lost mankind, but here is the difference. He died, but He rose again, and so *we* can be saved.

That is why, when we pray, we pray 'through Jesus Christ our Lord'. He is our Mediator, our middle-man, between us and God. In our sins we couldn't come into God's Presence, but Jesus has cleansed us from our sins, by taking them all on Himself - so we are free to enter in.

Oh, dearly, dearly, has He loved.

Did you ever manage to get hold of that little book I mentioned to you in the notes for January 30, C S Lewis' *Screwtape Letters*? Because, if you did, you might turn it up again to read how Lewis describes 'The Church'. He writes about all the funny people who join the Church: the ragged folk, the deformed ones, the blind, the deaf, the people with squeaky boots, and so on. Why should we be linked up with them? Because it is only the Church that welcomes them in - they find a home there, and we belong to them, as together we face the world and its hazards.

Some people think you can manage to be a Christian without belonging to the Church. But you cannot, because it is 'His Body'. If you are not in the Church, you are not in His Body either.

Because lots of people who go to church are just as much sinners as anybody else, some people say, 'Why should we go to church?' Yet it is lovely when they come, because they are under the sound of the gospel. Nobody ever said that the Church was perfect. How could it, since it is filled with sinners? Forgiven sinners! Unforgiven ones come who we hope will find forgiveness too.

Of course, the Church is not a building of bricks and stones - that is only the shelter that houses the Church. The Church is people, and Jesus Himself is the Head of the Body. And He is *perfect*!

Without having seen Him, you love Him; though you do
not now see Him, you believe in Him, and rejoice with
unutterable and exalted *joy* (1 Peter 1:8).

Peter, who wrote this letter, had of course seen Jesus for
himself. He knew what he was writing about. But most of the
people who read his letter then had not seen Jesus, and all who
read it today have never seen Him. I think Peter must have
overheard what Jesus said to Thomas: 'Thomas, because you
have seen Me, you have believed. Blessed are those who have
not seen, and yet have believed' (John 20:29).

We've thought about this before. But it's good to be
reminded continually, that we walk by *faith*. The invisible
God speaks right into our hearts and we experience His love.
We see what a difference it makes to other people too, when
they have found Jesus for themselves.

The real *me* is not just a body with a mind; God has given
us souls too, and it is the soul that lives on when the body dies.
One day we'll have new bodies. All the old aches and pains
will be gone, all the sorrows too, when we *see* Him face to
face. And He's promised that we shall: 'Now we see in a
mirror, dimly, but then - face to Face' (1 Corinthians 13:12).
And it's *His* Face we shall see.

It is a sign for ever between Me and the people of Israel that
in six days the Lord made Heaven and earth, and on the
seventh day He rested, and was refreshed (Exodus 31:17).

The Jews kept Saturday as their rest-day. We keep Sunday as
ours, because it is the day on which Jesus rose again from the
dead. The important thing is not so much *which* day, as that a
day needs to be set aside from ordinary work, so that every
person can get refreshment and renewal. It is because the
renewal needed is not only for body and mind, but also for the
soul, that we make it a very special day when we give more
time to our meeting with God and with His people - the
Church.

The so-called Continental Sunday is one that is very
similar to all the other days of the week, and here in Britain we
are in grave danger of following their example. It's not only
Christians that need a 'day of rest' - it's everybody's need.

Each one of us, not just the parson, has our part to play in
making Sunday the happiest and most refreshing day of the
week. The service in church can be dead and cold if we are not
praying about it. Your minister needs your prayers for him as
he leads the service, that he may truly speak God's Word to
the people, and that the whole service may be a joy and
refreshment to everyone present. It should be a place to which
we rejoice to bring our non-Christian friends, in the hope that
God's Word may reach them too.

And who were the 'hypocrites'? The Greek word *hupokritai* means an actor in a play. He would dress himself up to represent some other person, in the hope that people who saw him acting would think how very realistic he was - though of course they knew he was not really the person he pretended to be. He was just a 'make-believe'.

Jesus says that when we pray, we are not to try and show off how good we are. Nor are we to babble out long prayers so that people will think how religious we are. We need not try to impress God either!

In the parable of the Pharisee and the publican, you'll remember that the Pharisee stood and 'prayed with himself'. He wasn't talking to God - he was just swanking to God how good he was. The other man beat upon his breast, and cried out, 'God be merciful to me a sinner!' Jesus said that he was justified.

In our worship we should be unself-conscious, not trying to impress other people or God, but seeking to meet Him truly in our hearts, and to hear His Word to us. There is always a word for us in every service we attend, if we are truly listening to *God*.

February 27

Blessed is the man who does not *walk*
in the counsel of the wicked, or *stand* in the way of sinners,
or *sit* in the seat of mockers (Psalm 1:1).

Walk - stand - sit - what a wonderful way to start the very first of the Psalms! It matters where we walk, with whom we stand, and how we sit. In other words, the concern of the Psalmist is for the whole of a person's way of life.

Wrong company can soon totally destroy your whole outlook on everything. It gets you distorted from the truth as it is in Jesus. Obviously this doesn't mean that you must never meet wicked people, sinners, and mockers. Of course you will constantly meet them. But your own personal stand will not be in fellowship with them, your way of life will be different, your fellowship will be with Christians because that is where your strength lies - *in Christ*.

The rest of this short Psalm tells you where you really stand. Meditating in God's Law, drawing refreshment from the Water of Life, kept by the power of God. But all the time, you'll also be reaching out to those who are still in the wrong paths, seeking to introduce them to the One who said of Himself, 'I am the Way, the Truth and the Life.'

WALK - STAND - SIT with Him.

The Eternal God is your refuge, and underneath are the
Everlasting Arms (Deuteronomy 33:27).

These words were spoken by an old, old man - a centenarian,
Moses - when he was 120 years old. They were almost his
very last words to the Israelites, as he left them to go up to
Mount Pisgah to die. He was speaking to them as they were
about to enter the Promised Land. They had spent forty years
wandering in the desert, before they found their way into
God's Promise for them - years when they badly needed, and
found, God's guiding Hand upon them.

I wonder how often they recalled those parting words of
Moses: the Eternal God is your refuge? They still very much
needed God's Guidance, Presence and Protection. And in our
own daily journey through Life, we too need to be sure that we
have that same certainty. When things are difficult and the
way is hard, where do we turn for help?

I think David has a commentary on this in Psalm 139:7-10,
where he says of God: 'Where could I go to escape from You?
If I went up to Heaven You would be there. If I lay down dead
You would be there. If I fly out to sea, even there Your Hand
would lead me, and Your right Hand would hold me.'

That's a wonderful thought, isn't it? Wherever we are, we
are never far away from God. He is always close at hand. And
the Everlasting Arms are very strong!

Why don't you believe Me?
(John 8:46).

Can you imagine people listening to one of Jesus' stories or sermons - with all the marvellous love and strength He put into it, all His desire to reach them and draw them into the Kingdom - and yet turning away from Him? In fact, this crowd of Jews, when He had finished talking to them, tried to stone Him to death (John 8:59).

Yet we are surprised when our friends take the same line and refuse to come to Jesus or follow Him. We may think it is our fault - we have not prayed enough about them, or we have been clumsy in the way we have tried to reach them. But remember, Jesus was often rejected. And He told us, 'If they have rejected Me, they will also reject you.'

In His own district He could do no mighty work. *But* - yes - there were a few who were healed, a few who followed Him. We must not count success by numbers. Jesus said that many would go down the broad road to destruction and that few would find the narrow road that leads to Life. Yet He said in John 6:40: 'And this is the will of Him that sent Me, that every one which seeth the Son and believeth on Him may have Everlasting Life, and I will raise him up at the last day.'

So we know that His offer of life is open to all. Our business is so to present it that people are drawn to Jesus. And some will be, thank God. Keep Faith with Him.

Woe is me! For I am lost, for I am a man of unclean lips,
and I dwell in the midst of a people of unclean lips; for my
eyes have seen the King, the Lord of Hosts (Isaiah 6:5).

Isaiah, at this time, was a young man who loved and admired
his king, Uzziah, who, at the height of his triumphs, had
suddenly died. Isaiah was shattered; his dream-king was
gone. At *that* point, God spoke to him. Isaiah had the glorious
vision of God in His beautiful temple at Jerusalem. As he
gazed at God's glory, he realised his own unworthiness; he
saw himself as unclean, unworthy to be in God's presence.
That was the point where God could use him. Cleansing was
given and he was forgiven. Then God called him and sent him
out to serve.

If we are ever to be of use to God, we first have to come
to a sense of our own weakness, sinfulness and unworthiness.
Perhaps this will come *through* a sense of the majesty, glory,
wonder and love of God. A God who created all the myriads
of stars and universes and all the marvels of this beautiful
world, a God who still has time to care for one individual like
me! He loved me enough to send His dear Son to die for *me*!

Isaiah's response was, 'Here am I, send me!' What is my
response to be?

While we were enemies, we were reconciled to God by the
death of His Son (Romans 5:10).

So often when we meet people who are hostile to God and His
people, we write them off. But this is a wrong attitude to have.
It is often when they are most bitter against God that they are
closest to the moment when they are nearest to being touched
by His love. This was true of Paul. Jesus met him when he was
on his way to Damascus to persecute the Christians, and he
was soundly converted.

It was Ananias who introduced Paul to the Christian
fellowship, when he came to him in his blindness and called
him, '*Brother* Saul.' Saul must have been astounded to hear
a Christian calling him 'Brother'. His heart was melted and
the scales dropped from his eyes (perhaps washed out by
tears), and he recognised that he needed Jesus and His
followers - he was now one of them. 'Enemies - reconciled.'

It still happens today. When we find enemies - there's
God's chance.

March 3

I have swept away your transgressions like a cloud, and
your sins like the morning mist (Isaiah 44:22).

Sometimes early in the morning on a summer day, you come
out into the garden and the whole country seems shrouded in
mist. You think, 'Oh! dear, it's going to be a dull, cold day.'
But presently the sun peeps through and, before you know
where you are, the mist has disappeared and there isn't a cloud
in the sky. You're in for a really hot day and you go out and
bask in the sun; you feel on top of the world.

Isaiah tells us that that is just what it is like to be forgiven.
All the defeats and deadness and blackness of sin, which have
almost engulfed you, are suddenly swept away. God has
forgiven and cleansed you, and you just bask in the sunshine
of His love.

It ought to be like that always if you are a Christian. But
all of us have moods from time to time when we feel as if
everything is going wrong. The clouds may be there; but with
Christ, we are to rise above them into the sunshine. Let Him
fill you with His love today.

The dying thief said to Jesus, 'Lord, remember me when You come in Your kingly power.' And Jesus said to him, 'Truly, I say to you, today you will be with Me in Paradise' (Luke 23:39-43).

How long does it take to repent? Difficult to say. Jacob had to wrestle with the angel all night before he was truly right with God. But the thief on the cross did not have all night - his chance was only a matter of an hour or two. But the forgiveness was immediate, as it always is.

When we have wronged someone else, we should put it right with them as well as with God. It isn't always possible to put right the wrong that has been done. Certainly the thief had no time to restore anything he had ever stolen.

Zacchaeus promised to restore what he had taken wrongly. But I suspect he found it a difficult job to carry out. Could he ever remember all the people he had wronged? Maybe he kept a book, because he was dealing with money!

If we are not *willing* to put it right with *man*, can we expect *God's* forgiveness?

The unfolding of Thy Word giveth light; it imparts understanding to the simple (Psalm 119:130).

Paul writes in Ephesians 3:8 about 'The unsearchable riches
of Christ'; he says, 'His ways are past finding out.' I think one
of the exciting things about the Bible is that you can never get
to the bottom of it, there's always something fresh to find in
it. Jesus once said to His disciples: 'To you it is given to know
the secrets of the Kingdom of God' (Luke 8:10).

The Bible can be understood by simple folk and yet the
greatest theologians in the world can never plumb all its
depths. So a little child can understand enough and the
cleverest man can never know too much about God's Word.
If we are Christians, all of us are learners all our lives. 'Mary
sat at Jesus' feet' - the best place to learn (Luke 10:42).

From the front of the Bible given by Grannie –in her
handwriting:

The Scriptures
'I long for the husbandman to sing parts of them to
himself as he follows the plough, for the weaver to
hum them to the accompaniment of his shuttle, for the
traveller to beguile the tedium of journeying with
them' (Erasmus, 1500 AD from his introduction to his
translation of the Greek New Testament).

Pray at all times (Ephesians 6:18).

When you hear the word 'pray', what does it put into your mind? Does it make you think, 'Oh, dear, I suppose I ought to be praying more than I do', or, 'How long should my prayers last if I'm to satisfy God?' In other words, is it a burden to be borne? Or can we change the phrase and say that prayer is 'making friends with God'?

To make friends with anyone, you really need to meet fairly often. If you never meet, friendship is very difficult to keep up. You can write letters to each other, but unless you meet as well, letters can sometimes lead you astray, because you can't hear the tone of voice that is being used.

Now, this is one of our difficulties - we cannot *see* God. Nor can we *hear* His actual voice with our outward ears. But let me use an illustration from experience. If you live alone in a house, you have nobody to speak to, unless you go out or someone comes in or you use the telephone. If none of these are possible, what do you do? You speak to *yourself*. We do this because we need companionship, and we are imagining that someone is present to whom we speak.

I believe that is where God comes in. We can talk to Him about anything at any time, and especially when nobody else is there. We can listen to Him speaking to our inner ear - our mind, our conscience and our heart, if you like. The Bible is one way in which He speaks to us, it's like getting a letter from a friend.

Prayer does not have to be only at our bedside or in church, it can be anywhere at any time, long or short. We never cease to learn, the more we pray. Stand, walk, lie or sit - whatever suits the occasion.

Let another praise you and not your own mouth
(Proverbs 27:2).

This is rather a tricky one, isn't it? Because all of us like to be thought well of and to know that other people admire us. But if we suggest it to them, they will almost certainly think we are either bossy or too pleased with ourselves.

How does this characteristic show itself? In lots of different ways I think. Like this: if we hear someone else boasting of their achievements, we rather like to be able to cap it with our own. It's sometimes called 'One-up-man-ship'. When we hear it in other people, we don't like it very much. If that's so, we need to watch our own step very carefully.

But apart from anything else, we should remember that if we have any rather special gifts, either physically or mentally, they are 'gifts' from God. So we have nothing to boast about. If God has given us special qualities, we need to give them back to Him so that He can use them in us to His own glory.

Our business as disciples of Christ is to encourage other people to follow Him. So we should care more about them and their needs than of ourselves. But that doesn't mean that we should in any way despise ourselves. No, because God made us to His glory. The ambassador of a king should always be a gracious and attractive person, reflecting something of the majesty of his king. And that's true in Christian service.

How can I best praise God today?

You come to me with a sword and a spear ... but David
prevailed with a sling and stone (1 Samuel 17:45,50).

At this time, David was reckoned to be too young to be a
soldier. His brothers despised him. Yet, he was the only
person prepared to take on Goliath the giant. Did he think he
was stronger that Goliath? No, he didn't. But he was trusting
in God. Goliath had been blaspheming against God, and
David knew he must defend God's honour. The stone and the
sling, under God's mighty hand, overcame the sword and the
spear.

It was David's trust in God that enabled God to say that he
was 'a man after God's own heart' (Acts 13:22). God can take
the simple and weak qualities that most of us possess, and use
them to achieve His mighty purposes.

What a pity that David blotted his copy-book with his sin
against Uriah and Bathsheba! The occasion of that was when
he should have been fighting alongside his armies in battle,
but he was instead slacking at home with nothing to do. Satan
always finds mischief for idle hands to do.

A messenger for God needs to keep himself always close
to his Master.

PRAYER
Lord, keep my eyes fixed on You this day, that I may bring
honour to Your Name. AMEN.

March 9

In the world you have tribulation, but be of good cheer, I
have overcome the world (John 16:33).

Yes, every one of us is going to suffer at some time. But Jesus
says, 'When this happens, don't be depressed. I have overcome the world.' That's the antidote to be applied the moment
we feel depressed - it's the sign for remembering *His Victory*.

Tribulation takes different forms. Sometimes it is opposition by God's enemies. Sometimes it is physical sickness.
Sometimes it is just feeling alone, far from God's help.
Sometimes it is feeling we can't achieve our ambitions - we
try - but we see no light at the end of the tunnel. Sometimes we
feel it hard to pray, or we just want to take things easy and give
up.

That is the *point* where Jesus says to us, 'Cheer up, we're
winning this battle, together.' Remember this verse: 'A cheerful heart is good medicine' - 'depression makes dried bones'!
(Proverbs 17:22).

A little Holy Spirit oil on the dry bones today will get us
moving!

'Bless the LORD, O my soul ... who forgives all your iniquity, who heals all your diseases' (Psalm 103:2,3).

Have you noticed how, sometimes, when Jesus met with a sick person, He began by dealing with their sins before He tackled the disease from which they were suffering? I am sure that not all sickness is coupled with sin, but it certainly is sometimes. I suppose it's true to say that when our sins are forgiven and we are spiritually free, the whole personality is so refreshed by God that the physical sickness clears up too.

A case in point is the paralysed man in Luke 5:17-26. His friends carried him to the house where Jesus was teaching and healing. Because of the crowd, they had to lower him down through the roof. Jesus said to him, 'Friend, your sins are forgiven.' Only *later* did He say to him, 'Get up, take up your bed, and go home' ... and he went home, praising God.

Another case where sin is mentioned in connection with a man's healing is that of the paralysed man at the Pool of Bethesda (John 5:1-15). He'd been an invalid for 38 years and could get no healing anywhere. Jesus said to him, 'Pick up your bed and walk' (verse 8). And he did just that. Later he met Jesus again, and Jesus said to him, 'See, you are well again. Stop sinning, or something worse may happen to you' (verse 14).

I suppose the fact is that sin is a disease of the heart and mind and that the *whole person* needs cleansing by Jesus. I've just been reading *Freed for Life* by Rita Nightingale. She had been imprisoned in Thailand for smuggling heroin - but she was in fact innocent of the offence. There was tremendous rejoicing at her release, but long before her release she found her way to Jesus as Saviour. She was spiritually freed first.

You He made alive, when you were dead through the
trespasses and sins in which you once walked
(Ephesians 2:1,2).

Just as Jesus was able to resurrect the physically dead, such
as Lazarus, so He was, and is able today, to bring to new life
people who are spiritually dead. Sometimes when we talk
with such folk, we feel that there's almost nothing we have in
common with them, because as Christians we are living on a
different plane. And when we speak about spiritual things,
they just haven't a clue what we are talking about. To them it's
just foolishness.

But the marvellous thing is that those very people, when
God really touches them, can suddenly come to Life, and
immediately we are in fellowship with them. How? Well, it's
a miracle of God's grace, and nobody can explain it. This is
specially true for those who have not been brought up in a
Christian home. The contrast is greater for them. But the
necessity for the New Birth is equally great for all of us.

When we are born into the world, we are not committed to serving Christ, because we don't yet know Him. So we don't have a very good start; we need to be found by Jesus. When that happens, we immediately come under new management. We may not have been consciously serving the devil, but we have been pleasing ourselves. And the selfishness that engenders is something that needs to be dealt with by Christ, because now we are learning to serve Him.

All Christians know the tug-of-war that goes on in their hearts, when they want to do something that they know Jesus would not approve of. Paul put it like this: 'I have the desire to do what is good, but I cannot carry it out' (Romans 7:18). And he went on in verse 24 to say, 'What a wretched man I am! Who will rescue me from this body of death?' But he found the answer when he said, 'Thanks be to God through Jesus Christ our Lord' (verse 25). That struggle will be with us till we come to the end of our earthly days, and are face to face with God in Heaven. Only *there* is there no sin.

But in Christ, we are on the winning side. Our sins are forgiven. Jesus gives us strength to resist them, and He picks us up when we tumble. Paul knew this for he cried out in the next chapter, 'The Law of the Spirit of Life has set me free from the law of sin and death' (Romans 8:2), and he went on to say in verse 16: 'The Spirit Himself testifies with our spirit that we are God's children'. That's it, isn't it? Now we serve Christ. We belong to Him; we have turned right round to follow Him. He will keep us His *for ever*!

This is the motto for all Christians, isn't it? It's the great banner that flies over the big tent at the Keswick Convention each year, where Christians of many denominations meet together to have fellowship in Jesus, and the barriers that separate them are recognised as being less important than the truths that unite them.

It is also true in a Christian family, when all the family are believers, that the little things in one that annoy other members of the family take second place to the big truths that bind them together in Christ. This doesn't mean that we can conveniently forget our selfishness and not bother if we hurt others. No - it's just because we are 'brothers and sisters in Christ' that we must take care how we treat each other. They are just as important to God as we are, and He loves them just as much as He loves us. And it's inter-racial, too.

> Red and yellow, black and white,
> All are precious in His sight.

And this is the strength of the Christian Church today - we have one Master in common, Christ Jesus. So we need to 'live in harmony with one another' (Romans 12:16).

Commit your work to the LORD,
and your plans will be established (Proverbs 16:3).

Day by day we make all sorts of plans about what we are going to do: the things we shall make, the people we will meet, the lessons we will learn, the fun we will have; all the many things that are on our minds.

It is at that point that the Bible says to us, 'OK - but bring all these things, these plans, to the test of God's Word.' Ask His guidance for your schemes. Some of them may need to be altered, some perhaps to be dropped. We are under orders; we have a Leader who instructs us in the way in which we should go. Consult Him, therefore.

This same chapter of Proverbs goes on to remind us, 'A man's *mind* plans his *way*, but the *Lord* directs his *steps*' (verse 9). That's wise guidance. It is marvellous when you look back at the end of the day and can say, 'Today, God kept me from mis-managing my day; He helped me to keep it straight and to clear my hurdles properly. Thank you, Lord.'

March 15

Jonah was angry ... And the L<small>ORD</small> said,
'Do you do well to be angry?' (Jonah 4:4).

Obviously there are times when each Christian should be angry.
But there are problems connected with anger. What do we get
angry *about*? Is it about some imagined hurt that has been done
to us by someone else? Is it because we have been slighted by
another person?

Jonah's anger was twofold, I think. He had been sent by God
to warn the people of Nineveh that if they didn't repent of their
sins, God would punish them. First of all, Jonah didn't want to
go - hence the whale! But later, after he did go and preach to
them, the people did repent; but Jonah was angry because they
didn't get punished - he reckoned that the Ninevites would think
his prophecies didn't work! So he wasn't really trying to justify
God - only to justify his own prophecies. Jonah was not angry for
God's honour, he only thought of himself.

It helps to think of the occasions when Jesus Himself was
angry. Once was when He went into the Temple at Jerusalem and
found a mass of public trading going on, in place of worship of
God. He was angry for God's honour and glory.

He was angry when mothers brought their children to Him
to be blessed, and the disciples tried to keep them away.

He was angry when Peter tried to tell Him He must not allow
Himself to be crucified, for He saw it as a deliberate attempt by
Satan to thwart Him.

PRAYER
Keep us, Lord, from any kind of sinful anger,
but make us very concerned for your honour and reputation,
not for our own. AMEN.

March 16

They who wait upon the LORD shall renew their strength;
they shall mount up with wings like eagles,
they shall run and not be weary,
they shall walk and not faint (Isaiah 40:31).

Flying, running, walking - three ways of making progress! Flying is obviously the fastest way of getting about. Running is the most painful way, we get out of breath. Walking is in a sense the dullest, it's so slow! Well, here is Isaiah the prophet writing to remind us of all three.

I think when you first become a Christian, you feel on top of the world. Something new and wonderful has happened to you, and you know life will never be the same again. You are almost breathless with excitement - it's as though you were flying through the air! There will also come later occasions when you feel the same, and life will fly past.

But for most of us, these are not frequent occasions. In our early days, we truly *run* for the Lord. There will be many occasions when something special is on. An evangelistic meeting to which we can take a friend, and perhaps that friend comes to Christ - great joy. Or we ourselves come into some special blessing from Jesus.

But all of us know that the ordinary, everyday life may be more like humdrum walking. Nothing very special to get excited about, duties to be done, exams to be worked for, housework calling for help, beds to be made, washing up, getting up in time to have a proper Quiet Time with God.

Fly like eagles - run with zest - walk with patience. Whatever it is to be today for us, as we start with God, He has promised to give us all the strength we need.

The Race is on!

March 17
The Son of Man has come eating and drinking
(Luke 7:34).

Jesus had been talking with the Pharisees, who were determined to find fault with Him if they could. He reminded them that John the Baptist came fasting and didn't drink wine, yet they said, 'He has a devil'. But Jesus Himself ate and drank well, but they said He was greedy and friendly to wicked people.

The point is that a Christian will always be liable to criticism from enemies of the gospel, and we should expect this, though not to seek for it. What we have to do is to be natural, as Jesus always was. Sometimes rejoicing, as at a lovely wedding; sometime weeping with mourners at a funeral.

And we have moods, don't we? Sometime we're right on top, at other times we are defeated by sin. If life is difficult for us, so it was for Him. He knows and understands how we feel, He forgives when we repent, He encourages us all the way along. When we are ill, He reminds us that 'His strength is made perfect in our weaknesses', and He never lets go of us.

PRAYER
Whatever is Your plan for me today,
O Lord, keep me under Your powerful Hand,
and help me to be my best for You this day. AMEN.

March 18

Here we have no lasting city,
but we seek the city which is to come (Hebrews 13:14).

What a world of difference there is between those who are real Christians, and folk who really don't know God! The whole aims of the two are totally at cross purposes with each other. A Christian is in fact a 'man of two worlds'. He is both a citizen of this material world, but he is also a citizen of another world that he will come to in due course, after he reaches the end of this world.

When anyone dies, all that they have accumulated in this life is left behind, nothing can be taken into the next world. The worldly man, who doesn't believe there is another world, reckons he must get all he can and enjoy it in this life, and when he dies his family must have it. Maybe he'll try and help those less fortunate than himself, but he is not in any sense preparing himself for any *future* existence, he can only live for the present.

The Christian knows that God has placed him here to live for God's glory, and to prepare himself for an eternity with God in a new world where sin has no place. He knows he is living at present in a lost world, where man has come under the slavery of darkness and sin. He knows that people need to be rescued and brought to salvation in Christ, so that they may enter the New World that is yet to come, and see the King of Glory in all His majesty and beauty.

PRAYER

Keep our eyes fixed upon You, Lord,
and help us to be true citizens both of this world and the next.
For Your Name's sake. AMEN.

March 19
Called to belong to Jesus Christ
(Romans 1:6).

What a marvellous thing to happen, to be actually *called* to belong to the King of Kings! Sometimes I have thought what a wonderful thing it must be to be called to join the Royal Household at Buckingham Palace - what a privilege! How I would have to know all the etiquette, how to do the particular duties that were laid upon those there. And how I would love to be of service to the Queen herself.

But our calling as Christians is an even greater one than that; even the Queen herself is called to be a servant of the King of Kings! I'm not surprised that Matthew the tax collector 'left everything and followed Him' (Luke 5:27, 28). It is, after all, the greatest calling in the whole wide world.

In Romans 1 Paul says he himself was a servant, 'called to be an Apostle', and that the Christians to whom he wrote were 'called to be saints'. Called out of darkness - called into Light - called to His Glory; how can anybody ever refuse such a marvellous calling?

PRAYER
Lord, You have called me, You have chosen me;
help me to be faithful. AMEN.

Worship the Lord in the beauty of Holiness
(1 Chronicles 16:29).

There is a lovely hymn that has been written upon this verse. I'll just give you the first verse:

> O worship the Lord in the beauty of Holiness,
> Bow down before Him, His glory proclaim;
> With gold of obedience, and incense of lowliness
> Kneel and adore Him: the Lord is His Name.

When we come into the very Presence of God, we need to take time just to quiet our hearts and to remember to whom we are talking, and who is wanting to talk to us. This is why in Hebrews 12:28 it speaks of our 'offering God acceptable worship, with reverence and awe'.

I think if I were speaking to the Queen, I would be pretty scared lest I said the wrong thing or spoke out of turn. I wouldn't want to offend her in any way. How much more, when I am being received into the very Presence of Almighty God Himself, do I need to ponder before I speak. Above all I want to praise Him for all that He is, and all that He has done, and all that He has promised that He will do - My Saviour!

The fruit of the Spirit is Love, Joy, Peace, Patience,
Kindness, Goodness, Faithfulness, Gentleness, Self-
control; against such, there is no law
(Galatians 5:22,23).

What a basketful of nine pieces of such lovely fruit! And in
Galatians it follows on after a horrible bagful of seventeen
foul and evil things which spoil the lives of those who have not
yet become servants of Jesus.

I don't imagine that all those lovely nine characteristics
become the immediate possession of the Spirit-filled Christian; but I think that, like earthly fruit, they have to grow. And
I'm sure they take a whole lifetime, and then some, before
they all come to perfect wholeness.

But it's lovely to know that as we increasingly allow the
Lord Jesus to have His Way in our hearts and lives, so He
changes us that we become more and more like Him day by
day, until eventually we see Him face to face. He has promised that 'when we see Him, we shall be like Him' (1 John
3:2).

Sometimes as I look at myself, I wonder if I shall ever be
at all like Him. But that's a promise, and we can claim it for
ourselves. Certainly as I look at some people even now, I can
see the 'Family Likeness' in them.

No prophecy ever came by the impulse of man, but men
moved by the Holy Spirit spoke from God (2 Peter 1:21).

This is what makes the Bible so different from any other book
that has ever been written. Nobody has to believe what they
see written in a book if they don't want to. But if that book is
one that has been written down under the direction of God
Himself, it's a different matter.

This book is one we neglect at our peril. St. Paul tells us
that 'what was written in the past was written to teach us, so
that through endurance and the encouragement of the Scriptures, we might have hope' (Romans 15:4). It's our guidebook
to life, both this life, and to Life Eternal.

If you travel by car on an unknown road, you need to have
a map or you won't know where you are going. If you ask a
friend, 'Why did you come into the world?' - 'What are you
going to do in the world?' - 'Where will you go after this life?'
- they can only guess at the answers, unless they are true
Christians. But if you ask them, 'How can you get to Edin-
burgh from Birmingham?' they will tell you, 'Look at your
road map, and you'll see how to go.' If we need a map for that
kind of travel, how much more do we need one for our journey
through this life and into the next!

On my birthday in 1935, my dear Sylvia gave me a Bible,
and inscribed these words from George Herbert on the fly-leaf:

> It is the index to Eternity,
> He cannot miss of endless bliss
> that takes this chart to steer his vessel by,
> Nor can he be mistook,
> 'That speaketh by the Book'.

God has made everything beautiful in its time. He has also
set Eternity in the hearts of men (Ecclesiastes 3:11).

This really follows on from yesterday's reading about the
Guide Book. Mankind all over the world has always tried to
find out if this life is the only one we shall ever have. The
instinct is there that, somehow, there *must be* something more
to life than just this short span of around 70-80 years.

The other day, I was called to the bedside of an old lady
of 97 who was dying. She wanted to see me urgently. I had
known her for about twelve years, and she had always kept
away from spiritual things - she was a non-church goer and I
think a non-believer. But now, suddenly, she knew she was
going and she wondered *where*?

Was she too late? Could she face God, when she had
neglected Him all her life? Would He have mercy on her?
How could she find Him? She was far gone and I hadn't time
to say much. I reminded her of the dying thief on the cross. I
gave her just two verses of scripture - Revelation 3:20 and
John 5:24. I prayed with her and left. 1 asked the woman
looking after her to ring me at once if she wanted me again.
Two days later she was gone and the woman said she was at
peace with God.

But what a tragedy - to live to 97 without God and then to
turn to Him for only her last two days! For most people, that
would be too late - they'd be unconscious at that stage.
'Eternity in her heart?' Yes, I think so.

Do not be conformed to this world, but be transformed by
the renewal of your mind, that you may prove what is that
good and acceptable and perfect will of God
(Romans 12:2).

For our life in this world, we have a choice of two ways:
conformation or transformation. We can either find out what
the rest of the world wants to do, how they want to live and
behave, and throw in our lot with them - which they would
certainly want and expect us to do - that is what Paul means
by *conformation*. Or we can experience something quite
different, which Paul calls *transformation*. *Transformation* is
not something that we do, but something that God does, when
we let Him.

When we surrender heart and life to Jesus Christ, slowly
and steadily He begins to work in us. It doesn't happen all at
once, but from the very beginning our course is set in a different
way from that of the rest of the world. We are set, not to do what
we choose, but what God chooses for us. And, steadily, bit by
bit and day by day, we begin to become *like Him*.

Have you ever noticed how many old ladies seem to like
to have a little dog and when they've been together for some
time, they really begin to *look* rather alike; they have a set
pattern of life, and they both want to live it out.

Well, it's like that with people too. If they are set on
serving Jesus and living with and for Him, they begin to look
like real Christians; when you meet such people you say to
yourself: 'Just like his or her Master.' The opposite is also
true. When people live for themselves only, their very face
turns hard and bitter in time - like their master Satan.

'No man can serve two masters.'

'Son, why have You treated us so? Behold Your father and
I have been looking for You anxiously.' And Jesus said to
them, 'How is it that you sought Me? Did you not know
that I must be in My Father's House?' (Luke 2:48-51).

'Your father?' 'My Father?' Did they mean the same thing?
No, but His mother didn't understand that at first. It was a long
time before she understood who Jesus really was.

Obviously He had been brought up in a godly household
and - rightly - one of the rules of the house was obedience to
parents.

But there comes a point in every human life when a
personal choice has to be made, and that choice is not always,
or necessarily, one which has the full approval of one's
parents. Jesus was only twelve years old at that time, yet even
then He had begun to realise something of what His Heavenly
Father had in store for Him. He had stayed behind in the
Temple to talk with the Teachers of the Law and the Scriptures, questioning whether their interpretation of the Scriptures was a right one.

He went home with Joseph and Mary, and obeyed them
until He was older, helping in the home, and also in the
carpentry business in which Joseph was engaged.

He was thirty when His 'public' ministry began, but all
those years He was preparing for what was to happen in the
next three momentous years, years which were to change the
whole history of the world.

'My Father's *House*.' The Authorised Version here has
'My Father's *business*'. That is a business which is also the
concern of every Christian. We can serve Him in many
different ways, but we need to prepare for that service daily.

Search me, O God, and know my heart! Try me, and know my thoughts! And see if there be any wicked way in me, and lead me in the Way Everlasting! (Psalm 139:23,24).

There are times when we need to search our own hearts to see whether we are really being true to God. But it's a good thing to do this with an open Bible before us, otherwise we might very easily become despondent and discouraged at our falling so short of God's expectation of us. We don't find it difficult to find things that are wrong in us, but we have the promise of God's forgiveness: 'If we confess our sins, He is faithful and just to forgive us our sins, and to cleanse us from *all* unrighteousness' (1 John 1:9).

The Bible tells us that 'God is Love', and if the God who is love is living in our hearts and lives, 1 Corinthians 13 gives us a very good idea of how this will affect all our daily living and especially our behaviour towards other people. I am sure you know the acrostic on *joy*. It means,

*J*esus first -
*O*thers second -
*Y*ourself last -

and certainly that way of life is quite the most joyful, because it brings joy to all three: to Him first of all; to all the people who take precedence over our own needs and desires; and when we know we are pleasing Him and concerned for others, it also gives us the greatest Joy.

PRAYER
Lead me, Lord, in the Way Everlasting.

Do your best to come to me soon ...
Luke alone is with me (2 Timothy 4:9,11).

As he wrote this letter to Timothy, Paul was in prison. He was feeling very lonely, because other friends had left him, and one, Demas, had gone right back on his Christian faith. He would have been totally bereft, if it had not been for Doctor Luke! So he begs Timothy, his own 'son in the faith', the man he had led to Christ, to come to him soon.

Of course, Paul wasn't totally alone, because Jesus was with him in that prison cell, even though Paul couldn't see Him. But Paul was in great need of human Christian fellowship.

Whenever we see fellow-Christians in a lonely situation, we should always get alongside them to encourage them if we possibly can. As the writer of Ecclesiastes says, 'Two are better than one ... If one falls down, the other can help him up, but pity the man who has no one to help him up when he falls' (Ecclesiastes 4:9).

You never know when you yourself will need that kind of help. So look out today for anyone who is in need of a friend, you're almost sure to find someone to help.

I know your works: you are neither cold nor hot. Would
that you were cold or hot! So, because you are lukewarm,
and neither cold nor hot, I will spew you out of my mouth
(Revelation 3:15,16).

Lukewarm! What's that like? The dictionary says 'the un-
pleasant taste of *warm* water causes vomiting!' The Greek
word for 'hot' is *zestos*, from which we get our English word
zest. And that's a lovely thing to have about you - to be full of
zest, keen and ready to bring your best efforts to the job in
hand.

This church of Laodicea was just lukewarm, it made Jesus
feel sick! I like drinking cold water, and hot water too is nice
to drink if you think you've a cold coming on. But lukewarm?
Ugh!

Christians who are lukewarm are really no good to anybody. The church to which they belong is not helped because
they are just passengers. The world in which they live is not
influenced for Christ because they are not showing any signs
of Christlikeness; indeed they may even cause non-Christians
to say the church is no good. So Jesus says that He is going to
vomit them up! What a terrible thing to have said of you.

Have you ever gone to bed with a hot-water-bottle and
found in the middle of the night that it is just tepid? If so, what
do you do with it? Well, don't give God reason to do that with
you, and I trust He'll never have to do it with me either. Keep
close to Jesus, and then you will warm others also.

March 29
Open my eyes, that I may behold wondrous
things out of Thy Law (Psalm 119:18).

This 119th Psalm is entirely about God's Word, I think in almost every verse it refers to the Word of God. And it's also a wonderful acrostic. Every 8 verses in it begin with a different letter of the Hebrew Alphabet, so that by the end of the Psalm you have gone through most of the alphabet. The first 8 verses all begin with A, the next 8 with B, and so on. This of course is only in the Hebrew.

As you study God's Word, more and more you find out wonderful things about it. Every time you read it, even if you have read the passage many times before, you almost always find something fresh you had not seen before. The older you get, the more you find, yet you never reach the end when you can learn no more.

You can, of course, read God's Word mechanically, so that you take in nothing at all. It's a good thing to ask God to open the eyes of your heart and your understanding so that you don't miss the things God is wanting to say to you. If ever you get to the end of your portion for the day and have learnt nothing fresh, it is a good thing to turn back again and ask God to show you something you may have missed.

'Wondrous things' are certainly there to be had!

By faith we understand that the world was created by the
Word of God, so that what is seen was made out of things
which do not appear (Hebrews 11:3).

As I write, on my table I have a knobbly sort of ugly potato in
a pot which I have been watering every day. It has begun to
sprout and a huge long stem has shot up, and out of it this
morning have suddenly blossomed two most beautiful scarlet
lilies, each about 6 inches across, and the whole room is
transformed by the sight of them! 'What is seen was made out
of things that do not appear'!

How could this ugly potato produce such beautiful things?
Well, this is just a tiny part of God's handiwork. Man couldn't
do this. Oh, I know that man can doctor the bulb and make it
do wonders of growth - but the actual growth itself and the
texture of that lily and its colour is *God's* work.

What a marvellous world God has given us, and how easy
it is for man to spoil God's world. If we can do anything to
enable God's world to be its best and loveliest, that surely is
at least part of a Christian's calling.

If we have a garden, share it with others, and keep it tidy
and beautiful, so that people may praise - not us - but Him.
Have you ever studied under a magnifying glass the feather
off a wing of a butterfly? It's a wonderful sight. Man could not
produce such a thing in a thousand years. 'Even Solomon in
all his glory was not arrayed like one of these.'

Thank God for His world.

These are written that you may believe that Jesus is the
Christ, the Son of God, and that believing you may have
Life in His Name (John 20:31).

We sometimes wonder what were the things that Jesus did
that were not written down. There must have been very many
on which there has been no report. Why, for instance, have we
no report of His years from 12-30? Would not that be of
enormous interest to everyone? Yes, I'm sure it would and
perhaps one day we'll know all about those early days of His.
But John says, 'Lots of other things were done by Him which
we have not written down.' Why? Well, obviously they could
not have written everything down. So what did they choose?
John says they chose enough to enable us to put our full trust
in Him and find our way into His marvellous Life.

Nobody reading what *has* been written down can miss the
Way, if they really want to find it. John says, 'Read it, and
believe; and if your belief is *real*, everlasting life will be your
present and future possession.'

Lots of people put Him to the test: John, Peter, Thomas,
and many others. John heard and saw; Peter grabbed the hand
of Jesus; Thomas saw and believed, but Jesus said to him,
'Blessed are those who have not seen, and yet have believed',
and that includes you and me. We are blessed. No doubt about
that!

When Daniel knew that the document had been signed, he went to his house ... and he got down upon his knees three times a day and prayed and gave thanks before his God, as he had done previously (Daniel 6:10).

Daniel had learnt that loyalty to God had to come before everything else. And it was something that showed consistently in him on every occasion. Remember, he was a captive in a land that had taken him and his friends into slavery, and those slaves had somehow to try and show their captors what God was like.

1. He and his friends refused food that was harmful, and stuck to their own wholesome diet.

2. They insisted on worship of God alone, and refused to worship a human king, even though they knew this would involve being thrown to the lions.

So they knew they would be out of favour with the authorities, they knew they might well lose their own lives. Yet they held firm, when everyone else would have said they were fools. And God protected them (He doesn't always do so) and Daniel became the chief man in the land.

The same sort of temptations beset Christians today in every part of the world. Many are in prison for that loyalty, many cannot get a job because of making that stand for Christ. Young people are unpopular at school because of it - *but God honours those who are faithful*! And in the long run, *that* is what matters.

I have been crucified with Christ; it is no longer I that live,
but Christ who lives in me: and the life I now live in the
flesh. I live by faith in the Son of God, who loved me and
gave Himself for me (Galatians 2:20).

Yesterday I watched a film on TV of the life and death of Paul
and Peter. It was most moving, and I saw them standing for
Jesus right up to the last, and ultimately dying for Him - Paul
in the arena, and Peter crucified upside down. It was terrible,
but wonderful, especially when I knew it was *true*!

When Paul wrote this verse in his letter to the Galatian
Christians, he was recollecting all that had happened to him
since that day on the Damascus Road, when Jesus met him
and spoke to him, and Paul had that miraculous conversion.
He became the foremost missionary of his day - probably of
any day - in direct contrast to his earlier life of persecuting the
Christians. How could he manage to keep on, after all the
beatings, the shipwreck, the mockery, the hardships? I think
this verse gives the answer.

It was as though, in his sufferings, he saw them as being
part of the sufferings of Jesus. It was as though he had even
died on the cross. But there was a difference. In fact, his life
had been handed over to Jesus, and he reckoned that Jesus was
now in him, directing and controlling him, and in fact living
out His life in Paul.

What was true for Paul should also characterise the life of
every Christian. Jesus wants to live through us.

And Barnabas wanted to take with them John called Mark. But Paul thought best not to take with them one who had withdrawn from them in Pamphylia, and had not gone with them to the work (Acts 15:37-38).

Poor Mark - he had got scared when he was in the middle of Paul's first missionary journey, and gone home. It wasn't the first time he got scared, because he is reputed to be the young man who was present when Jesus was seized at night before the crucifixion, and who fled away naked when the soldiers tried to grab him!

In both cases, he knew he should have stuck it - but sheer fright drove him away. Thank God that Jesus understands our fears, and that they can be forgiven, and overcome.

Paul wouldn't take him on again. But Barnabas did - gave him a second, even a third chance. And it saved Mark for Christ. Because later Paul met him in Rome, and they were reconciled. And it was Mark who eventually wrote the first of the Gospels to be written down. Thank God for Barnabas, who could see that God really wanted Mark, and who wouldn't let him go.

People today are often scared to become Christians, or if they have become one, are too frightened to speak up for Jesus when they know they should. It's a wonderful rescue service if you know someone who's afraid, and you can stand alongside and encourage them. Keep your eyes skinned for someone like that today.

I was hungry and you gave Me food, I was thirsty and you
gave Me drink, I was a stranger and you welcomed Me
(Matthew 25:35).

This was part of a parable that Jesus told when He put into
parable form what was going to happen at the Second Coming. He was explaining how He would know the difference
between the real Christians and the sham ones. He called it the
difference between the sheep and the goats.

He said: 'The difference is this: When I was hungry, you
gave Me food; when I was thirsty, you gave Me drink; when
I was a stranger, you invited Me in; when I was sick, you
visited Me.' The 'sheep' answer: 'When did we ever see *You*
under these conditions?' Jesus replies: 'If that is how you
have treated other people, it's just as though you did it to *Me*.'
Then the goats say, 'But we never saw *You*!' And Jesus says,
'No, I came in human form, and you saw suffering people, and
you did nothing. It was *Me* you were neglecting.'

If we ever think it's a bore to be helping someone in need,
remember what Jesus said about it! You have a further
reminder of this in Hebrews 13:2: 'Do not forget to entertain
strangers, for by so doing, some people have entertained
angels without knowing it!' That's a thought, isn't it?

Therefore God has highly exalted Him and bestowed on Him the Name which is above every name, that at the name of Jesus every knee should bow, in heaven and on earth and under the earth, and every tongue confess that Jesus Christ is Lord, to the glory of God the Father (Philippians 2:9-11).

The passage I've selected has a prelude to it. Listen: 'Jesus ... made Himself nothing ... humbled Himself, and became obedient to death, even death on a cross.' *This* is what had to happen first. He had to become 'in the form of a *slave*', the lowest of the low, before God could exalt Him to be the Highest of the High.

Supposing He had decided to remain always in Heaven and in glory, what would have happened to us? We should be left still in our sins, never able to reach God's Heaven, because sin cannot come into His Presence. The only way to reach us was for Him to become one of us. And the reward we gave Him for that was to crucify Him!

'While we were still sinners ... and *enemies*, Christ died for us' (Romans 5:8,10).

> He died that we might be forgiven.
> He died to make us good,
> That we might go at last to Heaven,
> Saved by His precious Blood.

It's because of *that*, that we can join in that great 'Hallelujah Chorus'.

I will give them one heart, and put a new spirit within them; I will take the stony heart out of their flesh, and give them a heart of flesh (Ezekiel 11:19).

I suppose the heart is the very centre of a man's being. If it stops, the person is dead. It begins before you are born, and goes on without ever stopping for perhaps 90 or 100 years. Every second it beats, and if the beat become irregular, you are ill.

When you talk about 'getting to the heart of the matter', you mean you are finding out the secret of it. In Scripture, the heart is the sort of mainspring of life, but it is also the organ that decides how you will behave. Jeremiah 17:9 tells us that 'the heart is deceitful above all things, and desperately wicked. Who can know it?'

Now if Jeremiah is right, the outlook for us all is pretty poor. Something has to be done about it. It needs to be 'broken'. But if you break your heart, don't you die? Physically, yes, you would. But spiritually, no. The Psalmist tells us, 'A broken and contrite heart, O God, Thou wilt not despise' (Psalm 51:17).

So God wants to see us heart-broken for our sins, and *then* He can mend us. But He does even more - He gives us a New and Clean Heart. It is this New Heart that wants to put God first. The New Heart keeps the whole Person throbbing with New Life, new vigour and a new joy that is centred, not in self, but in Christ. So that we can say with St. Paul, 'To me, to live is *Christ*' (Philippians 1:21).

The fear of the LORD is the beginning of wisdom
(Proverbs 9:10).

Fear, in the Bible, is reckoned to be driven out by love. But fear, in the context of our readings today, is a good, not a bad thing. It is better described as 'Awe'. We should not be afraid of God, but we should have Him in awe. We should be afraid to offend Him. We should reverence Him. When we come into His Presence, we should humble ourselves before Him.

If I were invited to Buckingham Palace to see the Queen, I wouldn't go in my gardening clothes! Nor would I start chattering to my neighbours when I got there, if the Queen was present. I hope I wouldn't be scared of her, but I would hold her in great respect and would feel deeply honoured that she had invited me to see her.

So, when I come into God's Presence, I need to start by recollecting what I'm doing - to put away mundane, worldly thoughts, to remember that He is Lord of all the Universe; He made it all and I'm just a very humble member of His Creation.

I need to remind myself of His utter holiness, and that I am a sinner needing a Saviour. Perhaps the best sort of preparation that I can make for the occasion is the sort of thing Isaiah tells us about in Isaiah 6. 'I saw the LORD, seated on a throne, high and lifted up, and His glory filled the Temple ... Woe is me, I cried, for I am a man of unclean lips ... and my eyes have seen the King, the LORD of Hosts.'

If we come into His Presence like that, I believe God will be as gracious to us as He was to Isaiah on that occasion. He sent him out to serve.

Put on the whole armour of God, that you may be able to
stand against the wiles of the devil (Ephesians 6:11).

One thing we need to understand is that the devil is stronger
than *we* are. If we fight him in our own strength, we will lose.
His only real hope of winning is if he can stop us from putting
our trust in Christ. He likes to make us think we can manage
him on our own. But we cannot.

Paul tells us how we should arm ourselves against him.
Truth to surround us amidships. If we trust in the truth of the
gospel and ourselves speak the truth, the devil's spear won't
touch us. *Righteousness* is to protect our heart, not *our*
righteousness, but that of Christ. *Salvation* protects head and
brain. But if we're in a fight, what weapon of attack have we
to use? Only one - *the word of God*, which is the sword of the
Spirit.

So we need to learn how to wield the sword. And we
should do it as Jesus Himself did. When the devil tempted
Him, He answered by constant quotations from Scripture. He
knew His Bible. And to learn how to use the Bible takes us a
lifetime. We can learn much of it by heart; we can learn the
verses we need for special occasions. But we need to know
where to find them. Make a list of verses that you find to be
vital ones for different circumstances. And keep them in a
special booklet where you can easily locate them! But that
booklet cannot take the place of your own memory. And what
you learn before you reach age 25, you will never forget!

The god of this world has blinded the minds of the unbelievers, to keep them from seeing the light of the gospel of
the glory of Christ (2 Corinthians 4:4).

We who are Christians often find it very difficult to understand *why* non-Christians just cannot accept the gospel. We
know that it's the way of Life, both for this world and for the
next. And the answer is that they are *blind*. They don't know
they are, they think they know how to get through and enjoy
life. They look for plenty of money, lots of friends, lots of
amusements, a congenial job, and think *that* is the answer.
They think that to be a Christian is to be miserable, never able
to do what you want to do, always being told by God, 'Thou
shalt *not*'.

Yet for every negative God gives us, He replaces it by *two*
positives. Do you remember what happened when Jesus
spoke to the rich young man? He told him to sell all that he had
and give it to the poor, and *then* come and follow Jesus. And
the young man turned sadly away - he loved his money too
much. At that point, Peter spoke to Jesus and said, 'What
about us? We've given up everything for you.' And Jesus said
to him, 'Anybody who has done that will inherit Eternal Life,
but also God will give him all he needs and *much more
besides*.' What a pity the rich young man didn't wait to hear
that answer - he might have changed his mind.

We should pray for our non-Christian friends that their
spiritual eyes may be opened. And only God can do that.

I say to you that hear, Love your enemies, do good to those
who hate you, bless those who curse you, pray for those
who abuse you (Luke 6:27,28).

Those who think this is easy had better think again! I think it's
one of the most difficult things God has ever asked us to do.
How *can* you *love* the people who hate you, who are spiteful
to you, who are always trying to take the micky out of you?
Does He really mean we've got to *love* them? Why should
we?

Well, stop and think a minute. What would we like those
people to be like, the ones who hate us? We would like them
to love us, we would like them to become Christians, we
would like them to find their way to Jesus. Well - if that's what
we would like, hating them will only drive them further away
from Jesus. It will only make them say, 'Those Christians are
horrible to us, they hate us, and if that's what being a Christian
is, I'd rather not be one.'

A man who injured people in Uganda in recent years, was
Idi Amin, who was President there. Thousands of people were
murdered under his rule. He killed the Archbishop, and would
liked to have killed Bishop Festo Kivengere. Festo was
inclined to hate him for his evil deeds. Then suddenly he
remembered what Jesus said about loving your enemies. So
he sat down and wrote a book, which he entitled, 'I *love* Idi
Amin'. Now, whether Amin will ever become a Christian, I
don't know; but at least Festo encouraged him, because he
loved him, in spite of all he had done. The number of haters
of Christians who have been won by love must run into
millions. Paul himself was one of them.

Not to be served but to serve, and to give His Life as a
ransom for many (Mark 10:45).

When you stop to think what that means, and who said it, it is
quite contrary to everything that the world thinks greatness is
all about. Jesus had just told His disciples that He was going
to Jerusalem to be crucified. Immediately after He said it,
James and John asked Him if they could be given the chief
seats in His Kingdom! Jesus answered by telling them that
'the one who wants to be greatest must be the *slave* of all'. But
He didn't only say it, He acted it out also.

Do you remember when Jesus arranged to have the Last
Supper in the Upper Room, that there were no servants there
to wash the dusty feet of the disciples. Which of them would
think of doing it? It was the job of a slave. Jesus quietly picked
up a towel, put it round His waist, and set about washing their
feet. He, who was the Creator of the universe and had come
down from Heaven, was doing the humblest job that could be
done. Peter wouldn't stand for it. He said, 'Lord, You shall
never wash *my* feet.' Why not? Because it was not his
conception of what the Creator of the world *should* do.

I think we have to learn, not only to serve others, but also
to let others serve *us*.

PRAYER
Lord, what wilt Thou have me to do?

Even though I walk through the valley of the shadow of death, I fear no evil; for Thou art with me; Thy rod and Thy staff, they comfort me (Psalm 23:4).

I suppose this 23rd Psalm is the best-known and most-loved of all the Psalms. It reminds us, that under all circumstances, those who are Christians have the close Presence of Jesus with them at every step of the way, every single day until the very day that they pass from this life into the next.

Why are people afraid of death? I think it is because they are moving into an experience they have never had before. Nobody has ever yet come back from death to report what Heaven is like. Well - hardly anybody - Lazarus did. But the Bible doesn't record what he said about it, though it does say lots of people went to see him after he came alive again. The Pharisees planned to kill Lazarus, because his return to life had brought many others to Christ (see John 12:11). So if he reported anything of Heaven, it must have encouraged people!

But, of course, it is the fact of Jesus' own Resurrection that must encourage us most of all. Remember how He said, 'I go to prepare a place for you, that where I am, there you may be also' (John 14:3).

I like what David said about it; and remember Jesus hadn't even come when David wrote Psalm 73:23,24: 'I am continually with Thee; Thou dost hold my right hand. Thou dost guide me with Thy counsel, and afterward Thou wilt receive me to glory.'

So the Promises are there. We can trust our Master, Jesus.

Jesus said to Thomas, 'I am the Way, the Truth, and the Life; no one comes to the Father, but by Me' (John 14:6).

So often you hear people talking about religion and saying that all religions ultimately lead to God. But that is *not* what Jesus said. He said most clearly that there is no way to heaven except through Him.

When did He say it? In John 14 you find Jesus telling His disciples about the way to Heaven. He said, 'You know the Way to the place where I am going.' But Thomas jumps up and says, 'Lord, we don't know *where* you are going, so how can we know the *Way*?' The answer came at once, 'I *am* the Way.'

No other religious leader has ever said, 'I *am* the Way.' They say, 'This is the way' or 'Let me show you the way'. Islam says, 'Go to God, but Mohammed is His *prophet* - go through Mohammed.' But Jesus is not only the *Way* to God, He is the *Truth*. Not only does He speak truth, He *is* Truth. He is eternal *Life*, not just the way to life. So if we have taken Him as our Saviour, we are in the Way. And because He is the Way, He is with us. He is *truth*, so in Him, we cannot miss the way. And being in Him, we are also already *in* Eternal Life. He'll never let us go, so we are safe.

Elijah prayed fervently, 'O Lᴏʀᴅ my God, let this child's soul come into him again.' And the Lᴏʀᴅ hearkened to the voice of Elijah; and the soul of the child came into him again, and he revived (1 Kings, 17:21,22).

Elijah was, I suppose, the greatest of the prophets. He was one of the two men who were reported not to have died. Elijah went up to heaven in a fiery chariot! The other was Enoch, the father of Methuselah, the oldest man who ever lived. 'He was not, for God took him' (Genesis 5:24).

But Elijah was a tremendous man of faith. All the stories of him show that he completely trusted God. Another his adventures occurred during a famine, when God sent him to Zarepha, to be looked after by a poor widow. Elijah asked her to feed him, although she and her son were almost dying of hunger. In faith, she fed him first - and from that moment she never suffered shortage of food.

But there came a day when her son was taken ill and died. She complained to Elijah, and Elijah immediately took the matter up with God. Elijah took the boy up to his room, stretched himself over the boy on the bed, and begged God to bring him back to life. And that's exactly what God did.

Elijah's prayers were so powerful that they were even commented on by James in James 5:16: 'The prayer of a righteous man is powerful and effective.'

How little most of us know about real prayer. We have much to learn from Elijah.

Do your best to present yourself to God as one approved, a
workman who has no need to be ashamed
(2 Timothy 2:15).

This is an encouraging verse, especially to those who do not
think much of themselves! So often we think we aren't much
good to anybody, because we are not clever, not specially
good at games, not too bright in conversation; we reckon we
are outshone by most of our fellows. We tend to retire into our
shells, rather like a snail who has shut up shop for the day!

But all the time we are forgetting that God has made us
unique. There is nobody else in the whole wide world who has
exactly the gifts that we have, nobody else who could take our
place if we dropped out of the race. Truly, God can't *afford* to
lose us. What, *me* - when He has all the world to choose from?
Yes indeed - *you*. God has chosen you before the world began,
and given you something to do for Him and His kingdom
which cannot be done by anyone else.

What is that *something*? Ah! that you have to find out.
Nobody has ever been born who hasn't something to do for
God. So, don't let anyone demean you - you are (potentially)
an ambassador for Jesus Christ. How can you carry out that
task? By finding out what are your very special gifts, and then
dedicating them to Jesus.

Some years ago, Sylvia and I went to Israel to hold
services at the invitation of young Jewish Christians. We got
time off, and bathed in the sea of Galilee. There we discovered
pebbles under our feet and picked them up and brought them
back to England. I'm making a mosaic of these stones into a
Galilee fish, and it will decorate my room. Why? Well - it
could be a talking point with visitors! Opportunity!

Do nothing from selfishness or conceit, but in humility
count others better than yourselves (Philippians 2:3).

Is this an antidote to yesterday's reading. There we were
reminded of our own uniqueness. Here today we are reminded
that everyone else is just as important as we are. So we have
nothing to swank about. Not long ago I heard somebody say,
'I can't bear Mrs. So-and-So, because whenever I meet her
she always wants to talk about *herself*, whereas I want to talk
about *myself*.'

This I suppose is a form of 'One-up-manship' - we like to
make others think we are people who matter. But what Paul
is saying to us is, I think, something like this: 'Part of our job
as Christians is to encourage other people to be their very best,
so that they too can develop all their gifts. If our encouragement gives them a chance to realise that they are quite as
unique as we are, then we have achieved something for them,
and for God's Kingdom.'

So we don't always have to be showing how good or
clever we are; we can take a back seat and give other folk a
chance. By doing so, we shall not miss out, because even if
other people don't notice us, *God does*.

I think one of the greatest gifts anyone can have is to be a
good listener! Because it shows you *care* about the people
who are speaking to you. Look out for just such an opportunity
today. It could count for much.

In the shadow of Thy wings I will take refuge, till the
storms of destruction pass by (Psalm 57:1).

There come times in the lives of all of us when we find
ourselves buffeted by some great misfortune, and we wonder
whether we shall ever survive. Everything seems to be against
us and we don't know where we can turn for help.

Do you know the old hymn *Rock of Ages, cleft for me*? It
was written by a curate, Augustus Toplady, who was once
overtaken by a huge storm and, in his distress, he found shelter
in a crevice in a huge rock till the storm was over. At least that
is the story about him. But it is probably more accurate to say
that when he wrote his hymn, he was remembering the verse
in Isaiah 26:4 which speaks of 'The LORD Jehovah as the Rock
of Ages'. He would remember the story of the Rock which
Moses struck when the Children of Israel were in the wilderness and needed water, a passage which Paul picks up in 1
Corinthians 10:4, when he speaks of Jesus as the 'Cleft Rock'.

But it's true, isn't it, when our hearts accuse us and our
conscience condemns us, that we need to be rescued? It is to
Jesus that we turn for help and refuge. He is always ready for
us. We can hide in Him. Indeed we should be doing so not only
in times of danger, but always. He never fails.

The Grace of the Lord Jesus Christ, and the Love of God,
and the Fellowship of the Holy Spirit be with you all
(2 Corinthians 13:14).

How do you explain the Holy Trinity? Three Persons, and yet One God? So many mistakes have been made over the years in trying to explain God, especially to non-believers. It certainly isn't easy. One way is to think of your right hand: it is one hand but it has five fingers. Normally all five fingers know what any one of them is doing; they co-operate with each other. With our children we used to speak of the fingers as 'Thumbkin, Pointer, Big-man, Ring-man, and Little-man.' Each of them operates differently, but all are at the command of the hand.

Perhaps God is a little bit like that. The Father is our Creator, the Son is our Redeemer, and the Holy Spirit is our Counsellor. In the Grace, which we took as our verse for today, Paul reminds us of Grace, Love and Fellowship as being three separate attributes of God. Is this hard to understand? Well, if we could really completely understand God, I don't think He would be fully God. Never mind, we shall understand more one day.

Meanwhile, let us thank God with all our hearts for all He does for us in so many ways. He cares for us from the cradle to the grave, and a long long way beyond that! Praise Him!

Therefore, putting away falsehood, let everyone speak the
truth with his neighbour, for we are members one of another
(Ephesians 4:25).

I suppose lying is one of the biggest temptations that we have,
and I think it is often caused through *fear*. We do something
we know to be wrong, and perhaps we think we can get away
with it. Then, suddenly, we are faced by somebody with what
we have done. Panic! 'What can I do? How can I get out of
this? If I don't, I shall be punished. So - quick. Tell a lie.
Nobody will know.' And, maybe, they don't. Yet we still feel
uncomfortable, because we know we haven't told the truth. If
we're found out after that - we will be known as a liar. No one
likes to be called a liar. It means we cannot be trusted.

So what's the answer? Paul says, 'Tell the *truth* about any
wrong we have done.' Yes, it may hurt; yes, we may be
punished, but we deserve it; yes, it may mean people will
think we are wicked. *But* they will give us credit for telling the
truth. And if they know you always tell the truth, they will trust
you. Everyone likes to be trusted.

But Paul goes further than this. He says, 'We are members
one with another.' We are God's Creation, we belong together, we are brothers, children of the same Heavenly Father.
Brothers should not have lying coming between them. That's
the way hatred is bred. That's the way wars start. 'Those who
worship God must worship Him in spirit and in truth' (John
4:24). You can't do that if you are lying to your brother.

PRAYER
Help us, Lord, always to speak the truth to You,
and to each other. In Jesus' Name. AMEN.

O, Lord our God, save us from (Sennacherib's) hand, that
all the Kingdoms of the earth may know that Thou alone
art the Lord (Isaiah 37:16-20).

If you have time, read the whole of this prayer of King Hezekiah's, because I think it's an example of the sort of prayer we
ought to make when we pray to God.

Hezekiah and his people of Israel were threatened with total
destruction from their great enemy Sennacherib. He wrote a
letter to Hezekiah, telling him to read it to all the people so that
they would know they could not possibly survive an attack. He
had already destroyed all his other enemies so how could Israel
possibly survive?

1. *Hezekiah spread the letter before the Lord.* That was wise.
He and his people were in God's hands, they belonged to Him,
so they said in so many words, 'It's up to You, Lord.'

2. Hezekiah said to God: *'Sennacherib is insulting God.'*

3. Then Hezekiah said to God, 'Sennacherib has destroyed
all the heathen gods - and he thinks You're just another one.'

4. Hezekiah asked nothing for himself or his people, only
that God would bring glory to Himself, and prove to Sennacherib
that he cannot defeat the True *God*.

And Hezekiah got the right answer from God. God said: 'I
will defend this city and save it, for my sake, and for the sake of
David My servant' (Isaiah 37:35).

So when we pray, that's the kind of attitude we need - *God's
glory*. We need to be men and women of prayer, both on big
occasions and daily in the little things too. Have you something
special to ask for today? Would it be to God's Glory, if He gave
what you ask? That's what really matters.

April 21
You are the Salt of the earth ...
you are the Light of the World (Matthew 5:13-14).

SALT and LIGHT.
That's how God describes His people. It's what Jesus called His disciples. Why?

SALT?
Salt is a preservative. When we lived in Kenya, we used to go out occasionally and catch fish. If we had too many, we would salt some to preserve them - and they wouldn't rot. We could wash them later and they would still taste fresh.

Salt also adds flavour to what we eat, it brings out the taste. A meal with no salt can be very tasteless. That's what a Christian has to be in the world. He brings out the best in people, he adds a flavour to life, he cleans up wickedness where he can, he preserves what is best.

LIGHT?
Without the gospel and the Christian Faith, the world would be a desperate place to live in. There would be no hope beyond the grave. Evil would triumph. In many places today, the hope of the people rests fairly and squarely with those who are Christians, and their struggle for the truth is noticed by all the world.

Recently a policeman was shot in Bristol. Three of his teeth were knocked out - but those teeth stopped the bullet going further and killing him. He and his wife were pictured with their baby son and, as I looked at the photo, I felt they *must* be Christians, they looked like it. Next day, she spoke on the radio and told of their love for Jesus and their utter trust in Him. It was lovely to hear. *Salt* and *Light* - they were showing it.

That's what you and I must be always. The Light, of course, is not our own; we only reflect *His* glorious Light.

April 22

Indeed all who desire to live a godly life in Christ Jesus will be persecuted (2 Timothy 3:12).

I am sure you know that this really does happen. We have to expect it and not be surprised when it comes - but we do not have to encourage it. Sometimes when you ask people who have suffered, whether they would have gone on as Christians if they had known what was coming, they say they might not have. Yet when the time came, they were given strength to bear it and, looking back on it, they have often said they are glad that Jesus has given them the privilege of having suffered for Him.

Suffering takes different forms. Sometimes it is just that people despise us because we won't use the bad language that they do. Not long ago I spoke with a man who is a very good athlete and I asked if he might eventually get international honours. 'No,' he said, 'because all my games take place on Sundays and it would mean missing out on worship. I just can't do it.'

A man (or woman) may lose their job if they won't work on Sundays. In some countries it is difficult for a Christian to get a job anyway, and in many countries it is a hindrance socially to be a Christian. Some have even been killed for being believers - the supreme sacrifice. Jesus said this would happen.

When any kind of suffering for Christ comes to us, we can rejoice, because we are, even in a small way, sharing His suffering. And all the time He is with us.

Do you not know that your body is a
temple of the Holy Spirit? (1 Corinthians 6:19).

The moment you become a Christian, Jesus takes up His abode - His living-space - in you. It's an extraordinary thing to think that Jesus is actually living inside *me*!

And it's almost a frightening thing too. Because if it's true, and it *is* true if I am a Christian, then every time I misuse my body, I am fouling the house where Jesus lives. If I am a servant of Jesus, one of the jobs He gives me is to make a daily sweep of His house, wash it and clean it, and make it the kind of place where He wants to live. I must not let evil things come into it; I need to make it as perfect a place as I can so that He can enjoy His house.

God created me. Then He lost me. Then He sent His beloved Son to rescue me; Jesus bought me back to Himself, at the cost of His own life. He shed His Blood for me.

Obviously, this means that I must keep my body fit; it should be in as good a condition as I know how. The food I eat should be wholesome, the games I play should give me good muscles, strong arms and legs. I must keep my body up to the right weight and height and I want to be good to look at. Why? Because it is *His house*.

Paul gives us a good motto concerning our bodies. He says, 'I beg you therefore, brethren, by the mercies of God, to present your bodies as a living sacrifice, holy and acceptable to God' (Romans 12:1).

Witnesses who ate and drank with Jesus
after He rose from the dead (Acts 10:41).

Many people today discount the story of the resurrection of Jesus. They say, 'Yes, it's true He lived; but He could not have come alive from death; people don't. Probably the disciples stole the body.'

Paul gives us the evidence for Jesus' Resurrection in 1 Corinthians 15:4-7. He writes to Christians in Corinth to tell them that they can be certain of it. He says that Jesus appeared to Peter, to all the Apostles, to James (His brother), to more than 500 disciples at once, most of whom (says Paul) are still alive, people could go and ask any one of them. Jesus ate and drank with some of them. They touched Him. Some at first thought He was a ghost, but Jesus said, 'Handle Me and see; a ghost does not have flesh and bones as you see I have.'

If the disciples had stolen the body, why did they afterwards allow themselves to be put to death for believing in a lie? The Jews and the Romans had put a seal on the tomb, they guarded it all night; the stone was too heavy for a man to move. And yet the tomb was empty. If the guards had removed the body, they had only to produce it when the disciples said He was alive. But they didn't.

Certainly His body was different after the resurrection; He could appear and disappear at will, and could pass through closed doors. But ghosts don't eat fish, and Jesus did. Ghosts don't cook by a fire, but Jesus did.

Thomas didn't believe when the other disciples said they had seen Jesus. But Jesus came specially for Thomas a week later, so that every disciple could be absolutely certain.

'Death could not hold his prey.' Hallelujah for that! His Resurrection also makes yours and mine sure.

If you have raced with men on foot, and they have wearied
you, how will you compete with horses? And if in a safe
land you fall down, how will you do in the jungle of the
Jordan? (Jeremiah 12:5).

The Children of Israel had been rebelling against God, and
were trusting in their own strength and worshipping idols.
God spoke to them through Jeremiah and warned them that a
tough time was coming, far tougher than anything they had yet
experienced. They just would not be able to stand - perhaps
they then would learn to trust only in God's strength and His
protecting power.

When things go well with us, there is always the temptation to think we are quite capable of managing our own affairs;
but 'pride goes before a fall' and we so often have to learn the
hard way.

Life is not a bed of roses, even for the Christian. There will
always be difficulties and hardships to face. But facing them
with Christ can make the impossible become possible.

In one of his letters, the Apostle Paul says, *I can do all
things.* What a terrific claim to make for yourself! How dare
he say it? Ah! but he qualifies it by adding these words,
Through Christ who strengthens me. That makes all the
difference, doesn't it?

He gives power to the faint, and to him who has no
strength, He increases strength (Isaiah 40:29).

To all who received Him ... He gave power to become
children of God; who were born, not of blood, nor of the
will of the flesh, nor of the will of man, but of *God*
(John 1:12,13).

This is one of the most tremendous words ever spoken by God
to man. The main thought is this: here is a new beginning. The
Light that was in every man, which darkness could not put out,
came into the world; and when He came, His own people
didn't receive Him. His world didn't recognise Him. But He
began a new creation, and to everyone who did receive Him,
who did believe on Him, He gave the right to become God's
children. That is what the New Birth means. It is different
from physical birth, and it makes us *God's* children as distinct
from being just *man's* children. Jesus became one of *us* so that
we might become one of *His*.

The world rejected Him then and it still does, largely,
today. But some people received Him then and some still do
today. His salvation is on offer to all - He doesn't want to lose
any. Those of us who have found Him, He wants to use to
bring others to know Him too. And whether we travel overseas to do so, is for Him to decide. Either way, the need is very
great. 'The labourers are few' - but we are some of them. What
a privilege we have!

There fell a voice from heaven, 'O King Nebuchadnezzar
... the kingdom has departed from you, and you shall be
driven from among men ... until you have learned that the
Most High rules the kingdom of men' (Daniel 4:31-32).

How easily riches and power can make anybody think that
they can run the world and behave exactly as they like and get
away with it! King Nebuchadnezzar thought that and, because he lived in a palace of gold, he swanked and said, 'I have
built mighty Babylon, for my own glory - am I not clever!'
And he was reduced to living as a sheep put out to grass,
stripped of his royalty, even his clothes were taken away, until
he learned that God rules the world.

Many so-called mighty men have since thought as Nebuchadnezzar did. Hitler thought he ruled the world and that his
kingdom would last for 1,000 years. He ended up committing
suicide in an underground shelter as his country collapsed
around him.

My power, my wealth, my wisdom, if I have any of these
possessions, have come to me by God's permission and He
can take them all away at any moment. How do we use what
God has given to us? They are meant to be used for Him.

We should be very concerned for those who have power
or wealth, because so often they are totally out of touch with
God and the gospel does not get through to them. But when
they are Christian folk, as does sometimes happen, their
temptations are great. Their need of God is exactly the same
as yours and mine.

Pray for the Queen, the Prime Minister, and all our
leaders. They need our prayers.

By grace you have been saved through faith; and this is not
your own doing, it is the gift of God - not because of
works, lest any man should boast (Ephesians 2:8,9).

So often the world has a totally wrong view of what has
happened to anybody who has become a Christian. They think
they have suddenly become 'Pi', that they are really semi-
mental, that now they regard themselves as 'goodies' and the
rest of the world as 'baddies'. So they write us off.

How can we explain that they've got it wrong? As Paul
says, 'This is not your own doing, it is God's gift.' I cannot
earn my salvation - it comes from God. He offers it to all. I'm
no better than anyone else, indeed I may be worse than many.
Paul once described himself as 'the chief of sinners'.

Think of the jailer in Philippi. He had beaten Paul and
Silas, and they were bleeding in prison from their beating.
Then at midnight the earthquake came and the jailer was
frightened that he'd lose his job if the prisoners escaped. So
he comes trembling to Paul, saying, 'What must I do to be
saved?' And Paul replies simply, 'Believe in the Lord Jesus,
and you will be saved, and your family.' The whole family did
and were there and then baptised, amidst great rejoicing.

I suspect that the family and Paul and Silas had a real feast
that night - 'all one in Christ Jesus'! I'm sure the 'works'
followed and that this new family spread the light of Jesus.

Remember that you were once separated from Christ,
alienated from the commonwealth of Israel, and strangers
to the covenants of promise, having no hope, and without
God in the world. But now in Christ Jesus you ... have been
brought near in the Blood of Christ. For He is our peace
(Ephesians 2:12-14).

Contrasts - Before and After! The first part of this verse
describes the condition of all who do not yet know Jesus as
their Saviour. 'Separated ... alienated ... strangers ... hopeless
... Godless.' What a terrible condition to be in. Well, we were
too - once. *But now*, for us, things are very different. 'In Christ
... brought near ... and in peace.'

It is only Jesus who can make peace, real peace, for
anyone. We live in a world that is not in peace. The world is
full of wars and fightings and hatred and fear. But although we
live in this world, we have peace, because the Prince of Peace
rules in our hearts. And part of our job is to bring God's peace
into whatever situation we may find ourselves.

That means making friends. Making friends is not easy,
because people are suspicious and wonder what we're after.
Are we trying to get something out of them? No, we just want
to be friends and to share some of the good things we have.
What sort of things? Food, possessions, enjoyments, and
ultimately the gospel.

Making peace!

The seed is the Word of God. The ones along the path are those who have heard; then the devil comes and takes away the Word from their hearts, that they may not believe and be saved (Luke 8:11,12).

I think sometimes we forget just what we are up against. We are fighting an enemy who is desperate and who is also stronger than we are. John calls him, 'The prince of the power of the air.'

People are in the power of Satan unless and until they are in the power of God. Most people think they can pick and choose what they want to do and, up to a point, they are right. But Satan is very cunning. As long as he has got them where he wants them, he is happy. But when anyone turns to Christ, Satan realises he is up against a power greater than his own and that, ultimately, Christ will win. So at *that* point he brings all his wiles into play to prevent people accepting Christ, or if they have accepted Him, Satan tries to use all his power to stop them becoming effective Christians.

Temptation becomes stronger than they have known it before. Friends turn against them often when they become Christians. They fear they cannot stick it, and so they drift back and may eventually drop out. What can we do about it?

A lot. As soon as anyone we know becomes a Christian, that is when we need to pray hard for them that God may hold them. And we should keep close to them too, if we can - they need friends, Christian ones.

Pray that Jesus may bind Satan, so that his power is nullified. We are on the winning side!

May 1

I have done wrong ... I have played the fool ... I have erred
exceedingly (1 Samuel 26:21).

Three comments made by Israel's first king on his own
behaviour. Yet, as we study the previous history of King Saul,
we see that he had everything in his favour. We read that when
God first chose him he was a choice young man and a goodly;
he was the tallest youngster in Israel (1 Samuel 9:2). God
chose him, Samuel anointed him, and the people said, 'Is Saul
also among the prophets?' (10:12).

Everything was satisfactory about him. Then, *what* went
wrong? He had every backing, God had given him 'a band of
men whose hearts God had touched' (10:26).

The first wrong thing he did was to usurp Samuel's place
as a prophet (13:13).

Secondly, he passed a religious judgment on his son
Jonathan and condemned him to death (14:44).

Thirdly, he disobeyed God's command about the destruction of the Amalekites (15:1-35).

And finally, he was jealous of his God-appointed successor (18:6-9).

So it was a gradual slipping away from God.

We need to pray that we be kept from slipping. A godly
background is great, but we cannot rest on it. A good beginning is fine, but there has to be continuance. The only real
protection is a daily renewal by our Master, Christ Himself.

PRAYER
Lord, keep me this day walking in Your Way, and keep my
eyes upon You and my feet from falling. AMEN.

Whatever is born of God overcomes the world;
and this is the victory that overcomes the world, our Faith
(1 John 5:4).

One of the great problems facing us as Christians is how to have victory over Satan and evil in our daily lives. How easily we fall, how hard it is to win the battle, and how little different we are from the world around us. Yet we have all God's promises about victory.

I think if we examine this verse carefully, we may get a little light. John says here that *'whatever* is born of God overcomes.' He is not saying *Whoever*. It is the Lord Jesus Christ's New Birth in us that overcomes the world. You see, it is *His* power that makes us different, that makes victory possible to us.

The devil is strong, stronger than we are. But Jesus has defeated him, He is stronger than Satan. If Jesus is living in us, as we believe, then Jesus (in us) cannot be defeated. What is needed is our continuing trust in Jesus. And so it is that John can say, *'This* is the victory that overcomes the world, our *Faith.'* It is not the *strength* of our Faith that matters, it is the *Person* in whom we put our Faith. In his commentary on 1 John, John Stott puts it like this: 'Confidence in the Godhead of Jesus is the one weapon against which neither the error, nor the evil, nor the force of the world can prevail'.

I think this is something that we have to keep on learning in our day-by-day experience of the living Lord Jesus. The battle will be on until we find ourselves face to face with Him in Heaven - the final victory won.

Ezra opened the Book in the sight of all the people ... and
when he opened it all the people stood .... And they read
from the Book, from the law of God, clearly; and they gave
the sense, so that the people understood the reading
(Nehemiah 8:5,8).

This is a marvellous story and you must read the whole
account for yourself. The people of Israel had been in exile in
Babylon and their land had been ruined, the Temple destroyed
and the whole country was desolate. But Nehemiah got
permission from King Artaxerxes of Babylon to go back
home and help rebuild Jerusalem and the Temple, and eventually he brought more than 42,000 people back to help in the
rebuilding (Nehemiah 7). For years, during the Captivity, they
had virtually forgotten about God. So Nehemiah and Ezra the
scribe decided that before the place was rebuilt, they ought to
read God's Word to the people. And they did just that. They
built a huge open air pulpit, called all the people together, and
Ezra read from God's Word for about six hours non-stop.

As the people listened to the Word of God, they wept.
Nehemiah said to them, 'Don't weep. This day is a day of
Rejoicing, it's a Feast-Day. Don't grieve, because the *joy* of
the Lord is *your strength*' (Nehemiah 8:9, 10).

That put fresh heart into them and they rushed out and
built temporary shelters of shady trees (because there were no
houses). And they told everyone what God's Word said. They
truly came back to God, through the reading of His Word.

That Word is still the same today, and for us it is still
powerful. Read it!

Do not be anxious, saying, 'What shall we eat?' or 'What shall we drink?' or 'What shall we wear?' For the Gentiles seek all these things; and your heavenly Father knows that you need them all. But seek first His kingdom and His righteousness, and all these things shall be yours as well (Matthew 6:31-33).

When you come to think of it, most people are chiefly concerned about the three things Jesus mentions here - Food, Drink and Clothing. If they have enough to eat and drink, and can afford to wear the kind of clothes that will keep them in fashion with their friends, what else is there to worry about! Oh! yes, I know there are lots of other things today, such as a car, a television, a video, friends who think as you do, money enough to provide all you want; but, those three are the basics.

The word 'Gentiles' just meant those who were not Jews. We could apply it to all non-Christians. And Jesus is saying something like this: 'Don't think I don't know and understand all your needs. Of course I do; becoming a Christian doesn't mean you don't need food and clothes. But you leave that to Me; I'll see to them. Instead, put Me and the Kingdom first in your thinking and planning. You won't lose by it.'

It is truly marvellous how God meets our daily needs when we put Him first. We really don't need to worry. And as He meets *our* needs, we have something with which we in turn can help to meet the needs of *others* less well-off than ourselves.

Needs - and luxuries! they're not the same. But God in His goodness even gives us some of the luxuries too! And they too can be shared.

Jacob said, 'I will not let you go, unless you bless me.'
And he said to him, 'What is your name?' And he said,
'Jacob.' Then he said, 'Your name shall no more be called
Jacob, but Israel, for you have striven with God and with
men, and have prevailed' (Genesis 32:26-28).

Jacob is a strange character. From his earliest days he seems
to have played a fast one on his brother Esau. Yet Esau never
deserved his birthright, for he threw it away more than once.
Jacob was destined by God to become one of the great men of
Israel, so why did he have to try and beat his brother by
cunning? Finally he got his father's blessing by deceit - which
so much set Esau against Jacob that Jacob had to flee the
country.

Years afterwards, when Jacob decided to come home
again, his deceit of Esau and his slipping away from God had
been so great that it took all night for him to put himself right
with God.

But Jacob persisted and persisted in his wrestling with
God and eventually God answered his prayer and gave Jacob
the new name of *Israel*, a 'prince with God.' That name
became the name of the Jewish people right to this day - Israel.

When people have become estranged from God, it often
takes a long time for matters to be put straight with Him again,
there is so much that has to be forgiven and undone. But, thank
God, we can always have access to God through our Redeemer, the Lord Jesus; and, if we are His disciples, our sins
have already been cleansed away by the shedding of His
precious Blood.

May 6
The Blood of Jesus Christ, God's Son,
cleanses us from all sin (1 John 1:7).

There's a bit more to this verse than the quotation here given. There is a *condition* which applies before we can claim that the cleansing power of the Blood of Jesus applies to us. Here is the condition: 'If we *walk* in the *Light*, as He is in the Light, we have fellowship with each other, and the Blood of Jesus Christ ... cleanses us from all sin.' In other words, the cleansing is not automatic.

Sin cannot come into God's Presence. Sin is walking in darkness. We have to move over into a totally new life in Jesus - a life of obedience to Him. Does that mean that we will never sin again? No, it doesn't. But it does mean that if, and when, we sin, we must bring it straight to Jesus for cleansing, and we must ask for pardon. Sin must be abhorrent to us, as indeed it is to Jesus.

When we contemplate sin, we need to remind ourselves that it was sin (yours and mine and everyone else's) that brought Jesus to the Cross; and if we who are born again of God continue in sin, we are - as it were - crucifying Jesus afresh. (Hebrews 6:6: 'crucifying the Son of God all over again and subjecting Him to public disgrace'.) What a terrible thought!

'Walking in the Light'! Jesus Himself is the Light of the world, so we are walking in Jesus day by day. That's what Eternal Life is all about.

May 7

Jesus said to them, 'Render therefore to Caesar the things
that are Caesar's, and to God the things that are God's
(Matthew 22:21).

You will remember the context of this story. The Jews were
determined to catch Jesus out in the things that He said, so
they tried to trap Him into saying either that people should not
acknowledge Roman rule, or that they should. If He said they
shouldn't they would hand Him over to the Roman rulers as
a revolutionary and a rebel. If He said they should, they would
tell the people that they shouldn't trust Him as He was just a
puppet of the Roman government. Either way they reckoned
they had caught Him.

But Jesus asked for a denarius to be produced and then
asked whose head was on it. They said, 'Caesar's.' He
answered that whatever is due to Caesar must be paid to him
and whatever is due to God must be paid to Him.

In other words, we are citizens of two worlds. We have a
duty to the country or state in which we live, and we should
be good citizens of our country. But we also have a duty to
God. There are occasions when we cannot obey the state,
when it is asking something that we know is contrary to God's
Will. We should pray for those who live in countries that do
not recognise God's existence.

Thank God for our own freedom to worship Him, and pray
for our rulers that they may always recognise Him as supreme.

Jesus said, 'Take heed, and beware of all covetousness;
for a man's life does not consist in the abundance of his
possessions (Luke 12:15).

Some people are like squirrels, collecting everything they can
lay hands on, and then 'hiding them' so that other people
cannot get hold of them! Why, oh! why, do we keep so many
things put away and never really make proper use of them?

Making money is rather like that. Many people do it for
the sake of getting as much as they can, yet when they have
amassed a lot, they often don't know what to do with it.
Money, in itself, is quite valueless, it's only value is in what
it can *do*! That doesn't mean that we should be spendthrifts,
getting rid of it as soon as we get it. Nor does it mean that we
should give it all away, because if we did that, we would have
to depend on other people for our daily bread, our housing and
clothing.

Remember that Paul was a tent-maker, to earn money for
his keep. Some of the disciples were fishermen, presumably
selling fish to provide their daily needs. Jesus Himself worked
in a carpenter's shop, making furniture, before He began His
three years of Public Ministry.

Tithing our money, so as to give God a 'tenth' of what we
earn or what is at our disposal, is part of a Christian's way of
making his money useful for the Kingdom of Heaven. It's
good to keep accounts, so that we know where the money is
going and what it is doing. 'Treasure in Heaven' is everything
we do for God's glory and for the extending of His Kingdom
in the hearts and lives of people. It results in great happiness
to 'be content with what we have' (Hebrews 13:5).

Because He Himself has suffered and been tempted, He is
able to help those who are tempted (Hebrews 2:18).

Is it not marvellous that Jesus had just the same sort of
temptations that you and I get! If He had not, He would not
understand what we have to go through, never having been
tempted Himself.

Think of some of the temptations that came to Him. One
was to make a short cut - *make* people believe on Him by
performing some spectacular miracle such as throwing Himself off a pinnacle of the temple to prove that He could not be
hurt because He was God. Or to become a temporal King and
turn out the Roman power, and then force the world to accept
Him. Or to turn stones into bread because He was hungry.

I think, in our case, that many of our strongest temptations
come soon after we first make a stand as believing disciples
of Jesus. The reasons are twofold: one, because we have now
begun to resist temptation, whereas before we gave way;
second, Satan sees us beginning to struggle to get free from
him, and he is determined to get us back if he can - or at least
to make our Christian witness feeble.

If you fail and fall, don't stay down, but immediately
stretch out a hand to Jesus, asking His forgiveness and
restoration, and He will pick you up again and give you a fresh
start.

I am the Vine, you are the branches. He who abides in Me, and I in him, he it is that bears much fruit, for apart from Me you can do nothing (John 15:5).

This is the simple secret of bearing fruit for God's glory. Have you ever examined a vine in a large greenhouse? You will see how the gardener trains the branches to spread out in every direction, so that they get every possible ray of sun. He prunes the branches carefully, cutting out the weakly bits that will never bear fruit, so as to strengthen the others. He makes sure that the sap from the vine will flow freely into every branch. All dead bits are removed and burnt, all diseased branches are treated so as to cure the trouble, and the roots are kept watered and free from weeds. And the result? Lovely big bunches of grapes when the time comes, to bring joy and nourishment to all who taste them.

Jesus - the Vine. We - the branches. His 'sap' (the Holy Spirit) is provided by Him so that we can draw all the needed strength and be enabled to resist the attacks of the Evil One. Without the Holy Spirit, we could never stand up to the pressures that surround us. Thank God, we have a constant source of power at our disposal, but we need to draw strength from Him every day.

That way, we have peace of heart and mind. Whatever the turmoil in the world around us - because we are in Christ, and Christ is in us - 'He is our Peace.'

As for me, I am poor and needy; but the Lord takes thought
for me. Thou art my help and my deliverer; do not tarry, O
my God! (Psalm 40:17).

What a wonderful book is the Book of Psalms. It has a song
for almost every mood that is ours - for joy, for sorrow, for
sickness, for health, when we are feeling tempted or lonely,
when we are on top of the world! Study this 40th Psalm, it has
most of the moods in it.

Listen: 'God lifted me out of the slimy pit, out of the mud
and mire. He set my feet on a rock, and gave me a firm place
to stand. He put a new song in my mouth, a hymn of praise to
our God. Many will see and fear, and put their trust in the
LORD' (verses 2-3). What joy that has for us!

Or we have: 'Troubles without number surround me; my
sins have overtaken me, and I cannot see ... my heart fails
within me. Be pleased, O LORD, to save me; O LORD, come
quickly to my help' (verses 12,13). And He does, doesn't He?

This is the kind of Psalm for those who are having a
nervous breakdown, when all the world seems black and
dismal, and they don't know where to turn for help. This
Psalm would bring great encouragement to those who are in
prison for Christ - with its promise of ultimate deliverance
from the 'pit'. And it's when we begin to sing in praise, that
God leads us into a fresh life of victory for Him.

May that song be yours today!

And the vessel he was making of clay was spoiled in the potter's hand, and he reworked it into another vessel, as it seemed good to the potter to do (Jeremiah 18:4).

Some of the illustrations in the Bible make wonderful visual aids. Do you do pottery, or have you watched a potter at work? How carefully he (or she) uses his hands, taking an ugly lump of clay, putting it on the wheel, turning it and gently moulding it into a beautiful vessel, smoothing out lumps or excrescences, getting the curve of the neck exactly right, until he is satisfied with his handiwork. And if it isn't to his liking when it's done, he takes it up, squeezes it into a lump, and starts all over again.

And God sometimes does that with His people, and when it happens, it's a painful process. We don't like being, as it were, broken up and having to start all over again. And yet, it's always for our own good when it happens. 'A broken and contrite heart, O God, You will not despise' (Psalm 51:17).

He sometimes has to break us before He can make us what He wants us to be. But it's His remaking that turns us into useful human beings, people who can truly bring glory to His Name.

If we're willing to submit to the Master-Hand, we'll find it's a very gentle Hand that is upon us.

'Ah, Lord God,' I said, 'I do not know how to speak; I am only a child.' But the LORD said to me, 'Do not say, "I am only a child." You must go to everyone I send you to and say whatever I command you. Do not be afraid of them for I am with you and will rescue you,' declares the LORD (Jeremiah 1:6-8).

When we are young, we often reckon that we cannot speak about God or Jesus to others, because they will not listen to us. So we keep quiet and hope someone else will do what we cannot.

Don't be too sure! Look at the many occasions in the Bible when a youngster did things that grown-ups were afraid to do.

Remember how Jesse's youngest son, David, was only a shepherd-boy when his big brothers went off to the war? But when Goliath challenged the Israelite army, all the people were afraid of him. And they mocked David when he offered to fight Goliath. He had no sword or spear or axe - only a sling and a stone - yet he won the battle. You see, it was God who had David in hand - and that made all the difference.

Moses was the same, he was scared of Pharaoh. 'But I will be with you,' said God. And that made all the difference.

You never go in your own strength, but in God's. We read that 'His strength is made *perfect* in weakness' (2 Corinthians 12:9). Not my strength or yours, but His, and that makes all the difference!

Let no one say when he is tempted, 'I am tempted by God';
for God cannot be tempted with evil; and He Himself
tempts no one; but each person is tempted when he is lured
and enticed by his own desire. Then desire when it has
conceived gives birth to sin; and sin when it is full-grown
brings forth death (James 1:13-15).

In the Lord's Prayer, Jesus taught us to say, 'Lead us not into temptation, but deliver us from evil.' It is true that God does allow His people to be tested, as Abraham's faith and Job's sincerity were tested. These testings may be used by Satan to try and turn us from God and to do evil, and then to blame God for it. Satan told Jesus that he wanted to have Peter so that he might 'sift him as wheat', but Jesus told Peter that He had prayed for him that his faith would not fail when the testing came.

James reminds us that it is not God who is the author of sin, but man's own sinful desire and thought. It is we who are to blame when we sin - not God. Certainly the devil puts it into our minds, as he did to Adam and Eve at the very beginning of time. But they didn't have to say yes to Satan, any more than we have to. They could have said, 'No', and so can we. It is when we become disciples of Jesus that we are given strength to resist.

What the devil offers us may look desirable, but its conclusion is always *death*. Thank God for New Life in Christ!

Men who have turned the world upside down
(Acts 17:6).

That was how the Jews described Paul and Silas when they arrived in Thessalonica on their missionary journey! Certainly wherever the gospel is preached faithfully and lived effectually, things begin to happen and it creates publicity. Paul and Silas had been speaking in the local synagogue for three Sabbaths, preaching the death and resurrection of Jesus, and pointing the people to the Way of Salvation. Turning the world upside down?

Of course it was really the exact opposite. The world has been turned upside down by sin and Satan, and what Paul and Silas were doing was turning it right side up again.

People so easily get into a mess when they try to run things for themselves in their own way. It is necessary for them to turn to the Lord Jesus Christ in order to get right again - right with God, right with the world in which God has placed them, right with one another, right in their own hearts and lives.

What is our brand of the Christian Faith doing to 'turn the world right way up again'? The world where we live, the home we inhabit, the schools we go to, the places where we work - are they feeling the effect of our Christian living? It all depends on how far we are allowing the Holy Spirit to have His way in our lives, so that we are effective servants of Jesus.

Blessed be the God ... of all comfort, who comforts us in
all our affliction so that we may be able to comfort those
who are in any affliction, with the comfort with which we
ourselves are comforted by God (2 Corinthians 1:3,4).

Quite often, when somebody has been bereaved by the loss of
a loved one, their friends keep away from them because they
are a little frightened to talk to them at such a time. And yet,
that is the time when they most need comfort and help.

What's the best way to give help? Often, it is not necessary to speak - just a quiet squeeze of the hand can convey far
more than an actual word. Sometimes a sympathetic letter can
make all the difference. I have some marvellous letters which
I received when my own dear wife was taken to heaven, and
I treasure these.

But often the comfort needed is on an occasion when
something has gone wrong, or some sin has been committed,
or some friend has failed, or there is loneliness and depression.

What does the word 'Comfort' mean?

It comes from two Latin words, 'Con' and 'Forte'. They
mean 'bringing strength to a person.' We feel weak and are in
need of strengthening. So a good friend can help us to feel
strong again, enable us to face the world afresh with a brave
face, knowing that God is with us and friends around us.

Do you know someone in need of 'comfort' today? What
can you do to help?

When I bring clouds over the earth and the bow is seen in the clouds, I will remember My covenant which is between Me and you ... and the waters shall never again become a flood to destroy all flesh (Genesis 9:14, 15).

The rainbow is one of the most beautiful sights in the world. Yet it is so fleeting - usually only there for just a few minutes before it fades away. We talk about 'all the colours of the rainbow' when we try to explain some exquisitely beautiful colouring, maybe in a flower, or a bird, or a sunset. The rainbow is a constant reminder of God's Promise to us, a visual aid to tell us that He will never again drown the world.

Remember other visual aids in the Bible: Blood, stones, bread, a cup - all simple and common things, yet all having a significance of the many and great Promises that God has made to us, His people. Promises of salvation, protection and His presence with us; the guarantees are there for us to see.

We may not see Jesus Himself at present - though we will do so one day - but we can see His guarantees. It's good to remember that this is what they are, when we see, touch, and eat.

'I will never leave you nor forsake you,' He said.

Blessed be the God and Father of our Lord Jesus Christ!
By His great mercy we have been born anew to a living
hope through the resurrection of Jesus Christ from the
dead, and to an inheritance which is imperishable, unde-
filed, and unfading, kept in Heaven for you (1 Peter 1:3,4).

Yesterday we were looking at God's Promises. Today we
have what is, I suppose, one of the greatest of them - the
ultimate fulfilment of all our hopes in a totally indestructible
inheritance in Heaven.

Have you ever thought how far people will go to make
sure that their property is absolutely safe? They lock up their
treasures in a strong box at home, with locks and iron bands
on it so that thieves cannot break in. Or they put them away
into a strong room at the bank. But a thief can pinch the box
and a robber can rob a bank, a moth can destroy a beautiful
garment, a fire can burn your house down, a business can go
bankrupt and even a government can fail! So, nothing is really
safe. Somebody may even promise to leave you some money
in their will, yet when they die, it may be found they have
nothing to leave!

But look at what God has promised to us. An inheritance
which is quite indestructible, which is absolutely pure and
true and good, which cannot dissolve or disappear. It's under
the absolute care, protection and keeping of God Himself.
And there's no doubt about who it's for - it's for *you*!

Hearken to your father who begot you, and do not despise
your mother when she is old .... The father of the righteous
will greatly rejoice ... Let your father and mother be glad,
let her who bore you rejoice (Proverbs 23:22,24,25).

All parents have an anxious time as their children are growing
up; they wonder how their children will eventually turn out.
Has their family upbringing been right for them, will the
whole family flourish, or will one go astray?

Influences outside the home today are often very destructive of family life, with children encouraged to go their own
way. Many homes are divided, the parents divorced or separated, and the home suffers.

How can we make the best of the home that we have,
whilst we are young enough to be dependent upon it? Is it the
kind of home that we would like to have when we marry and
move into a home of our own making? Would we want our
children to quarrel with each other, or to disobey us?

What was the home of Jesus like when He was young? We
don't know much about it, but we get a tiny glimpse in Luke
2:51, 52 where we read, 'Jesus went down to Nazareth with
them, and was obedient to them ... And Jesus grew in wisdom
and stature, and in favour with God and men.'

'Listen to your Dad, back up your Mum,' that was the
advice from Proverbs, and I'm sure Jesus knew that advice
and followed it - how wise.

I commend you to God and to the Word of His Grace,
which is able to build you up and to give you the inheritance among all those who are sanctified (Acts 20:32).

This was the parting word of Paul to his friends in the church
which he had founded at Ephesus. He knew he would never
see them again, and they knew it - so every word he said on
that occasion was of very special importance. They wept as he
said goodbye. They were only a few people - their life at
Ephesus would not be easy - but it was their job now to spread
the gospel and pass on the good news of Jesus' Salvation to
the unbelieving populace there. How would they manage?

Paul put them back into God's Hands. He knew they'd be
safe there. But He also reminded them that they had a
Guidebook which could train them in the way they had to go,
a Book they could trust. That Book is now nearly 2000 years
old and yet it is still the most-read Book in all the world. It is
not out of date, nor will it ever be out of date, for it is timeless.
Through its study they would grow up as strong and true
Christians. It would guide them all the way through life and
right on into Eternity itself. They would never come to an end
of it, for every time they read it they would find something
new and fresh.

You know the Book, and so do I - the BIBLE, the written
Word of God. We need to 'read, learn, and inwardly digest it'.

For we are His workmanship, created in Christ Jesus for
good works, which God prepared beforehand, that we
should walk in them (Ephesians 2:10).

Yesterday we were reading the farewell message of Paul to
his friends at Ephesus. Today we read a word he wrote to
them. The letter may have been a circular, such as missionaries today write to their friends, meant to be passed round the
neighbouring churches. But it would have covered Ephesus
as well.

I like the phrase 'we are His workmanship'. God made us
to begin with but He also re-made us when we became
Christians; we became 'new creatures' (2 Corinthians 5:17).
Spoilt by sin, He has taken us in hand all over again and now
we are truly *new*. Each of us is Hand-made, with the author's
copyright on us!

He knew what His purpose for each of us was when He re-
made us: 'good works, that I should walk in them'. What sort
of good works? Each Christian has a general pattern and a
special pattern. The general one we find laid down in God's
Word. The special one He will only reveal bit by bit, because
no two patterns are alike. We have to find our speciality from
Him, and that is quite an exciting process!

To you who believe, He is precious, but for those who do
not believe, the very stone which the builders rejected has
become the head of the corner (1 Peter 2:7).

The NIV has for 'the head of the corner' - 'the capstone'. The
capstone is, I think, the 'keystone' or 'the coping-stone'.
Unbelievers would like to have Christianity without Christ!
But, if they did, the building would fall down. So to Christians, the very centre of their Faith is the Lord Jesus Christ
Himself. Without Him, faith is useless, meaningless. We
cannot build up a Faith which is just constructed on decent
behaviour or a civilised way of life. Faith is putting your trust
in a Person, not a thing.

Take the keystone out of a great stone arch, and the whole
arch falls to the ground. You may jack it up with props, but it
will still be totally unsafe. It's the keystone that draws the
whole erection together. What holds Christians together is
Jesus Christ. 'We love, because He first loved us' (1 John
4:19). Christianity without Christ is a contradiction in terms.
But a church flourishes where Christ is recognised as Saviour,
Redeemer, head of the Church, and central to all activities,
because 'He is the head of the corner'.

What a lovely thing it is to be able to begin each day with
Him - it means He is with us all day. And in all our activities
we can share our concerns with Him - He is our constant
companion.

Whoever knows what is right to do, and fails to do it,
for him it is sin (James 4:17).

Some people think that the Christian Faith is just a series of
negatives - 'Don't do this, don't do that, don't do the other.'
And a series of 'don'ts' is certainly boring, isn't it?

Here's a bit of advice that is positive. James is saying, 'If
you know what you ought to do, go and get on with it.' And
that's definitely not negative, is it? But have we ever really
thought of it as sin when we fail to do something that we know
we should? Often it's what we do rather than what we say
which counts most with non-Christians, indeed with anybody, and quite certainly with the Lord.

Do you remember the illustration that Jesus gave of this?
He spoke in Matthew 25:14-30 about the people to whom God
gave talents, or gifts, that they might use for Him. Those that
used them were rewarded by being given greater responsibilities. But the man who hid his talent in the ground was
condemned - not for the evil he had done, but for the good he
could have done and didn't.

If you have a capacity for doing something well, and fail
to use your gift, it eventually dies on you, out of sheer disuse.
An artist who never puts brush to paper soon loses even the
desire to paint.

Similarly, if you have a gift for making friends, use it to the
full for God.

Delilah said to Samson, 'Please tell me wherein your great
strength lies' (Judges 16:6).

What a marvellous champion Samson was to Israel. I suppose
he was one of the strongest men who ever lived. He was able
to pick up the very gates of a city and carry them away on his
shoulders! He slew 1000 men with the jawbone of an ass. No
wonder the Philistines hired a woman to see if she could find
out the secret of his strength.

The secret was in the fact that he had committed his life to
God, and God had told him never to shave his head - it was to
be the sign of his might.

What did Samson do about it? He fooled with his strength.
He made friends with a Philistine girl when he should have
known better than to tie himself to a 'heathen' woman. She
enticed him. At first he only pretended and each time it made
her cross with him. She begged and begged, and at last he gave
way and told her the truth.

When he awoke, his strength was gone. 'He did not know
that the Lord had left him' (verse 20). The Philistines took him
and blinded him. But he was spiritually blind long before that
- from when he first started to play around with women.

When God gives us any special gift, it is to be used for
Him. And if we misuse God's gifts, they will be taken from us,
as Samson's was. Yes, I know God did give him one more
chance, but by then he was blind. He died in his final effort,
yet at the same time helping Israel in his destruction of the
Philistines.

Lord, help me to use any gifts You have given me for Your
glory. AMEN.

For Thou hast delivered my soul from death, my eyes from tears, my feet from stumbling; I walk before the LORD in the land of the living (Psalm 116:8,9).

David is thanking God for His continuing mercies. What David is referring to is an experience that belongs to every Christian. You have so much for which you ought continually to be thanking God. What sort of things?

1. When you became a Christian, you were for ever delivered from *death*. Until that moment, death was a certainty for you. But now, you are in the clear - for time and for eternity. God will keep you whilst you live on earth, and will take you to Himself when the time comes for you to leave!

2. *Tears*. It doesn't mean you will never have any, but that when they come, they will soon be wiped away. And in heaven, there will never by any at all! Some tears anyway are tears of joy.

3. *Stumbling*. When you cannot see your way, you can easily stumble and fall. But in Christ, God keeps your feet straight. You can see the Way and you avoid the snares, God keeping your feet.

And when you have begun to experience this kind of treatment from God, you can say with the Psalmist, 'I walk before the LORD in the land of the living.' It's a daily walk you have with Him, and what joy to know you are never alone. You can walk with confidence and security when you walk with Jesus.

Thank Him today for all His love, showered upon you.

I do not pray that Thou shouldest take them out of the
world, but that Thou shouldest keep them from the evil
one. They are not of the world, even as I am not of the
world (John 17:15,16).

This is part of the prayer that Jesus made to His Father just
before the Crucifixion. It was a prayer for all His disciples -
not just the Twelve, but for all those who were going to
become His disciples in later years, and that includes us.

It's very easy for us to imagine that this life, which is the
only one we know, is all there is, and that it's therefore very
important. Certainly it's important, because it's a preparation
for the much greater life that is yet to come. And it's what
happens to us here and now that determines our future life
with Christ in Heaven.

So we find Jesus praying very earnestly for us that we may
be kept out of the power of the Evil One - the devil. We are
certainly in the world, but we don't belong to it, we belong to
God. So it is that we have to think of our time here on earth
as a sort of pilgrimage, a journey from earth to Heaven.

Have you read Bunyan's *Pilgrim's Progress*? If not, you
should - it will help you grow into being one of the friends and
servants of Jesus. As you read it, you can see how it is in fact
describing your own journey through life. This is what Bunyan says about his book:

This book will make a traveller of thee,
If by its counsel thou wilt ruled be;
It will direct thee to the Holy Land,
If thou wilt its direction understand.
Yea, it will make the slothful active be;
The blind also delightful things to see.

You have died, and your life is hid with Christ in God.
When Christ who is our Life appears, then you also will
appear with Him in glory (Colossians 3:3,4).

If you have a very precious piece of jewellery, like a gold
clock or a ring set with diamonds and pearls, and you want to
be sure of keeping it safe - how do you set about that? To
insure it doesn't help - because all you would get would be its
value, not the thing itself. To put it in the bank or a safe would
have some risks. No certainty anywhere.

But when our new life has begun in Christ, it is absolutely
safe. How safe? Firstly, it is *with* Christ - and it's *hidden in*
Him, so nobody could prise it out of His care. Secondly, it is
also hidden with Him *in God*. And that makes it doubly safe.

Paul reminds us that at the Second Coming of Jesus, when
He comes back to our world, we shall come back with Him
and we shall be a part of His new world in Glory. What a future
we have! And our future is as certain as the Promised Return
of Jesus.

Now if that be so, then our present ought to be spent to the
very best advantage of His Kingdom. What shall I do with my
life? The best possible answer to that question is to give my
life back to God who made it, and let Him guide as to how it
can best be spent. It will never be wasted if He has hold of it.

The men marvelled, saying, 'What sort of man is this, that
even winds and sea obey Him?' (Matthew 8:27).

Some years ago I was in East Africa at the time the great Jinja
Dam over the Nile was about to open and the engineers
showed me round. The Queen came out to open it a week after
I was there. The dam was to harness the waters of Lake
Victoria and direct the great River Nile so that it played a very
large part in the industrial development of East Africa. In the
event, it was to provide all the electricity needed by Kenya,
Uganda and Tanzania - I suppose one of the biggest and most
powerful jobs ever done by any river in the world.

But the disciples of Jesus witnessed an even greater power
being exercised - the wind and waves being harnessed to obey
the direct command of their Maker. No wonder that they
'marvelled' when they saw what He could do. But His Power
was greater than that of the Nile, for His pertained also to the
healing of men and women, as well as the control of the forces
of evil. And His power still does - He is the 'same, yesterday,
today and forever'.

Through His death, Jesus destroyed the one who has the
power of death - the devil. That is difficult to understand. It
means that His Resurrection has removed Satan's power once
and for all from us, and guaranteed our immortality once we
are 'in Christ'.

What a Saviour we have!

Peter began to say to Him, 'Lo, we have left everything
and followed You.' Jesus said, 'Truly, I say to you, there is
no one who has left house or brothers or sisters or mother
or father or children or lands, for My sake and for the
Gospel, who will not receive a hundredfold now in this
time ... and in the age to come Eternal Life'
(Mark 10:28-30).

That was a tremendous Promise for Jesus to make, but there
are countless thousands of people who can bear out the truth
of those words; people who have gone overseas with the
gospel, who have given up wealth and human prospects to
serve God, often under difficult conditions, in lonely places,
often in poverty, in persecution and suffering sickness. And
it is quite unbelievable what recompense has been theirs, even
in this life.

David Livingstone, William Carey, Eric Liddell, Mother
Teresa, Festo Kivengere, Carey Francis, and hundreds of
others you could name would all bear testimony to the fact that
they received far more back from God than they ever gave to
Him. They are just a few of those who have experienced the
truth of the Promise that Jesus made to Peter.

One thing you can be sure of: God always keeps all His
Promises. As you seek to serve Him, you will be able to add
your own witness in due time. What a pity the 'rich young
ruler' didn't stay to hear that promise - 'he went away sadly,
for he had great possessions.' And Jesus had longed to have
him.

Not in plausible words of wisdom, but in demonstration of
the Spirit and power that your faith might not rest in the
wisdom of men but in the power of God
(1 Corinthians 2:4,5).

Paul often decries himself. He calls himself the chief of
sinners; he says that he has a 'hindrance' which he asked God
to take away, but God did not. Here Paul says he came 'in
weakness and fear, and with much trembling'. Often when we
speak about Christ to people we are scared as to what they will
think. Well, Paul was like that too. And yet - he spoke 'with
power'.

He may have reckoned he wasn't much of a preacher, yet
when he spoke about Jesus, the Word went home and people
were converted. How did that happen? It was because God
was taking hold of a weak and fearful, trembling creature and
pouring out His power through him to people.

What he did with Paul, God still does today with similar
scared and weak folk just like ourselves. We don't have to be
clever or physically strong for God to use us; we have only to
be faithful and true.

I have met a woman who was soundly converted through
the trusting faith of a little girl. I have known boys who have
led their fathers to Christ. One of the biggest crowds ever to
attend a missionary funeral was there because the missionary,
who said he 'couldn't preach for toffee', was more like Jesus
Christ than any other man the African converts had ever met.

'Not in the wisdom of men, but in the Power of God,' said
Paul. And he was right.

As they were stoning Stephen, he prayed, 'Lord Jesus, receive my spirit.' ... And when he had said this, he fell asleep (Acts 7:59,60).

Two things I note about Stephen's martyrdom. One is that after the Resurrection of Jesus, we do not often read of Christians 'dying'. No, like Stephen, they 'fall asleep'. Death is done with, because they are alive in Christ, either in the flesh or in the spirit. The second thing I note is that 'Saul was there, giving approval to his death.' This must have been very much one of the turning points in Paul's life. He could, I am sure, never forget the look on Stephen's face: 'All who were sitting in the Sanhedrin looked intently at Stephen, and they saw that his face was like the face of an angel' (Acts 6:15). He could not forget a sight like that, especially when he was assisting at killing the man concerned.

It is unlikely that for us there will be the fate that overtook Stephen, that of stoning - but there is mockery, criticism and disdain for the Name of Christ. Stephen had courage enough to die for Christ; have we got the courage to live for Him? I think perhaps we can do so if we see what Stephen saw that day: 'I see the heavens opened, and the Son of Man standing on the right hand of God' (Acts 7:56). That sight would give him the certainty that Jesus had hold of him and would never let him go. Nobody else saw that vision that day - it was private to Stephen.

The story doesn't end with the death of Stephen - it ends with the fact of Saul who later was to become Paul, one of the greatest ever exponents of the Faith.

June 1

According to the riches of His glory, He may grant you
to be strengthened with might through His Spirit
in the inner man (Ephesians 3:16).

Christians sometimes get very despondent about their capacity to live the Christian life to the full. They know they are weak and that they often fail; therefore they think, 'Well, some Christians are built to be strong and brave, and some of us to be weaker people; we just can't help it; that's the way we are made.'

That is sheer nonsense, because we do not generate our own strength, we *receive* it, it is God's gift to us. How strong is God's Might? Well, Paul tells us it is far stronger than the strongest human being, because it is drawn out of 'the Riches of God's Glory'.

The Spirit of God dwells in us from the moment we receive Jesus as our Saviour. And the Spirit doesn't offer a tiny bit of Himself to some and a fullness to others - He comes in His fullness to all of us.

If Jesus is in your heart, so is the Spirit and so is the Father. In Ephesians 4:15, Paul tells us that 'we are to *grow up* in every way into Him who is the Head, even Christ'.

Ah! that's what is wrong with us - we are not 'growing up'. God has given us His fullness, we are not taking advantage of His gift, we are content with just a fraction of what God has given us. The fault lies with us, *not* with Him.

Often in the Bible you read that someone was 'filled with the Spirit' on some particular occasion. Then later on you read that the same person on another occasion 'was filled with the Spirit'. Let us dig deep into our inheritance.

The word of the Cross is folly to those who are perishing,
but to us who are being saved it is the power of God
(1 Corinthians 1:18).

Crucifixion was the most degrading death that anyone could
be given under the Roman occupation of Israel. It was
reserved for the worst of criminals. I suppose it was the most
cruel death that could be inflicted, taking several hours for the
sufferer to die, usually in the heat of the blazing sun. The
criminal was hanged in the full view of any people who cared
to watch, having first been stripped of all his clothes and
brutally beaten before being crucified.

No wonder that Paul could say that non-Christians reckoned that the Cross was 'foolishness'. But when Jesus was
crucified, He turned the Cross into a thing of Glory, because
it was through the Cross that He wrought out our Salvation.
Indeed today, when you mention crucifixion anywhere, people think of Jesus - even if they're not themselves Christians.

Do you know John Bunyan's lines about Christian as he
came to the Cross?

> Thus far I did come laden with my sin;
> Nor could aught ease the grief that I was in,
> Till I came hither: what a place is this!
> Must here be the beginning of my bliss?
> Must here the burden fall from off my back?
> Must here the strings that bound it to me crack?
> Blest Cross! Blest sepulchre! Blest rather be
> The Man that there was put to shame for me!

That's what the Cross means to us Christians. We thank
God for the Cross, and Jesus calls us to 'take up our Cross
daily and follow Him'.

Blessed be the Name of the LORD from this time forth and for evermore! From the rising of the sun to its setting the Name of the LORD is to be praised! (Psalm 113:2,3).

There's a lovely story in the Old Testament, in 2 Chronicles 20:19-25, of how, when the Israelites were attacked by their enemies, the then King, Jehoshaphat, called the people together to sing and praise the Lord. When they 'began to sing and to praise, the LORD set ambushes against their enemies, and the Israelites won the battle, and had to spend three days getting in all the spoil!'

You know, I think it's still true, that when we begin to praise, God gives us the victory over our old enemy, Satan.

Singing, too, is one of the best ways of spreading the gospel, for people will often listen to a singer rather than to a preacher!

Most people love a good song, and if it has a good swing about it, they'll sing all right. Even at football matches, people will sing one of the old well-known hymns, and the whole ground will ring with *Amazing Grace* - which must touch some hearts for Christ.

So start today with a song of praise, and it will stay with you all day.

Praise the Lord.

The Father Himself loves you, because you have loved Me,
and have believed that I came from the Father
(John 16:27).

I suppose one of the earliest memories any of us have is of a
very loving father and mother who ministered to our every
need, and to whom we turned whenever we were in any kind
of need. The best of them feed their children, teach them to
stand, to walk and to run. They play with them, introduce them
to other children, and explain the wonders of the world in
which we live.

In our verse today, Jesus is telling His disciples something
of the qualities of their heavenly Father, whom they have not
yet seen, but who is even closer to them than any earthly father
could ever be. 'He loves *you,*' He said, 'because you love
Me.' In other words, our relationship to Jesus introduces us to
a close fellowship with the Creator of the Universe. The God
who created the planets and stars, and the millions of people
who live on this planet, that Almighty God has become my
Friend, just because I love His dear Son.

Some folk love to collect autographs of famous people
and show them to their friends: 'Look, I have the Queen's
signature here, here Sebastian Coe has signed, and the Prin-
cess of Wales!' When we come to know God intimately, He
also puts His signature for us: the rainbow, the wind, the sun's
warmth, the beauty of His world and His Holy Spirit into our
hearts - with the Promise that He will meet our every need.
Only the Christian can know God like that. And it's because
we love His Son, who gave His very life for us. Praise the
Lord!

How can a young man keep his way pure? By guarding it according to Thy Word (Psalm 119:9).

Impurity is one of the biggest temptations that most of us have to face. It comes at us in so many different ways. Suggestive pictures and indecent books can allure us into evil thoughts, and evil thoughts into immoral actions. Sometimes friends will lead us astray, until eventually our whole lives become twisted and corrupt.

The world in which we live is full of this kind of corruption - it shouts at you from street hoardings, newspapers, videos and television. What hope have we of resisting its attraction?

The Psalmist puts his finger on the answer from our verse: 'Guard your way, your life, your thoughts, your imagination, your behaviour, by a daily resort to the Word of God'. The Bible is a mine of great wisdom, a very precious source of spiritual guidance which will never lead us astray. It constantly brings us into touch with the Living Word of God, the Lord Jesus Christ. Each day as we read some portion of God's Word prayerfully, pondering its message to us for the day, we will find it fresh and clean and purifying. There will always be something new in the reading that we had not seen in it before, and nearly always relevant to the needs of the day we are facing.

It's not the *length of* the portion we read that matters, it's the special thought for the day that counts, and often during the day we may find our minds refreshed by what we have read.

Open Thou mine eyes, that I may behold wondrous things out of Thy Law (Psalm 119:18).

Work out your own salvation with fear and trembling; for
God is at work in you, both to will and to work for His
good pleasure (Philippians 2:12,13).

At first sight, this advice from Paul seems to contradict the
teaching of Jesus. Jesus always taught that salvation was
God's free gift to us when we accepted Jesus as our Saviour,
and that we could never earn our own salvation, nor could we
invent it for ourselves. So what does Paul mean?

Read a bit further into the verse. Paul says that '*God* is at
work *in* us'. So, what God works *in*, we have to work *out*. And
that makes sense.

'To work out' is Paul's challenge to us not to stop half-
way. If God is to give us His power, we have to do our part too.
Firstly, we can work it out by regular study of God's Word,
which feeds our prayer-life. Secondly, we need to work it out
in fellowship with others. If we don't share our spiritual life
with others, it soon gets stagnant - like the Dead Sea. If we are
out of touch with God, share that need with another Christian.
We can find our way back.

But what about the 'fear and trembling'? I think this: we
have no goodness in ourselves apart from God. That quality
comes from Him. We can only work out what *God* puts in. Are
we afraid we cannot manage? That's good - because apart
from God, we can't. But if we continue to *obey* Him, He will
continue to work in what we have to work out.

God make you perfect in every good work to do His will,
working in you that which is well-pleasing in His sight.

And He will!

The Light shines in the darkness, and the darkness has not
overcome it (John 1:5)

Darkness is a horrid word, isn't it? Except when you are
asleep, you need to be able to see, and if you cannot see, you
fumble and stumble, and you could easily damage yourself.

Both Paul and John saw this world of ours as a 'dark'
world, in a darkness that has persisted all through history. If
you walk into a room that is completely dark, you go very
carefully, because you cannot see your way. But if you have
any sense, you will take a torch or candle with you and,
however dark the room may be, that tiny light will penetrate
to the furthest and darkest corner and destroy the dark.

There are two lights. The first is the light of man's
conscience. Every man has it, all know the difference between
right and wrong. That light has never been destroyed by
darkness - even if men do not obey their conscience.

But I think John was also thinking about the coming of
Jesus into our world of darkness. He said of Himself, 'I am the
Light of the world; he that followeth Me shall not walk in
darkness, but shall have the Light of Life' (John 8:12).

Earlier, when Jesus talked with Nicodemus, He had said,
'This is condemnation, that light is come into the world, and
men loved darkness rather than light, because their deeds
were evil' (John 3:19).

Every Christian is a pin-point of light in a dark world. Let
your light *shine*!

Jesus rebuked him, and the demon came out of him, and the boy was cured instantly. Then the disciples came to Jesus privately and said, 'Why could not we cast it out?' He said to them, 'Because of your little faith' (Matthew 17:18-20).

This is a difficult story about a sick boy - difficult because we cannot believe that God wants people to remain in that condition, and yet we see so few people really healed of epilepsy. 'Why?' asked the disciples. And Jesus replied, 'Because of your lack of faith.'

The boy was helpless - so was his father - so were the disciples. Ultimately, they went to Jesus. 'Bring him here to *Me*,' said Jesus. And in a few moments, the boy was healed.

Perhaps that was the whole answer. Of course, Jesus was not there when the disciples first met the boy. So they tried to cast out the demon, but failed. I wonder *what* they tried to do to him? Did they try to cast out the demon in the Name of Jesus? Obviously the doctors had failed with him too. Jesus told them they were not really *expecting* the boy to be healed - they didn't really trust God over it.

Does God always heal people who are sick, if they are prayed for? No, I'm sure He doesn't - but He does *care*, and He does sometimes heal too.

When we are ill, and the doctor cannot cope with it, do we ask Jesus about it? We should do, even if the doctor *can* do something, because the ultimate healing of anyone rests with God - not with us.

Often God has to heal the *mind* of a person before He can heal their bodies. When a person's mind is right with God, this has a great influence on their bodies too.

June 9

I appeal to you therefore, brethren, by the mercies of God, to present your bodies as a living sacrifice, holy and acceptable to God (Romans 12:1).

Yesterday's reading referred to the *mind*: today's is about the *body*. The Christian knows that his (or her) body belongs to God just as much as the mind or the soul, and that Christian service involves the body. If the Holy Spirit lives in my body, then He has come in in order to do His work through me.

So Paul says to each of us, 'Take your body with all that you have to do every day - at school, in the shop, the factory, the office, or wherever you work - and offer your whole service for the day to God.'

Is the typing dull? Are maths a bore? Is the washing-up something I really hate? Ah! but if I'm doing it not only for my earthly boss, but also for (and with) my Master in Heaven, that makes a difference! We do it together, and we don't skimp it because it's part of presenting my body to Him.

So look out for the distasteful job today, and remember you're doing it with Him, because that changes the distaste into sheer joy! And *that* is real worship, the offering of your everyday life to God.

PRAYER
Lord, bless this day,
and use me in it to serve You faithfully. AMEN.

As Jesus drew near ... behold a man who had died was being carried out, the only son of his mother, and she was a widow .... And when the Lord saw her, He had compassion on her, and said to her, 'Do not weep' (Luke 7:12,13).

I think Jesus always had compassion on any who were in sorrow, especially when a loved one was dead. Here, He spoke first to the mother and said, 'Don't cry.' There was a huge crowd with her, so she must have been a well-known and loved person. Jesus knew what He was going to do. So - 'Don't cry.'

Then He spoke to the dead young man, just as though the dead man could hear Him! 'Young man, I tell you, arise.' Could the man *really* hear? Yes, of course he could. His body was dead, but *he* wasn't. Whenever Jesus raised the dead, He always spoke to them. 'Lazarus, come forth.' 'Little girl, arise'. He'd known Lazarus before. Lazarus would recognise His voice. Had the others ever met Him? I don't know. But there was never a Voice like *His* voice.

Sometimes when people are deeply unconscious, the friends and relations will bring a familiar voice into the room and speak or sing something which the unconscious person would recognise, if they heard. And that voice revives them. Who knows what an unconscious person can hear? But these three were actually *dead*. And only the voice of Jesus could raise the dead. They heard. What joy that must have brought to that widowed mother! And everyone present spread the news all over Judea!

Life for evermore - in Christ!

Barnabas took Paul, and brought him to the apostles, and declared to them how on the road he had seen the Lord, who spoke to him, and how at Damascus he had preached boldly in the Name of Jesus (Acts 9:27).

There's some back history to this story. Saul (Paul) had left Jerusalem, where he had assisted at the stoning of Stephen, to go to Damascus and get all the Christians he could into prison. There had occurred his great conversion on the Damascus road, followed by some three years away in the Arabian desert. Then he returned to Damascus, and preached Christ there. The Jews there tried to capture him, but the Christians came to his rescue and he was let down in a basket over the wall at night, and so got away.

Now, back in Jerusalem, he sought out the Apostles - who were scared of him. I'm sure they must have heard of his conversion, but then he had disappeared for three years, so they must have wondered what he was up to. Was he really a Christian?

It's at this point that Barnabas comes into the story. He had been with Paul in Antioch and Damascus - he could speak for him. Barnabas reassured the apostles that Paul was a true disciple and could be trusted. But for Barnabas, Paul might never have been heard of again. Yet he was to become the most famous apostle of them all!

When you know of someone who has unexpectedly become a Christian, you need to back them up and get behind them, so that they develop into the kind of disciple God means them to be. Your backing might be the means of some person becoming a famous worker for God in days to come.

When you hear of wars and rumours of wars, do not be
alarmed (Mark 13:7).

In the first part of this chapter, Jesus was telling His disciples
that in the near future there would be persecution and the
destruction of the Temple - the latter of which took place in
A.D. 70. But He went on to speak of the things that were to
lead up to His Second Coming. Matthew, Mark and Luke all
record this talk, which was given shortly before the Crucifixion.

So, from what He said, we are to expect troubles, wars,
earthquakes, and many people turning against God before He
comes again. We are not to be anxious when we hear these
things - but to be ready and looking forward to meeting with
Him then.

Many people have tried to fix the date, but Jesus Himself
told us we could not do that. Nobody would know till He
actually came - but when He does come, all over the world,
people shall know at once. So it's a waste of time guessing -
but it *could* be any time.

The gospel had first to be preached to all nations, and I
think we can say that has now been done. Not that everyone
has heard - but some in every nation have. Wars and earthquakes and famine are certainly with us now (and we have to
do all we can to relieve sufferers). But also, we have to be
telling people about Jesus and persuading them to accept
Him, as far as we are able.

Most of all, we have to live our ordinary lives, doing our
duty as we see it - 'until He comes'.

Since all have sinned and fall short of the Glory of God,
they are justified by His Grace as a gift, through ... Christ
Jesus (Romans 3:23, 24)

There is a great temptation for most of us to compare ourselves with other people, especially other Christians! Then
we can say, 'Well, I'm not as bad as so-and-so, so I think I can
manage.' Paul is, however, quite clear about the truth concerning every one of us. 'All', he says, 'have sinned and come
short.'

If you were a good athlete and hoped to aspire to the
Olympics, there is a standard which any would-be aspirant
must reach, if he is to be considered. You might be an
excellent high jumper but if you cannot measure up to the
standard, you will not be considered. Say it is 6 feet, and you
can do 5 feet 11 3/4, you still will not qualify. 'But,' you may
say, 'I'm much better than so-and-so, who can only do 5 feet
6, so ought I not to be given a chance?' The answer is 'No. 6
feet is the standard. You don't measure up.'

However good we may think we are in God's sight, we are
still sinners. And *all* sinners are excluded. One sin keeps us
out. There is only one way into God's Kingdom and that is the
way of God's Grace, offered to us as a free gift, through the
Redemption won for us by Jesus on Calvary's tree. That is the
only way man may be judged just before God. As Jesus told
us, 'No man comes unto the Father, *but by Me*' (John 14:6).

But when we have received Him, we are cleared of sin.
We are still sinners, but we are now *forgiven* sinners, and that
makes all the difference.

What love He has poured out on us!

And the son said to him, 'Father, I have sinned against
heaven and before you: I am no longer worthy to be called
your son.' But the father said to his servants, 'Bring
quickly the best robe, and put it on him: and put a ring on
his hand, and shoes on his feet' (Luke 15:21,22).

The story of the Prodigal Son is, I suppose, one of the best-
known of all the wonderful stories Jesus told. It follows on
from yesterday's reading, doesn't it? The sinner, who had
roamed off far from home and spent all his money on riotous
behaviour, finally became destitute, and only then did he
realise what he had lost.

He comes back in penitence and sorrow, and begs his
father to take him back, no longer as a son, but as a servant.
But the father comes more than half-way to meet him, and
receives him with open arms.

'There is joy in heaven among the angels of God over one
sinner that repents.' It's a great privilege to be with someone
when this happens to them, and to share the inexpressible joy
that comes with the realisation that all is forgiven, and a totally
new life has begun with Christ. On goes the 'new robe' of
God's righteousness and the newcomer joins all those who
'have washed their robes and made them white in the blood of
the Lamb' (Revelation 7:14).

This is a life worth having, isn't it? And it goes right on
into all Eternity, with Him.

June 15

The years of our life are threescore and ten, or even by
reason of strength fourscore; yet their span is but toil and
trouble; they are soon gone, and we fly away
(Psalm 90:10).

When we are very young, thirty seems old, but as we get older
we usually reckon that an old person is about ten years older
than we are. I remember hearing my mother talk about an old
friend of hers as being 'a nice girl' when, in fact, she was over
eighty! Time seems to go slowly when we are young, but as we
get older, it flies.

Here is the Psalmist telling us just how long we may
expect to live. Seventy, perhaps eighty, but after that it is a
burden and, anyway, it is nearly finished. What he is really
saying is this: we have just a short time to live in the world as
we know it, and there is so much we may want to achieve
whilst we are in it - so don't waste it.

What most of us would like to be able to do, I think, is to
leave this world a rather better place just because we have
been in it. That is a big ambition, isn't it? Because the world
is so vast and each of us is just one tiny person in it; how can
we expect to influence all the world?

Your *world* is in fact the place you live in, amongst the
people where you are. There's probably quite a lot you can do
there to bring a bit of joy and happiness to other people. There
are certainly plenty who don't know God or Jesus as you do.
There are lonely people, sick folk, unhappy people. Can you,
today, think of one to whom you could bring a little joy? The
Psalmist qualifies what he says in this verse by another: 'So
teach us to number our days that we may get a heart of
wisdom' (Psalm 90:12). Go to it!

Built upon the foundation of the apostles and prophets,
Christ Jesus Himself being the chief cornerstone, in whom
the whole structure is joined together and grows into a holy
temple in the Lord; in whom you also are built into it for a
dwelling place of God in the Spirit (Ephesians 2:20-22).

Our verses today make a good deal of sense of yesterday's
reading. It puts us in God's perspective. The picture is of a
great Temple, a very beautiful building, all centred upon Jesus
Christ. But every single little bit of the building has a special
place and purpose. Jesus is the centre and everything else
there is to point to *him*.

Somewhere in that building is yourself. As what? A brick
in the wall: 'built into it for a dwelling-place of God in the
Spirit'.

No Christian is left out. There is a nook for every single
one of us, and together we help to make up the beautiful
whole, with Jesus Christ holding us all together in Him,
bringing glory to His Name.

With just one of us out of place, the building is imperfect.

PRAYER

Lord, You have called me into Your Temple. Show me my
corner; make me obedient to You; help me truly to live for
You, this day. AMEN.

At my first defence, no one took my part; all deserted me.
May it not be charged against them! But the Lord stood by
me and gave me strength to proclaim the Word fully
(2 Timothy 4:16,17).

As he wrote these words, Paul was in prison, chained up (as
he says in 2:9). He was suffering greatly because of his
preaching of the gospel. But what caused him more grief than
anything else was the fact that, at this time, all his previous
helpers had just faded away. Demas, having loved this present
world, had given up his Christian profession altogether. Luke,
Crescens and Titus had all gone elsewhere and even Tychi-
cus, who had helped him a lot, had now set off to Ephesus. So
poor Paul was lonely.

When he had to stand trial, he was alone - 'everyone
deserted me'. Yet even then he begged that God would not
condemn them for it.

All alone? No, not really, of course. His heart began to
warm again, as he remembered: 'The *Lord* stood at my side
and gave me strength'. That just made all the difference. God
has always promised to do this for any of his friends. Paul was
very near his own end and he knew it. He said, 'I am already
being poured out like a drink offering, and the time has come
for my departure' (4:6). As far as we know, he died for his
faith.

If you and I have to suffer for our faith, will we be able to
stand? That is a problem we cannot face in advance. But when
the moment comes, we shall not be alone, for Jesus promised:
'I am with you always, even unto the end of the world'
(Matthew 28:20).

The Kingdom of Heaven is like treasure hidden in a field,
which a man found and covered up; then in his joy he goes
and sells all that he has, and buys that field
(Matthew 13:44).

This is one of the many parables of Jesus and we may well
wonder how to interpret it. Does it mean that a Christian can
sell all that he has and buy salvation? No, because salvation
is a free gift of God to man. We cannot buy it.

I think the 'man' who finds the treasure is God. We know
that 'the field' represents the world (verse 38). So God goes
into the world and finds a treasure. What kind of a treasure
would God be willing 'to sell all that He has' to buy it? I think
only one kind of treasure and that is 'man'. As John 3:16 says,
'God so loved the world that He gave his only-begotten Son'.

Does God really think of sinful man as 'treasure'? Yes, I
think He does. When He created man He said, 'Let Us make
man in our own image ... and let him rule over all the earth'
(Genesis 1:26). And then man sinned and was driven out of
the Garden of Eden where God had walked with him - the
treasure was lost. But God found him again when He sent His
only-begotten Son (the best that He had) down into our world,
to give His life for us and 'buy' us back to Himself. God's
world is to come back to Him again, because He has redeemed
us, and that purchase will be made complete when Jesus
comes again.

What a prospect is ours! You and I have our part to play
in helping the Man recover that field.

At the Name of Jesus every knee should bow, in heaven
and on earth and under the earth, and every tongue confess
that Jesus Christ is Lord, to the glory of God the Father
(Philippians 2:10,11).

We thought about this verse once before, on April 5th to be
exact. But I want to take a different line about it this time. This
verse brings us to the utmost peak of submission, praise and
glory to our Lord Jesus Christ. And not just yours and mine,
but the ultimate bowing of every knee to Jesus - people from
all over the world, of every tongue and nation.

This, in fact, is going to take place one day. When? Who
can tell? But it will be the ultimate day when the whole world
is back in His hands. What will bring that day to pass? Jesus
told us that the date lay in His Father's hands, and that nobody
could foretell it.

But one thing is sure - you and I and every Christian is
called upon to play our part to that end. We have a hand in
'bringing back the King'. From today, every person who is a
true believer in Jesus will help to bring that day nearer. So it
means, for you and me, a steady trust in Him, a bending of all
that we are and do and think and say, to the glorification of
Jesus our King.

No, it does not mean watching the sky for His coming, or
sitting down and waiting; it involves our usual daily life -
every bit of it, school, home, church, friendships, business,
recreations, thoughts and prayers - all to be put under His
guidance and control, and kept there continually.

'O use me, Lord, use even me,
    Just as Thou wilt, and when and where'

June 20
They devoted themselves to the Apostles' teaching, and to
the fellowship, to the breaking of bread, and to prayer
(Acts 2:42)

Christian people often ask whether we ought not to try and get
back to the kind of way the first Christians used to live and
behave. What was it like in those days just after the Church
was first formed, how did they behave, and what made the
Church grow as fast as it did then?

Here is the answer or, at least, part of it. It's a description
of what the tiny church was like, just after Peter had preached
his great sermon on the Day of Pentecost (Whitsunday) when
3,000 new Christians were added to the church that very day!
These were the rules they kept:

1. *The Apostles' teaching*. For that, we have the whole
New Testament to guide us, as well as its frequent references
back to the Old Testament. This means that we really must
give time to reading and studying the Bible for ourselves. It's
a good thing to have a private notebook in which we can
record what we've read and when and what we learn from our
study. It need not be a lot to begin with - just a note or two -
but record it.

2. *The Fellowship*. One cannot be a Christian in isolation,
all on one's own. Each must have at least one fellow-
Christian, and that will lead to others. All should be in God's
House at least every Sunday, worshipping together.

3. *Breaking Bread*. The fellowship meal is for us all - as
soon as we are full members of His church. We feed upon
Christ, together.

4. *Prayer*. This is the life-line of every Christian, both a
regular time of prayer, and in any time of need wherever we are.

All that is Primitive Christianity!

June 21

Thy Word is a lamp unto my feet and a light to my path
(Psalm 119:105).

When we were missionaries out in Kenya, a good many years ago now, there were very few main roads, but hundreds of little tracks. I often used to get called out in the middle of the night to visit some seriously ill person. There would be a knock at the door and an anxious man saying that he had a very sick wife or baby at home, could I please come at once. I would quickly slip on a warm sweater and a pair of gum boots, and off we would go (on foot). No street lights, and when there were no moon or stars, it was very dark indeed. And to guide us? Just the light of a paraffin storm lamp. One step at a time, one gleam of light on the track, till we got safely there.

God says that life's journey is like that, and in the dark, we need a light. He has given us one, His Word. As we study the Bible, God uses it to shine up the Way for us, and we need it so as to navigate safely all our days.

Take for an illustration this wonderful 119th Psalm. 176 verses long - the longest Psalm. Each verse has something to say about God's Word, His Law, His teaching. The whole Psalm is divided into sections, each section being 8 verses long. Each section has a heading, and the headings are the Hebrew alphabet (Aleph, Beth, Gimel, Daleth, He, etc.). The first word in each section (in Hebrew), i.e. 8 words each time, begin with *that* letter of the alphabet. In the first section, each verse begins with A = Aleph. So it's an acrostic Psalm. And the whole Psalm is very full of spiritual meat! What a book!

Now I, Nebuchadnezzar, praise and exalt and glorify the
King of Heaven, because everything He does is right, and
all His ways are just. And those who walk in pride, He is
able to humble (Daniel 4:37).

We had the first part of this story of Nebuchadnezzar on April
27th, and we saw how God had to humble him, and how he lost
his senses and was put out to grass like an animal. But, after
a time, God restored his sanity, and then he praised God with
all his heart (verses 34, 35 give us the song of praise he sang).

It's a wonderful thing when this happens - that men who
have boasted of their own powers and then experience a
tremendous downfall really come right back to God and find
Him to be the answer to all their needs. It happened to Paul,
who in his early life was a tormentor of the Christians.
Suddenly, on the road to Damascus, he was stopped in his
tracks and temporarily blinded. It took him three days before
he was ready for God's restoration of him. But what a change
came over him! His sight of the glorified Lord Jesus was the
last thing he saw till Ananias came to him in his blindness and
said to him: 'Brother Saul! '

The marvellous thing is that at the moment we come to
Christ, we come right into the whole fellowship of believers
all over the world - 'All one in Christ Jesus' (Galatians 3:28).
So we have much for which to praise God today.

It is full time now for you to wake from sleep. For salvation is nearer to us now than when we first believed; the night is far gone, the day is at hand. Let us then cast off the works of darkness and put on the armour of light (Romans 13:11,12).

When Paul wrote this letter, he knew that time was short. He had opportunity *then* to preach the gospel, but who could tell when persecution would greatly limit the possibility? The letter was written from Corinth around A.D. 60. Four years later was the Jewish revolt and Roman persecution of the Christians, and Paul sensed this coming, I think. Also he was looking forward to the end of this age - which did not come in his day and has not yet come, but that could take place at any time. So for us too - the time is short.

'Wake up!' says Paul. When Jesus comes again, the opportunities will have finished. A well-known missionary, Carey Francis of Kenya, once said: 'When my time comes, I want Jesus to find me with my work in order, my jobs done, and me hard at it to the last.' And that was, in fact, what happened to him. He took his lesson that morning, was due to fly to England on furlough next day - and God took him sitting at his desk. Four thousand Africans attended his funeral, and the Kenya Parliament was closed for the day. He was ready.

These days are days of crisis. But we should be encouraged. Jesus once said, 'When you see these things begin to come to pass, then look up, lift up your heads; for your redemption draweth nigh' (Luke 21:28).

Are we ready? 'Put off darkness - put on the armour of light.' We're in a battle!

June 24th

Why then did you go out? To see a prophet? Yes, I tell
you, and more than a prophet .... There has risen no one
greater than John the Baptist (Matthew 11:9,11).

This is what Jesus said about the man who was His forerunner.
How was it that Jesus could say that John was more than a
prophet, and that no one greater than he had yet come?

John was, in a sense, the last of a long line of prophets, all
of whom had in some measure prophesied the coming of the
Messiah. It was John who was to usher in Jesus - he was the
great herald of the King of Kings. John was 'A Voice'. He
belittled himself, in order to magnify Jesus. He said he was a
nobody, unworthy even to touch the shoes of Jesus. He was
to decrease - Jesus was to increase. As you read the story, you
find John pointing his own disciples to Jesus, and they left him
and followed Jesus. That was what John wanted.

John was, in a sense, the end of the Old Testament and the
beginning of the New. He stood between the two. That was
how it was possible for Jesus to say that one who was least in
the Kingdom of Heaven was greater than John. Up to that
point, nobody had yet come into Christ's Kingdom - but John
showed the way. Obviously John himself was also to come in.
'The prophets and the law prophesied *until John*' (Matthew
11:13).

What a rough life John led - out in the deserts, living
rough, and always pointing, pointing to Jesus! His life ended
with his beheading by Herod. That was his entry into *life*
eternal!

To be a pointer - what a privilege is ours - to point to Jesus.

Those who are wise shall shine like the brightness of the firmament; and those who turn many to righteousness, like the stars for ever and ever (Daniel 12:3).

The Book of Daniel is a strange book, part history, part prophecy. This verse comes near the end of the visions about the future that Daniel had. Daniel was told not to try and worry out the meaning of his visions. They would be understood by the people who would be around towards the end of the age. Many people have tried to puzzle them out.

But this little verse stands out as a pure gem, applicable to all who are trying to win others to Jesus. It's the reward Jesus promises to those who are giving their lives into His service; people in many walks of life: missionaries, ministers, godly men and women in business, humble people little known outside their own immediate circle, others with famous names, boys and girls faithful to Him - all sorts. What's the reward: we shall 'shine brightly like stars for ever and ever.' What a lovely thought, isn't it? Of course, the brightness comes from Him - the Light is His, but reflected by us.

I would like that promise to be mine and yours. It can be.

Let us rise, and shine, and give God the glory;
Let us rise, and shine, and give God the glory,
Let us rise and shine.

And the king said to me, 'Why is your face sad, seeing you are not sick? This is nothing else but sadness of the heart .... For what do you make request?' So I prayed to the God of Heaven. And I said to the king, 'If it pleases the king .... that you send me to Judah, to the city of my fathers' sepulchres, that I may rebuild it' (Nehemiah 2:2, 4, 5).

Nehemiah was a captive in Babylon, and his country had been ruined and ravaged by their enemies. The temple was destroyed and the city walls broken down. Nehemiah himself had been given a post in his kingly captor's household - he was the cupbearer to the king. What could he ever do for his own country in such a position? Well, he was a man of prayer; and he kept his eyes open for any opportunity that might come his way.

And one day, come it did! The king spotted his sad face and asked what was the matter. Opportunity! 'So,' says Nehemiah, 'I *prayed* to the God of Heaven, and I *said* to the king ...'.

This happened all in a flash. He shot up an arrow prayer: 'Quick, Lord! Help me! What shall I say?' I expect it didn't take him as long to pray it as it has you to read it! And I'm sure the king didn't even notice his hesitation, if there was any.

When you have a little time, read through the book of Nehemiah and see how many other 'arrow' prayers you can find in it. You'll be surprised. And then, try it out for yourself next time you're in a fix and have to decide quickly. It still works! Remember where Jonah prayed! (Jonah 2:1).

The fruit of the Spirit is love, joy, peace, patience, kindness, goodness, faithfulness, gentleness, self-control;
against such there is no law (Galatians 5:22,23).

Paul is describing the result of the Holy Spirit's occupation of
the heart and life of a believing Christian. As you look at the
list, you wonder: 'Am I really expected to acquire all that? I
might do something about love. But I should be a sort of
plaster saint if I managed all nine of those virtues?'

I think I would agree with you in thinking that you cannot
grow these bits on to your character. God does this in you, and
He doesn't do it all at once, any more than grapes can ripen on
a vine in ten minutes. It's a slow and steady progress, going
on all your life, as you come increasingly under the Holy
Spirit's power.

LOVE here means that however much a person may
injure or insult us, we will always want their highest good.

JOY is based in God, not in possessions, triumphs, even
friends.

PEACE is happiness of heart, knowing that our way of life
is safe in God's perfect hands.

PATIENCE means being slow to anger with people, as
God is constantly patient with us.

KINDNESS was shown by Jesus to Mary when she
washed His feet.

GOODNESS is strength to resist and rebuke evil - not
ignoring it.

FAITHFULNESS is being trustworthy,

GENTLENESS is being open to God's guidance,

SELF-CONTROL is keeping your body and mind and
spirit mastered by Jesus Christ.

Jesus answered Nicodemus, 'Truly, truly, I say to you, unless one is born anew, he cannot see the Kingdom of God.' Nicodemus said to Him, 'How can a man be born when he is old? Can he enter a second time into his mother's womb and be born?' Jesus answered, 'Truly, truly, I say to you, unless one is born of water and the Spirit, he cannot enter the Kingdom of God' (John 3:3-6).

How does anyone become 'born of the Spirit'? Is this something different from being baptised and being a church member? Yes, it is more than those two things. It is making my relationship to Jesus Christ *real*. In Revelation 3:20, we hear Jesus speaking to the *church* in Laodicea, a church which was cold and dead, and saying this: 'Behold, I stand at the door and knock. If any man hears My voice and opens the door, I will come in to him, and eat with him, and he with Me.'

You don't just invite *anyone* to come into your house, do you? To come in and share your house should only be on offer to a person you can trust and love. Jesus knocks - He will not force His way in. *You* have to open the door to Him.

When you do, new life begins. Sin in your life has to be dealt with. Every person is a sinner, and we all need God's cleansing and forgiveness. But Jesus died for our sins, and through His death we may be forgiven. 'He bore our sins in His own Body on the tree' (1 Peter 2: 24).

If you take the step of personally inviting Jesus into your heart, you should tell a Christian friend, because it helps to have a friend who knows you have made a start. And if you are not already a church member, make a start there too.

Opening the door to Jesus is the first step on the ladder that leads to Heaven.

Jesus said to him the third time, 'Simon, son of John, do you love Me?' Peter was grieved because He said to him the third time, 'Do you love Me?' And he said to Him, 'Lord, You know everything; You know that I love You' (John 21:17).

Peter, the impetuous spokesman for the rest of the apostles, has a little private talk with Jesus, after Jesus had cooked them a breakfast of fish and bread on the beach. He not only cooked it, but He also served it to them - the Master becoming the Servant again.

As Jesus began to talk to Peter, He asked if Peter loved Him. Twice Peter said he did. But the third time, his mind went back to a day, not so very long ago, a day of which Peter didn't want to be reminded. The day when he had three times denied that he even knew Jesus. And Jesus had looked at him as the cock crew. That look caused Peter to burst into tears.

And now Jesus has touched that sore spot again, and Peter's heart turned over! Three denials - three loves. Which was it to be? All the barriers were down now. Forgiveness was complete.

When Jesus and Peter first met, Jesus took him off the fishing and told him He would send him to catch men. I believe this breakfast morning was Peter's commissioning by Jesus to go out and care for His sheep, His lambs. It was to be Peter who was to be the break-through for Jesus into the Gentile world.

He asks you and me today: 'Do you love Me? If you do - feed My Sheep.' What shall we answer Him?

And Zacchaeus stood and said to the Lord, 'Behold, Lord,
the half of my goods I give to the poor; and if I have
defrauded any one of anything, I restore it fourfold'
(Luke 19:8).

Two days ago, we were thinking about the meaning of what
Jesus called 'The New Birth'. We saw the necessity of it
happening, if we are to be truly His disciples. Today we have
an illustration of just what happens when a person is 'born
again'.

Zacchaeus was a tax-collector and such men were notori-
ous cheats, which was why they were so much hated by the
general public. Zacchaeus was himself a very rich man. But
he was a little chap, and was very anxious to see this great
Preacher who was passing through Jericho. He couldn't see
over the heads of the crowd, so he shinned up a tree, which
gave him an excellent observation-post. But he hadn't bar-
gained on Jesus seeing *him*! 'Come down, Zacchaeus, for I'd
like to come to tea with you!'

Down he scrambled, and off they went together - amid the
mutterings of the crowd, who couldn't think why the great
Preacher should associate with such an evil man. We don't
know what Jesus said to him at home. But we see the result.

Jesus said, '*This day* is salvation come to *this* house.' And
Zacchaeus announced that he would put right all his cheating
of the public as far as he knew, handing back four times what
he had taken, and then giving half his property to the needy.

When a person is born again, it shows in their behaviour.
If it doesn't, you wonder if their New Birth was genuine.

Lord, help me to live out what I profess.

O Lord, who shall dwell on Thy holy hill? He who walks blamelessly, and does what is right, and speaks truth from his heart; who does not slander with his tongue, and does no evil to his friend (Psalm 15:1-3).

Living in this present world, as you look at the picture of the world to be when it is under the total control of Jesus, doesn't it seem virtually impossible that anybody can ever qualify for a place?

Even the very best people we know could never match up to the standard that God sets, could they? Do they always 'walk blamelessly'? Do they always 'do what is right'? Do they always 'speak the truth'? Do they never 'slander' anybody? Have you never 'done evil to a friend'? I can't match up to those standards, I know.

Yes, the standards are clear enough. That's what we are aiming at. But I haven't forgotten that even Paul had to say that he hadn't reached perfection - yet. He was facing the right way, he was on the road. Listen to what he said: 'Not as though ... I were already perfect: but I follow after ... Forgetting what is behind and straining towards what is ahead, I press on towards the goal to win the prize for which God has called me heavenwards in Christ Jesus' (Philippians 3:12-14). Not already perfect - but facing the right way. That doesn't mean we can ever be satisfied with our attainments - there's always something better ahead. But we keep Jesus in sight all the time. And His forgiveness and cleansing are constantly available.

Lord, keep my eyes in the right direction today, and in my living, let me glorify You. AMEN.

Suffering produces endurance, and endurance produces character, and character produces hope (Romans 5:3,4).

I suppose all of us hate suffering when it comes. We dread the pain, whether it is physical, mental, or spiritual. We shrink from having to undergo it, and we pray to God to deliver us from it. But in this passage, Paul is saying - 'this is how God brings out the best there is in us - this is what it takes to make us strong - this is really when we begin to grow spiritually.'

If you are a gardener, you may well have a greenhouse in which to start off your seedlings. Once they have begun to grow, you put the pots outside for the seedlings to harden off, and eventually transplant them into the soil of the garden. The wind, the rain, the cold, all put pressure on the seedling, but it soon grows strong and sturdy. If you leave it always in the greenhouse, it will grow leggy and thin, and probably fail to produce its flowers or fruit.

It was hard to be a Christian in Rome in Paul's day. So Paul writes to them not to worry when pressure comes - it is meant to stimulate them into resistance and fresh hope. William Barclay describes what Paul means by his use of the word *dokime* for 'character': *Dokime* is used of metal which has been passed through the fire so that everything base has been purged out of it. It is used of coinage as we use the word 'sterling'. The character which has endured the test always emerges in hope.

So, when suffering comes your way, hold your head high. Remember, every step of the way Jesus Christ is with you.

Lord, teach us to pray (Luke 11:1).

Isn't this one of the biggest problems that any Christian has to face? We know so very little about real prayer, we find it hard to concentrate, we tend to drift into just asking for 'things'. We would like to be praying people, but we're not quite sure HOW.

Look for a moment at this verse in its context. 'One day Jesus was praying in a certain place. When He had finished, one of His disciples said to Him, "Lord, teach us to pray, just as John taught his disciples".' Was He praying with His friends then, or had He gone aside and was praying alone? Obviously, they were watching Him at prayer. They wanted to be able to pray in the way they had seen Him praying.

But they had also seen how John the Baptist taught his disciples to pray. When it came to 'HOW', Jesus gave them a model prayer - what we call the Lord's Prayer. In fact, of course, it is not His, but a model for us to use. His prayers we have, ideally, in John 17.

After giving us the model, He gives us an illustration - the man who goes to a friend at midnight and asks for three loaves to feed a visitor who has come. He gets what he asked for by persisting in his request.

It's a good thing to keep a regular prayer list, which you will keep adding to and subtracting from; when you get a clear answer from God, it's good to note that down. When God answers our urgent prayers, do go back and thank Him.

What do you want to put into your prayer-list? Your time for prayer is limited, so obviously you can't possibly pray for all your concerns every day - some should be weekly or monthly.

Christ has entered ... into Heaven itself, now to appear in
the presence of God on our behalf (Hebrews 9:24).

When Jesus returned to Heaven, He had completed his work
on earth for us. He had taught us what God is like; He had
redeemed us from our sins; He had done away with the Old
Testament sacrifices, having made the one perfect sacrifice
for sins for ever. Before He left, He told the disciples that He
was going into Heaven to prepare a place for them, that they
would one day be with Him there for ever.

Hebrews reminds us that Jesus is able to save to the
uttermost those who come to God through Him. As someone
once put it, 'He is saving us from the guttermost to the
uttermost.' So He is bringing back the human race into God's
Presence.

He is our representative before God. Our link with Heaven
has been restored and we can now come into God's presence
unashamedly because Jesus bore the penalty of our sins and
wiped them off our slate. We have become citizens of Heaven.

Yes, we are still citizens of earth. But that is a temporary
phase for we are ultimately to dwell with God for ever.
Meanwhile we are part of the Body of Christ on earth and our
purpose here is to be His witnesses to all who don't yet know
Him.

We have our fellowship with all those who are in Christ,
of *whatever* race or colour. For instance, once we were
holidaying in Switzerland and we found ourselves on a train
with a banker and his wife from East Germany. We knew no
German, they knew no English. But we each had a New
Testament, and sharing that, we were united in Christ.

Now the elder son was in the field: and as he came and drew near to the house, he heard music and dancing. And he called one of the servants and asked what this meant. And he said to him, 'Your brother has come, and your father has killed the fatted calf, because he has received him safe and sound.' But he was angry, and refused to go in
(Luke 15:25-28).

In the story of the Prodigal Son, most people concentrate on the boy who ran away and spent his father's legacy on riotous living. But there was this elder son, who stayed at home and worked for his father, and had never rebelled against him.

When the younger son came back, the old father was overjoyed and heaped blessings on him. But the older son was angry and jealous: 'I never did anything wrong, yet you never made a feast for me! Yet as soon as this ne'er-do-well son of yours comes back, you make a huge feast for him!' Anger - but self-righteous anger, and jealousy.

When someone does something that makes our rage rise, what do we do about it? Do we want to fly off the handle? If so - why? We need to examine our motives. The elder son wouldn't even call him 'my brother' - it was 'this your son'. Yes, truly the youngster had been wicked, but now he had repented and come back.

We should rejoice if a former 'enemy' of ours suddenly turns to Christ in repentance and faith. He has become a 'brother' in Christ, and if God forgives him, shouldn't we do the same? 'Forgive us our trespasses, as we forgive those who trespass against us', we say as we pray the Family Prayer. If we can't forgive, how can we expect Christ to forgive us?

Elisha said, 'Fear not, for those who are with us are more than those who are with them.' Then Elisha prayed, and said, 'O LORD, I pray Thee, open his eyes that he may see.' So the LORD opened the eyes of the young man, and he saw; and behold, the mountain was full of horses and chariots of fire round about Elisha (2 Kings 6:16,17).

You really need to read the background to this story! Elisha had been advising the King of Israel about his enemies who were trying to destroy him. Eventually the King of Aram discovered what Elisha was up to and sent an army to capture him. The army surrounded the city where Elisha was, and his servant became scared that his master would be captured. Elisha told him to trust in God. And lastly, he prayed that the eyes of the servant would be opened and they were. Then he saw and his fear was gone. Next Elisha prayed that the eyes of his enemies might be closed and God also answered that prayer. The army was captured - but was later released - and there was no more war!

Do you ever get a scare that it's almost impossible to live the Christian life because of the hostility of others? That you aren't strong enough? That there's nobody backing you up? That temptation is too strong? Understandable: but that's where you need to pray for opened eyes. If you're 'with Christ', you're on the winning side. The ultimate victory is His. The heavenly legions are surrounding you, and He won't let you go. The battle is His - not yours. You can stand by and watch, as He takes over.

Open my eyes, that I may see.

He is the expiation for our sins, and not for ours only, but also for the sins of the whole world (1 John 2:2).

One of the things for which we thank God every single day is that, through the death on the Cross of the Lord Jesus, all our sins are forgiven. It takes an enormous load off our minds to remember this wonderful truth. But there's another fact that comes out of this verse, which is that the sins of every person can also be forgiven - as and when they receive Jesus.

Much flows from this. Just pause and think for a moment: of all the people you know, especially those whom you most dislike? Have you any enemies at all? Christ died for them too.

One of the great Christians of Uganda was Bishop Festo Kivengere. He did much to help and rescue the thousands of children who had been orphaned through the murder of their parents by Idi Amin and his men. Festo has written the story of these happenings and of how he very nearly lost his own life at the time when Amin murdered the Uganda Archbishop Luwum. Festo wrote a book entitled *I Love Idi Amin*. How can you love such a man? But Jesus once said, 'Love your enemies: do good to those that hate you and despitefully use you' (Luke 6:27, 28).

He loved Judas who betrayed Him. Does that thought give you someone to pray for today? Hating people is purely destructive; loving them could turn enemies into friends. Remember Paul's conversion.

July 8

I have learned, in whatsoever state I am, therewith to be content. I know how to be abased, and I know how to abound; in any and all circumstances I have learned the secret of facing plenty and hunger, abundance and want (Philippians 4:11,12).

'To be content.' That is something that most of the world today knows little about. Writing in 1 Timothy 6:8, Paul says, 'Food and clothing - that's enough.' The basics of contentment! Yet from our earliest days we spend time and effort in striving for much much more than that. What must we have today? A car, a fridge, a video, a bigger salary, a colour TV, a comfortable home?

Most of our world is living not above, but below the breadline. Millions are half-starved, while we in the Western world are comparatively well-off. Even the unemployed in Britain are better off than millions in Asia and Africa. How much does our Government give to aid starving refugees in Asia? Yes, something is being done, but not nearly enough.

What can I do to change things? No, I can't feed all the starving, but I can do something through Christian Aid, Tear Fund, or a missionary society to help. I can ask my member of Parliament to press our Government to increase Aid to the Third World. Almost certainly I can do something to help someone worse off than myself. So do it *now* while I have time and opportunity. Remember what Jesus once said about His own possessions: 'Foxes have holes ... but the Son of Man hath not where to lay His head' (Matthew 8:20). God Himself with no home? In helping someone else, I am helping Him.

He is Lord of lords, and King of kings, and those with Him
are called and chosen and faithful
(Revelation 17:14).

Some people think that they can decide whether or not to
follow Jesus. In fact, of course, the first move is with God, not
with us. He seeks for us before we ever begin to think about
following Him. It is when we feel His drawing power that we
can begin to respond.

1. We are Called
God calls in different ways. Sometimes from our earliest
days, if our parents are believers. Sometimes through a friend,
a book, an evangelistic service. How did He call you?

2. We are Chosen
Just as He chose the Jewish Race to be the recipients of His
Grace and the spreaders of the Good News, so He chooses us
to be His friends and servants. Don't ever think you haven't
been chosen.

3. We are Faithful
If we are Called and Chosen by God, then in the purpose and
plan of God, we shall be Faithful. No, it doesn't mean that we
are bound to stand firm or that our innate strength will keep us.
But we are in safe Hands, and it is His Hands that will enable
us to be true to our Calling. He will not let us go. If we slip, He
will rescue us. We are His. So keep *faith*.

It is for freedom that Christ has set us free. Stand firm,
then, and do not let yourselves be burdened again by a
yoke of slavery (Galatians 5:1).

Am I good enough to get into Heaven? The answer clearly is
'No'. Nobody is. All men are sinners, and no sin can enter
God's heaven. 'The way of Law,' says Paul, 'makes Salvation
dependent on man's achievements. If you go by Law, you
have to be totally innocent.' Nobody that has ever existed
(apart from Jesus) has ever been totally sin-free. So the only
other way of finding our way to Heaven is by God's free
Grace. We cannot earn it, we do not deserve it, but Jesus offers
it to us freely as His gift to us. Our sins are forgiven by His
death on the Cross where He took our sins upon Himself and
bore the penalty for us.

That doesn't mean that, since Jesus has forgiven us, we
are now free to sin as much as we like. It has been said that the
Christian principle is 'Love God and do what you like.' But
that really means that if we truly love God, we shall only want
to do what pleases Him. We don't do things that we know will
grieve our best friends.

The late Dr Howard Guinness wrote a chorus which runs:

Free, Free, Free!
For He carried my sins on the tree;
And He lives in my heart,
So sin must depart,
And I'm Free, Free, Free!

That is Christian Freedom.

As for what was sown on rocky ground, this is he who hears the Word, and immediately receives it with joy; yet he has no root in himself, but endures for a while, and when tribulation or persecution arises on account of the Word, immediately he falls away (Matthew 13:20,21).

This parable of the Sower and the Seed and the Ground which Jesus told is very well known by people who read the Bible and attend some form of worship.

Sometimes we find a friend who has never made any profession of faith in Christ suddenly apparently making a very good start. We rejoice when we see it - he or she seems really to have entered upon the true Christian life. But a little later on, they either drift gradually away or for some reason suddenly drop out - and we wonder what has happened. It may be something like this. Yes, they were certainly attracted to the Christian Faith when they began. But they hadn't realised that becoming a Christian would involve disapproval from non-Christian friends.

'How can you link up with those narrow-minded people? (they think) You'll have to drop all your former amusements and interests, and just attend some dull church with a lot of old people who have nothing better to do. For goodness sake, come off it.' And then they're scared. 'Did I just rush into this because it sounded exciting and new? On second thoughts I wonder if I was wise. Let's go gently.' Yes, they heard the Word with joy - but they cannot face the music. 'Tribulation or persecution from friends is too great.' 'I wish I had your faith,' they say. 'But perhaps this is not really for me.'

The Word has not taken root, it's not for keeps. God's Word must grow in our lives, if we are to be *real* disciples.

Do not neglect to show hospitality to strangers, for thereby
some have entertained angels unawares. Remember those
who are in prison, as though in prison with them: and those
who are ill-treated as if you yourselves were suffering
(Hebrews 13:2,3).

Have you ever heard the phrase, 'Getting inside another
man's skin?' None of us are going to be very much use to other
people unless and until we can understand at least a little bit
of what it is like to be them. Obviously you cannot be someone
other than yourself; but you need to imagine what it is like to
be living the sort of life that other folk live, especially if you
are wanting to win them for Christ. You can't begin to get
them into God's new world, until you at least understand the
sort of life and background that is theirs now.

So often people are won to Christ, not so much through
preaching, as by the living example of Christ set by Christian
people. 'It is not so much what you say as what you are.'

Entertaining strangers can be quite embarrassing sometimes and you may easily be taken in by fraudulent people.
But better to run the risk of that than to refuse aid to those in
need. Yet how many people there are who have at some time
taken in a student or other visitor from overseas and only later
have discovered that their visitor has developed into becoming a king, a Prime Minister, or a leading Christian in their
own country when they have returned.

Abraham and Lot entertained angels, though they didn't
know that when they first offered them hospitality - they
found out later.

Who is my neighbour? (Luke 10:29).

O Jerusalem, Jerusalem ...! How often would I have
gathered your children together as a hen gathers her brood
under her wings, and you would not! (Matthew 23:37).

Jesus was on His way into Jerusalem for the last time before
His crucifixion. He had longed and longed to bring the people
of Jerusalem to Himself, but they had rejected Him and now,
as He looked down upon the glittering turrets of the city, He
wept over them with love.

I never read this verse without remembering something
that happened when we were missionaries in Kenya. We used
to keep a few chickens, and one of them had built her nest
outside the run, and was sitting on a dozen eggs. One night, a
swarm of soldier ants came right through the mission premis-
es, eating anything that was edible for ants. In the morning,
when I went out, I discovered the ravages of the night. When
I got to the nest I found the mother sitting on the nest and the
eggs untouched. But the mother-hen was just a bag of feathers
and bones, the ants had eaten her as she sat, and she never
moved. She cared - and died at her post.

Jesus went down the hill into Jerusalem and ministered
there the early part of that week. But eventually they took Him
and put Him to death - the Man who loved them so much that
He gave His very life for them - and for us - and for all His
world. God incarnate dying for a world that rejected Him.
'God so loved the world, that He gave ...'.

How much do I love Him?

And he commanded the chariot to stop, and they both went
down into the water, Philip and the eunuch, and he baptised him. And when they came up out of the water, the
Spirit of the Lord caught up Philip; and the eunuch saw
him no more, and went on his way rejoicing
(Acts 8:38,39).

Isn't it strange how people from opposite ends of the world
seem to meet, apparently by chance? The eunuch in this story
was the financial secretary of the Queen of Ethiopia. He was
travelling home after a visit to Jerusalem, where he had
evidently bought a bit of a scroll of the prophet Isaiah.

Philip, a deacon of the early church in Jerusalem, had been
sent down to Samaria to conduct a Mission. There he was
spoken to by an angel (in a dream?) and told to leave Samaria
at once, and go to the Jerusalem-Gaza Road, to the desert.
Why? He didn't know. But he went. From the ministry to the
crowds, to a ministry to one man. His path and that of the
eunuch crossed, and God said to Philip, 'Go and link up with
the chariot.' God was preparing both of them for that interview.

The eunuch was reading the Isaiah scroll and obviously
didn't understand a word of it. Philip knew that Isaiah had
prophesied the coming of Jesus as Messiah. And 'he preached
unto him Jesus' (verse 35).

Philip baptised him in a tiny oasis. Then they parted:
Philip to Azotus, the eunuch to Ethiopia, and the Gospel came
to Africa! A chance meeting? God's 'chances' are perfectly
planned, down to the very last detail. The upshot? Rejoicing!

Do all things without grumbling or questioning; that you may be blameless and innocent, children of God without blemish in the midst of a crooked and perverse generation, among whom ye shine as lights in the world (Philippians 2:14,15).

This last week I've been watching the tennis from Wimbledon. It has been fascinating to see how the various competitors behave during their games. When I saw that some make no complaints, have no arguments with the umpire, never query a line decision, but accept with a good grace what is decreed, I began to wonder if those folk are Christians. And quite often it turns out that they are. They smile, take their defeats well, and are concerned if their opponent falls.

These are just some of the graces that should characterise a Christian. They are most attractive when they are there; the person concerned stands out and everyone notices it.

That's what St Paul is writing about in his letter to the Philippian Christians. There will often be occasions about which one could grumble and most people would normally do so; but Paul says, If you're a Christian, take it in your stride. 'Crooked and perverse' characterises the generation in which we live today. And it was so in Paul's day too.

Christians are different because they are committed to serving a Master who 'when He was reviled, reviled not again' (1 Peter 2:23). Their job is to 'shine as lights in a dark world.' The light that shines from us is the reflected glory of the Lord Jesus Christ.

July 16

One of the lepers, when he saw that he was healed, turned
back, praising God with a loud voice; and he fell on his
face at Jesus' feet, giving Him thanks. Now he was a
Samaritan. Then said Jesus, 'Were not ten cleansed?
Where are the nine? Was no one found to return and give
praise to God except this foreigner?' (Luke 17:15-18).

Gratitude. Only one in ten said a proper thank you - and he a
stranger. Jesus had healed them all of the dread disease of
leprosy and they could now return to normal society.

Some Christians keep a little book of requests that they
make to God from time to time. As the prayers are answered,
a little thanksgiving should always be inserted! We cannot
just take God's answers for granted.

Always in our daily time for prayer, there should be an
expression of grateful thanks to God for all His provision for
us - our health, our homes, our friendships, His Word to guide
us, His Spirit to refresh us, His Presence to keep us, His joy
to fill us, His strength to restore us. A Christian needs to keep
praising.

A great Bible king, Jehoshaphat of Judah, was beset by
enemies, but he appointed 'men to sing to the LORD and to
praise Him for the splendour of His holiness ... and as they
began to sing, the LORD set ambushes against their enemies,
and they were defeated' (2 Chronicles 20:21-22).

So, start today with a song of praise to the Lord.

The Word of God is living and active, sharper than any
two-edged sword, piercing to the division of soul and spirit
... and discerning the thoughts and intentions of the heart
(Hebrews 4:12).

What a marvellous Book is this Bible - the very Word of God.
In John 1:14, John speaks about Jesus as the 'Living Word'.
But in Hebrews the writer is referring to the written Word,
which reminds the readers of the danger of exclusion of the
unbeliever from God's rest, and the promise that the true
believer can enter.

But this Word is not just a dead word; it's alive, it's
powerful, it gets right down into the inner recesses of a man's
heart and life, treating him as a surgeon treats a sick body,
cutting into it and removing from it the diseased parts and
applying healing and curative medicine where this is needed.

How often we read or hear of people picking up a torn page
of Scripture and reading it, and through it finding their way
into the life and liberty that there is for all who are in Christ.

I have a copy of a Breeches Bible, printed in 1599, and the
translation of Psalm 119:105 reads like this:

Ev'n as a lantern to my feet,
So doth Thy Word shine bright,
And to my paths where'er I go,
It is a flaming Light.

That's nearly 400 years old. But the whole Bible has been
written for nearly 2000 years, and it's still the most read book
in the world. Dig deep into it.

July 18

Therefore take the whole armour of God, that you may be
able to stand in the evil day, and having done all to stand ...
Above all, taking the shield of faith, with which you can
quench all the flaming darts of the evil one
(Ephesians 6:13,16).

We looked at this terrific problem of temptation on January
16, so just peep back at that to refresh your memory.

I think the important thing is that God doesn't leave the
Christian unprotected when the devil is trying to turn him off
course. Paul knew all about this, which is one reason why he
wrote about it in his letter to the Ephesian Christians.

Have you noticed how a good tennis player may find
himself on top of the world by winning a set, but in the next
game he suddenly flops. Why? The reason is that he thinks
he's got there and can afford to slacken his efforts. With a
Christian it is often similar. All is going well and he thinks he
need not bother quite so much.

It's better to take our illustration from a river-fish. If you
watch them, you'll see they are always facing upstream.
Why? Because if they didn't, the water would get in behind
their gills and they would suffocate. A fish floating down-
stream, on its back, is always dead!

The Christian cannot float, he has to swim, and always
against the general stream of the world. So when Satan says,
'Take it easy, you're OK,' BEWARE! Keep your fire-extin-
guisher (of faith and trust in Christ) always at the ready!

Now there are varieties of gifts, but the same Spirit; and
there are varieties of service, but the same Lord; and there
are varieties of working, but it is the same God who
inspires them all in every one (1 Corinthians 12:4-6).

Isn't it exciting to think of all the hundred of thousands of
people all over the world who are serving the Lord Jesus
Christ in dozens of different ways? Think of some of them:
prophets, teachers, preachers, joyful givers, fishermen, mag-
istrates, mothers, fathers, schoolchildren; almost every profession you can think of will have people who belong to Christ
working there.

St Paul was a tent-maker, and earned his money that way.
Jesus was a carpenter until His last three years when He was
given solely to teaching and preaching and healing.

Obviously there are some trades in which you cannot
serve God because they are working against Him. But no
Christian who is in one such would stay, each would have to
change his or her job.

I remember an engine-driver who was a train-spotter. I
asked why he had joined a boy's sport like that. He replied,
'I'm train-spotting for Christ!' He would take boys into the
cab of his train, show them round, and give his witness for
Christ as they left.

If you're an athlete, that too can be used for Christ. Your
job, your hobby, your skills, all these can play in on your
Christian profession. 'Varieties of gifts, but the same Spirit.'

If we walk in the Light, as He is in the Light, we have fellowship with one another, and the Blood of Jesus God's Son cleanses us from all sin ... If we confess our sins, He is faithful and just, and will forgive our sins and cleanse us from all unrighteousness' (1 John 1:7,9).

We thought about this a bit on May 6, so today we pursue it a bit further. 'If we walk in the Light', we are not the only people doing so, but by doing so ourselves, we are linked up with all the others who are also walking in the Light. That means Christian Fellowship which covers many denominations, over-riding the differences of belief that we hold, because serving Christ is not limited to a particular brand of worship.

Notice that our fellowship is also 'with the Father, and with His Son Jesus Christ' (1 John 1:3), and that we have also 'the fellowship of the Holy Spirit' (2 Corinthians 13:14). The very fact that we have fellowship with God's people helps to keep us walking in the Light.

God doesn't just cleanse us from sin once. He keeps on cleansing us. The tense used here is the continuous tense. Whenever we sin, as we do, we need to keep coming back to Christ for forgiveness and cleansing. You cannot be a Christian in isolation - you could not keep it up - so God has given us a fellowship. And in the company of other Christians, with Jesus in our midst, 'all things are possible.'

Now Samuel did not yet know the Lord, and the word of the Lord had not yet been revealed to him ... And the Lord came and stood forth, calling as at other times, 'Samuel! Samuel!' And Samuel said, 'Speak, for Thy servant hears' (1 Samuel 3:7,10).

I think one of the fascinating things about Samuel is his age when he first began to serve God. He was still only a child, but although he was already serving in the Temple, he didn't yet know God to speak to.

His parents had dedicated him to God's service as soon as he was born. His education under the priest Eli cannot have had much spiritual life in it, for we read that 'in those days the Word of the Lord was rare' (1 Samuel 3:1), and Eli himself cannot have been much help to him. But God kept this little boy clean and good, awaiting the day when God spoke to him personally. And it came, in the middle of the night!

There were no conflicting voices around to distract him and, clearly in the dark, God's voice rang out into his conscience and mind: 'Samuel, Samuel!' Startled, he woke up and ran to Eli, saying, 'You called me?' Three times that insistent call came until at last Eli recognised that the call was from God.

So the little boy, who heard God's call and obeyed, gradually grew into the great prophet who was to be the spiritual leader of his people.

This story should be the inspiration of every Sunday School teacher and of all who work amongst children. Who knows when or how the Lord may speak personally to any one of them.

Pray for those who teach.

Let us run with perseverance the race that is set before us,
looking to Jesus the pioneer and perfecter of our Faith
(Hebrews 12:1,2).

The writer of this passage was obviously thinking of the great
Olympic Games and the way in which the winners had to
throw all distraction to the winds and concentrate hard on the
goal that they could see in the distance. Any deviation, any
looking at the other runners, any carrying of unnecessary
garments, would destroy any hope of victory.

So in the Christian Race. It is Jesus who started us off. It
is Jesus who runs with us every step of the way. It is Jesus who
will welcome us into His heavenly Kingdom with His 'Well
done, good and faithful servant' when we come to the end of
the race. There is no retiring in the Christian Race, we have to
'keep right on to the end of the road'.

What a motto for any Christian: 'LOOKING UNTO
JESUS'. And it is as we look at Him we begin to become more
and more like Him. Isn't it marvellous how often you can
recognise a Christian as soon as you see him or her? There's
a little verse in Acts 4:13 which I think illustrates this: 'When
they saw the courage of Peter and John, and realised that they
were unschooled, ordinary men, they were astonished, and
they took note that these men had been with Jesus.' What a
lovely testimony to have!

We beseech you, brethren, to respect those who labour among you and are over you in the Lord and admonish you, and to esteem them very highly in love because of their work (1 Thessalonians 5:12,13).

This is a word that needs saying because so often we criticise our ministers for not being to us all that we require of them. How often do you pray for your minister? Because if he's not doing his job properly, is it partly your fault for not praying for him?

I can see this from both sides, having been a minister for over 50 years and now for having been 'on the receiving end' for 13. Certainly no minister is perfect and there are always lots of things we 'have left undone' and some that 'we ought not to have done'.

But we do know when people are praying for us, it certainly comes through. And that should be part of your 'fellowship in the Gospel' with them. A minister does not 'make the Church' - the Church is the minister and people together.

And if you are asked to do something, you are not doing it for the minister but for the Church of which you are an integral part. A minister's job is to lead the Church, but not to do everything himself! So he is not the only 'visitor' in the parish, every Christian in the congregation should also be looking people up and inviting in those who never come. It has been said that 'the Church is the only club that exists for non-members'. Let it never be said that it's just a hidy-hole for comfortable Christians!

Many of His disciples drew back and no longer went about
with Him. Jesus said to the twelve, 'Will you also go
away?' (John 6:66,67).

Most people at some time or other begin to wonder if they can
possibly keep up being a Christian. The going has become
pretty tough and is it worth the struggle?

Jesus had been talking about the need to 'feed upon Him'
constantly if we truly want to understand what it means to
have Eternal Life. I think perhaps some of them had been
thinking that once they had decided for Christ, they could just
sit down and take it easy. They hadn't realised it was going to
be a lifelong struggle. So they began to drift quietly away.
Jesus knew that if the Twelve also pulled out, His whole
Mission could become a failure, there would have been
nobody left to carry the Gospel into all the world.

This was the moment of crisis. What would they say in
answer to His challenge? Peter, always the spokesman for the
others, came back with the words: 'Lord, to whom shall we
go? You have the words of Eternal Life. We believe and know
that You are the Holy One of God.'

And Jesus answered, 'Have I not chosen you, the Twelve?
Yet one of you is a devil.' He knew that Judas was 'out'; he
wouldn't go on, he would ultimately betray Jesus to His
enemies; yet he'd pretend up to the very last.

Peter was to deny Him, but he came back. Thomas was to
doubt, but not after he saw and touched the Risen Lord. All of
them were to run away, but ultimately they were to stand firm,
because Jesus never left them without help. And He won't
leave us, either. 'I am with you all the days ...'.

God chose what is foolish in the world to shame the wise,
God chose what is weak in the world to shame the strong
... so that no human being might boast in
the presence of God (1 Corinthians 1:27-29).

I find this verse one of the most encouraging in the whole
Bible. It is the opposite of the world which sets store enor-
mously by the people who it thinks are the great ones, brilliant
minds, strong athletic bodies, beautiful people whom everyone admires.

Can you think of anyone you know who fits God's bill? I
can. I think of a very humble African man. His name was
Mwangi. I don't know if he is still alive. He could read and
write, but not very well. He had no home of his own, no wife
or children, no money. But he was a true believer, and he was
a marvellous story-teller. He would go to market and sit down
with little boys and girls and tell them stories. And soon
grown-ups would come round too to hear him and then he'd
preach the Gospel in terms any African could understand.
Hundreds of people came to Christ through Mwangi. When
he'd finished his stories, he'd move on - anywhere in Africa
you might find him. If you offered him money, he wouldn't
take it, but he'd be glad of a meal. Any clothing he had was
second-hand, he never used shoes, just shorts and a shirt,
nothing else.

I have his photo - he doesn't look anything. But that man
is a giant for God. When we get to heaven, I would happily lick
his boots - but he won't have any!

We shall certainly get some surprises when we get to
heaven. Meanwhile, let us take courage, God can use even
you and me.

That through death, He might destroy him who has the
power of death, that is, the devil, and deliver all those who,
through fear of death were subject to lifelong bondage
(Hebrews 2:14,15).

Fear of the unknown is, I suppose, one of the most difficult
fears to overcome. We cannot talk with anybody who has
been through the experience of death and then returned to tell
us all about it. So how can we face up to the totally unknown?

Only as we study what Jesus Himself has to say about it
- for He did exactly that. Presumably the Body in which He
returned was recognisably similar to the Body in which He
died, for He was able to show His disciples the marks of His
wounds. Perhaps they did not at first recognise His face, for
they were not expecting Him to be alive. But His voice was
utterly recognisable, for Mary Magdalene almost jumped out
of her skin when she heard Him speak to her by name.

Of more recent writers, John Bunyan in his *Pilgrim's
Progress* gives a lovely description of Christian's passing
into heaven: 'Christian broke out with a loud voice, "Oh, I see
Him again; and He tells me, When you pass through the
waters, I will be with you; and through the rivers, they will not
overflow you." Thus they got over, and they saw two shining
men waiting for them ... but they left their mortal garments in
the river. So they went up through the regions of the air
sweetly talking as they went, comforted because they had
such glorious companions to accompany them ... till the King
commanded to open the gate ... and all the bells in the city rang
for Joy." ' And Bunyan says: 'I wished myself among them!'

No fear, only Joy.

Whatever your hand finds to do, do it with your might
(Ecclesiastes 9:10).

Hands are a very expressive part of our body, aren't they? Sometimes goods advertised as being 'Handmade'; they are probably of beautiful workmanship and, therefore, are more expensive.

Examine the carvings in many old churches in the land and marvel at the beauty of the exquisite shapes that have been in the past produced all by hand. These things cannot be repeated today; men have largely lost the art, machinery has taken over, but the machinery cannot copy what men have done by hand.

A great artist can leave behind very beautiful paintings which will adorn the world long after the painter has gone to his rest. Your hands can bring joy and refreshment to many needy people over the years. So it is that the writer of the book of Ecclesiastes says: 'Whatever your hand finds to do, do it with your might.' It will not only bring joy to others, you too will be blessed in the doing.

A handshake is a token of friendship. The touch of a hand may mean a wealth of understanding to a person with leprosy or one suffering bereavement, and a squeeze of the hand can bring strength to a sufferer. The use of the hands in the pulpit can be a visual aid to the preacher, expressing welcome or power or gentleness.

In what ways can you make use of your hands for God?

Looking to Jesus the pioneer and perfecter of our faith, who for the joy that was set before Him endured the Cross, despising the shame, and is seated at the right hand of the throne of God. Consider Him who endured from sinners such hostility against Himself, so that you may not grow weary or faint-hearted (Hebrews 12:2,3).

Jesus started us off in the Faith. He will also take us right through to the very end. So the writer here is suggesting that we need to see how He coped with all the problems and temptations that came to Him, how He survived the enmity of evil men and the weakness of His friends, but ultimately came right through to victory and to the very throne of God. That Saviour is alongside of us at each step of our way all through life and will never let us go.

Yes, we too will have much to endure throughout our life - opposition, hostility even, temptations to slackness, to take the easy way, to avoid the cross. To keep clear of unnecessary distractions will not be easy, sometimes they are very attractive sidelines.

But if we keep 'Looking unto Jesus' every day, we shall not go far astray from the path of Faith.

Turn your eyes upon Jesus,
Look full in His wonderful face,
And the things of earth will grow strangely dim,
In the light of His glory and grace.

Let no evil talk come out of your mouths, but only such as
is good for edifying, as fits the occasion, that it may impart
grace to those who hear (Ephesians 4:29).

Sometimes if you are telling a story about something that has
happened, it makes it a bit more interesting if you exaggerate
a bit, it's more fun! Yes, but if you are giving evidence in a
court of law, you are told to stick strictly to the facts. Why?
Because the truth is much more important than the stirring of
interest.

But here Paul is concerned with the way your speech helps
the person to whom you are speaking. He says it must be
'edifying', that is, it should 'build them up', not depress them.
Obviously this doesn't mean we should always choose all our
words carefully, because that would make what we say stilted
and ponderous. We don't have to be continually thinking
about the effect of our words, because that would make us
self-conscious.

I think our general behaviour should be friendly and
welcoming to others. We want to make them feel at home with
us. And if you can be a friend to a person who has no friends,
that is wonderful.

Bad language is, of course, 'out' for the Christian, partly
because it cannot possibly 'minister grace to the hearer'. But
also because it is perfectly possible to express what you mean
without swearing. Jesus once said, 'Swear not at all ... but let
your "yes" be "yes", and your "no", "no"; anything beyond
this comes from the Evil One' (Matthew 5:34-37).

You were sealed with the promised Holy Spirit, which is
the earnest of our inheritance until we acquire possession
of it, to the praise of His glory (Ephesians 1:13,14).

I think sometimes there is a danger that we preachers may give
the impression that all we need is to be filled with the Spirit
and then all in the garden will be lovely! If people think that
bliss and ecstasy will always surround us, they'll be disap-
pointed. No, on earth there's going to be much sadness and
frustration. But we have the 'Earnest'. One day the sadness
will be over.

But what is the 'earnest'? It's one of the great words of the
New Testament, but it only occurs three times, here, and in 2
Corinthians 1:22 and 5:5. The Greek word is *arrabon* and in
Classical Greek it means caution money that a purchaser
deposits when a bargain is struck, which is forfeited if the
purchase is not completed. A woman was selling a cow and
she received 1,000 drachmae as an *arrabon* - a deposit - that
the rest would be paid in due course.

Paul's use of the word is always as a description of the
Holy Spirit. He is saying that God's gift of the Spirit to us is
an instalment, a guarantee, an advance foretaste of the life that
the Christian will some day live when he lives in the presence
of God. 'Though now we see through a glass, darkly, we shall
some day see face to face' (1 Corinthians 13:12). The Holy
Spirit gives us a tiny taste of what God has in store for all His
faithful disciples. We are 'His purchased possession' and
ultimately He will take full possession of us.

Then the disciples came and said to Him, 'Why do you
speak to them in parables?' And He answered them, 'To
you it has been given to know the secrets of the Kingdom
of Heaven, but to them it has not been given'
(Matthew 13:10,11).

At first sight it looks as though Jesus is deliberately trying to
stop non-believers from ever knowing the truth. But we know
this cannot be so because His stated aim was that 'all men
should know the truth'. So what does Jesus mean here?

I think this. He is saying, 'You are my disciples. I have
chosen you, and you have received me. You can understand
and they cannot, yet. They can hear the earthly story, but they
won't understand its heavenly meaning. Until they have
received Me, they won't know what I'm talking about. When
I heal someone from an evil spirit, you know that this is God's
touch on him. But the unbelievers think I'm doing it under the
power of the devil, or that's what they say. They just can't
understand. But perhaps the story may lead them to Me, and
then they'll begin to understand.'

If you ask an unbeliever what it means to be a Christian,
he can only make a guess at it, he won't know. He can only
know when he becomes one himself. Meanwhile his guess
will be a caricature of the real thing, because he just doesn't
understand.

And whenever you hear unbelievers describing Christians and what they are like, you'll know what Jesus meant.
They haven't a clue what it really means to be a Christian,
because you only learn this when you have started on the
heavenward Way.

Was it not necessary that the Christ should suffer these
things and enter into His Glory? (Luke 24:26).

Guess who it was who said this! It comes out of one of the
loveliest stories of the New Testament. You may remember
the story. Two days after Good Friday, two disciples were
travelling home from Jerusalem with sad hearts, for their Lord
and Master Jesus had been put to death. As they travelled, a
stranger drew up beside them and began to walk with them,
asking what they were talking about. They assumed he must
be a foreigner, so they told him about the death of Jesus, whom
they had hoped was to be the Messiah. The stranger rebuked
them for not believing what the Old Testament Prophets had
written about Him: 'And, beginning at Moses and all the
prophets, He explained to them what was said in the Scriptures concerning Himself' (Luke 24:27).

Wouldn't you have loved to be there to hear Him referring
them back to prophet after prophet. Dr Campbell Morgan has
a lovely note on this: He was David's King, 'fairer than the
children of men', and in Solomon's day 'the altogether lovely
one'. He was Isaiah's Child-King, with a shoulder strong
enough to bear the government. He was Jeremiah's Branch of
Righteousness, Ezekiel's Plant of Renown, Daniel's Stone
cut out without hands, Joel's Hope of the People, and the
'turning again' of which Micah spoke. He was the 'Sun of
Righteousness' of Malachi's dream.

And that night they suddenly knew, as He blessed and
broke the bread. Not surprisingly they said, 'Did not our
hearts burn within us as He talked with us in the way, while
He opened to us the Scriptures.'

'Lord, open Thou mine eyes.'

I have laid up Thy word in my heart, that I might not sin
against Thee (Psalm 119:11).

How frequently the Scriptures reiterate the absolute necessity
for every Christian to study and learn by heart the Word of
God. The reason is obvious. We are put into this world in order
to come to Christ ourselves, and then to lead others to Him.
The Scriptures lead us to Him. And we cannot lead others,
unless we know God's Way as revealed in His Word.

When David wrote this wonderful Psalm, he knew very
well that knowing and understanding and drinking in God's
Word is one of the very sure safeguards against drifting into
sin. As we do so, we can claim God's promises for ourselves.

During the Mau Mau troubles in Kenya around 1953/4, a
school teacher and his wife, who started their day by reading
the Scriptures, had come to the passage, 'The Name of the
LORD is a strong tower; the righteous runneth into it, and is
safe' (Proverbs 18:10). After breakfast he went down to
school and began to teach. Suddenly the school was invaded
by armed men, who immediately fired at the teacher. He stood
still and cried out: 'Jesus! Jesus!' and they missed. They fired
again, and he shouted, 'Jesus, tower'. And the men left. One
of the boys asked the teacher, 'Why did you cry out "Tower"?' 'Did I?' said he. Then he remembered his reading of the
early-morning; the Tower had stuck in his memory, and he
thanked God for His protection that day.

Who knows when part of the Word of God may bring us
courage in a sudden emergency? To store our minds with His
Word helps to build us into strong and trustworthy men and
women of God.

Peter said to Jesus, 'Lord, how often shall my brother sin
against me, and I forgive him? As many as seven times?'
Jesus said to him, 'I do not say to you seven times, but
seventy times seven' (Matthew 18:21, 22).

Seven in Scripture is a sacred number. It was the number of
times (maximum) a good Jew was expected to be willing to
forgive someone who had wronged him.

So Peter must have been staggered when Jesus said to
him, '70 x 7'. Do you think he started to do his sums, and
reckon that really meant 490 times! No, because he would
never be able to keep count of all that amount. However many
times his 'brother' had wronged him and later said, 'Sorry' -
he was to be forgiven.

So, every time we pray the Lord's Prayer, we need to
remember this petition: 'Forgive us our trespasses, as we
forgive'. If you ponder this one out, how many times do you
think Jesus has had to forgive us? We couldn't count, could
we? And neither does He. True repentance to Him will always
bring true forgiveness.

Jesus followed His dictum by a parable: the man who
owed 10,000 talents and was totally forgiven, but then tried to
strangle a friend who owed him 100 pence. Incidentally, it
indicates that you should not lend if you want to keep a friend
- far better to give outright if you possibly can. Then the
question of ultimate repayment just doesn't arise, so there is
no underlying grudge.

Lord, make us generous, both in gifts, and in forgiveness
- as You have treated us. AMEN.

Therefore, if any one is in Christ, he is a new creation
(2 Corinthians 5:17).

I wonder what Paul was thinking about when he wrote these words in his letter to the Corinthians. Was he remembering his own conversion on the Damascus Road, when he himself was utterly changed from being a persecutor of the Christians into being a totally dedicated disciple and apostle of Jesus? Or did he know the story of Jesus' interview with Nicodemus, a religious leader of the Jews, who suddenly discovered that to be a Christian, he had to be 're-born' spiritually! Until that took place, he could not 'enter' the Kingdom of God.

Paul's conversion was sudden, Nicodemus's more gradual - but by the time of the crucifixion, Nicodemus knew where he stood. People today speak quite glibly about 'born-again' Christians, but no one can really understand what it means unless and until they have experienced it for themselves.

How can you explain it? It's like joining the army. When you do so, you are under a new regime, you don a special uniform, get into directed training daily, make sure you are physically fit to carry out your orders and lead a disciplined and directed life. You don't go on strike, you serve your Queen. And, ultimately, she pensions you off.

Put that into spiritual terms. Christ has enlisted you, has given you a new life to live, no longer for yourself, but for Him. He trains you daily, privately, and with others who have been enlisted, and you have a Guide-Book of instructions to follow. No outward uniform distinguishes you, but the inward life of your Master shines out through you. But there's no retirement with Him!

You're a New Creation - His.

Then a maid, seeing Peter as he sat in the light and gazing at him, said, 'This man also was with Jesus.' But he denied it, saying, 'Woman, I do not know Him'
(Luke 22:56,57).

It was a lie, of course. But Peter was frightened, and to save his skin, on the spur of the moment, very thoughtlessly and in panic, he denied his Master. Yes, it was just at the moment when His Master was on trial for His life, a moment of great need.

A moment later, Jesus looked at His impetuous disciple and Peter burst into tears. What had he done? How could he? And could he ever do anything to put it right? Poor Peter, he must have suffered agonies over that; and then to see his beloved Master go to the Cross! 'Was it my fault? Could I have saved Him? Can God ever possibly forgive me?' I am sure the devil must have told him many times over that he had committed the unforgivable sin; that he was now in Satan's hands; that he had better give up trying to be a Christian; that God had forsaken him; he had better go back to his fishing job.

Satan was always the 'father of lies' (John 8:44). Forgiveness is always there for the disciple who has sinned. And every one of us sins daily, and God forgives us daily as we come back to Him. He has said, 'I will never leave you nor forsake you' (Hebrews 13:5). We sin in thought, word and deed - at least three different ways. And whatever way, we need His forgiveness constantly.

Peter was forgiven and re-commissioned, and his lie will never be held against him. No more will yours or mine - as we too come back to God.

I have fought the good fight
(2 Timothy 4:7).

Paul was very near his end, his martyrdom, and he knew it. So this was his farewell to his beloved son in faith, Timothy. He is summing up his life since he first became a Christian. At first glance it may look as if he is boasting about his Christian behaviour.

But no, he is not saying, 'I have fought a good fight.' He is saying, 'I have fought *the* good fight' - God's Good Fight against the devil and all his works. All Christians are in that Fight from the moment each turns to Christ. Often they have sinned and slipped in the battle, often they have failed their Master, and just as often they have been picked up by Him again and forgiven, and set on the battlefield afresh.

Never despair, never give up, never think you cannot live the Christian life. Whilst the devil does everything he can to weaken you, Jesus is always with you to hold you and empower you and keep you. You may sometimes feel lonely or defeated or friendless - Paul often knew his weakness. He writes to the Corinthian Christians: 'I was with you in weakness and in fear' (1 Corinthians 2:3); but he also wrote to them: 'God has chosen the weak things to shame the strong' (1:27).

Paul continued to Timothy: 'I have finished the race, I have kept the Faith - now there is in store for me the Crown ... and not only for me, but for all who long for His appearing.' That means you and me too. What a glorious Race to be in! And what a Leader we have!

August 7
God richly furnishes us with everything to enjoy
(1 Timothy 6:17).

What a marvellous world God has provided for us to live in.
Think of its beauty, its fertility, its sun and its rain, its animals,
birds, fish, insects - and its people who mostly still do not
know Him. Every new generation that is born into the world
is a pagan generation, whatever their background. The Christians in each generation have the task of winning their
generation to Christ. If they fail in that, they shall come under
judgement.

We are not responsible for the previous generation or for
the next, but for this one. Do we really understand that the
Gospel could entirely disappear if the whole of this generation
went pagan?

No, don't take the whole burden upon your own shoulders. You are not responsible for the world, but you are for a
small section of it. Paul wrote about this to Timothy: 'The
things you have heard me say in the presence of many
witnesses entrust to reliable men, who will also be qualified
to teach others' (2 Timothy 2:2). Yes, that's how the Gospel
is spread, isn't it? Passing it on to others, as we have opportunity.

'Everything to enjoy.' We should be joyful Christians in
whatever circumstances God puts us in. The less we concentrate on ourselves, and the more on others and their needs, the
more joyful we shall be. Christian Joy is very infectious, it's
easily caught. It bubbles over to those who have no joy.

The 'Joy of the Lord is your strength' (Nehemiah 8:10).

His brothers threw themselves down before Joseph .... But Joseph said to them, 'You meant evil against me; but God meant it for good' (Genesis 50:18-20).

If you read the early story of Joseph, you find almost everything against him from the beginning. His brothers were jealous of him and sold him into slavery. He was the youngest but one of his family. He might have just bemoaned his state, saying 'Everyone is against me', but he put his trust in God - the safest way to live even today.

Potiphar's wife tried to entice him into immorality, and when he refused, she accused him to her husband, and Joseph was sent to prison. But all the time, the Lord was with him and Joseph kept faith with God.

Ultimately Joseph's troubles ended and he became the man who, under God, saved the land of Egypt from complete starvation.

If you put your trust in other people, they can let you down and you might become disillusioned. God never lets His people down, even if things appear to be against them. We have to hang on in faith - God doesn't misuse His tools.

But the treatment meted out to us by others is often God's way of allowing us to grow through adversity - it throws us constantly back upon Him. So, if ever you feel you are maltreated, take it (if you can) with a grain of humour and don't worry too much: it may be part of your training!

Keep me smiling, Lord.

Come to Me, all who labour and are heavy-laden, and I
will give you rest (Matthew 11:28).

John the Baptist was one of those who were 'heavy-laden' at
that time, for he was in prison for his life (verses 2-19). The
great cities had refused the Gospel (verses 20-24), and Jesus
turned to prayer to His Father, and said, 'I thank you that you
have hidden these things from the wise and learned, and
revealed them to little children' (verses 25-26).

Do the clever people know everything? Of course not, but
sometimes they behave as though they have all the answers.
Jesus is just saying that simple folk like you and me can
equally understand the Gospel, and often we don't make it
quite so complicated! A real understanding of the Gospel is a
matter of God's revelation to us, not something we have to
puzzle out for ourselves. Some people say, 'If I can't explain
a thing, I won't accept it as true.'

There is much in the Christian Faith that cannot be
explained, because it is spiritual, not physical. We can accept
it, even if we can't always explain it. I don't know how
electricity works, but I can use it, by pressing the switch. What
causes it to put a current through a wire, I can't explain.

So Jesus puts it simply to us and says 'Come to Me'. And
I come because I need refreshment and strengthening. I come
because I am weary. As I rest in Him I find the zest and
quickening that I need to start afresh, filled with His joy and
His Life. We need a daily refreshing and He is always
available to give it to us.

He was oppressed, and He was afflicted, yet He opened not
His mouth .... They made His grave with the wicked and
with a rich man in His death, although He had done no
violence, and there was no deceit in His mouth
(Isaiah 53:7,9).

Some people say, 'I believe in the New Testament, the Old
Testament is not for us.' Yet Jesus Himself made it perfectly
plain that the Old Testament was equally the Word of God.
And it is borne out in Isaiah's great prophecy concerning the
death of Jesus. It was written 700 years before Christ, yet it
cannot be interpreted of any other man or nation.

'The wicked' - the two thieves. 'The rich' - the grave was
provided by a rich man, Joseph of Arimathea (Matthew
27:57). 'He was oppressed' - He was beaten. 'He was afflicted' - they mocked and tormented Him.

The centurion who presided at the Crucifixion could say
at the end: 'Truly this was the Son of God' (Matthew 27:54).
Back to Isaiah (verse 5): 'He was wounded for our transgressions, He was bruised for our iniquities; the chastisement of
our peace was upon Him, and with His stripes we are healed.'

Of whom else in all history could these words be said?

'He did it for *me*.' And because He did it, my sins are all
forgiven; His death gives me Life. God incarnate dying in my
place, that I may live.

Lord, help me to live out my life for You.

Put on then, as God's chosen ones, holy and beloved,
compassion, kindness, lowliness, meekness, and patience
.... And above all these put on love, which binds all
together in perfect harmony (Colossians 3:12,14).

Paul has a lot to say about 'putting on the New' - because this
is what has to happen, and be seen to happen, once we have
taken the first great step into Christ as our Lord and Saviour.

We are, in fact, new people. Then let us behave as such.
The characteristics that identify a Christian are given as a
reminder of what the new man is like. This is how we shall
recognise him (or her). These are the garments of the believer
in Christ. Kindness to others, humbleness in ourselves, for-
bearance with those who annoy or provoke us, no insistence
on our own rights, giving way when there's no principle at
stake. And refusing to retaliate! Sometimes that is very hard.

When you have put all your new clothes on, don't forget
your overcoat - that covers all the rest - *love*! 'The bond of
perfectness.' It is the life-blood of all the other virtues, and it
is love which makes the rest acceptable to God. Read 1
Corinthians 13 again to let that sink in.

What a recipe for holy living! We shall fail it again and
again, but forgiveness is still there. Our repentance too will
draw us closer, not only to God, but also to our fellow-men.
And His Peace will be upon us.

Dear Lord, remould me again in Your perfect likeness.
For Jesus Christ's sake. AMEN.

Thine, O Lord, is the greatness, and the power, and the
glory, and the victory, and the majesty; for all that is in the
heavens and in the earth is Thine; Thine is the kingdom, O
Lord, and Thou art exalted as Head above all
(1 Chronicles 29:11).

This wonderful paean of praise was uttered by Israel's greatest king, David, as he handed over the kingship at the very end
of his reign to his son, Solomon. He had ruled for forty years
and Israel had greatly prospered under him. David was not
without his faults; he had committed murder and adultery
amongst other sins. But always he had come back to God in
repentance and had received forgiveness.

Paul speaks of him in Acts 13:22 as 'a man after God's
own heart', and certainly David knew something about the
meaning of praise. The highest praise that people could give
Jesus was to call Him, 'Son of David', and we think of Jesus
as 'Great David's Greater Son'.

David didn't write all the Psalms, but in order that they
should receive due notice and recognition they are called 'The
Psalms of David', and many of them are certainly from his
pen. Every Sunday, in the Church of England, we begin our
praises with David's great 95th Psalm: 'Let us come into His
Presence with Thanksgiving'.

To begin the day by praising God is to take the first step
on the road to victory, because we are setting out hand in hand
with the King of Kings Himself.

It is not an enemy who taunts me - then I could bear it; it is
not an adversary who deals insolently with me - then I
could hide from him. But it is you, my equal, my companion, my familiar friend (Psalm 55:12,13).

Poor David had suffered one of the worst things that can
happen to man - the infidelity of a close personal friend. They
had known and trusted each other, they hid nothing from one
another. But now, his great friend has let him down and
betrayed his trust. What can he do? He could cope with the
hatred of his enemies, but not the disloyalty of a friend.

Who has not known this kind of thing? It happens to all of
us at some time - but it is very distressing when it comes. What
can we do? It seems as if our world has suddenly become
meaningless.

We would never treat anyone like that, would we? We'd
stick by them through thick and thin, we'd not be so dastardly
as to let down a real pal. Wouldn't we?

Jesus knew all about that. He had eleven close personal
friends. He could trust them, they'd never betray Him, never
forsake Him. But when He most needed them, 'they all
forsook Him and fled'. Yes, even John the Beloved Disciple,
even Peter and Andrew and James.

That must have hurt more than being arrested on the say-
so of Judas. He knew Judas was a wrong one - but the others
- no! Let's be honest, how many times have we too let Him
down? Too often to count. Yet He still forgives, still calls us
back. The only totally utterly faithful Friend is Jesus Himself.

Lord, keep us loyal always.

They all alike began to make excuses .... 'I have bought a field' .... 'I have bought five yoke of oxen' .... 'I have married a wife' (Luke 14:18-20).

Excuses! This parable of Jesus is a most searching one. If you are invited to some great occasion, there must be a valid reason why you don't accept. And if you are honest, you will give it. But excuses! These are never the real reason. Look at these three:

1. 'I have bought a field, and I must go out and see it.' Some years ago I bought the house in which I now live, but not before I had seen it! It might have been a poky little place, falling into ruin. Without seeing it, I couldn't possibly buy.

2. 'I have bought 10 oxen, and must go to prove them.' A similar situation. Whoever heard of a man buying cattle to work for him, before he had seen them at work and knew of what they were capable? How stupid can you be?

3. 'I have married a wife, and therefore I cannot come.' But surely the invitation included the wife too? It wasn't a stag party! But it was an important occasion.

What were their real reasons? The first was his property: he was so busy with that, he wasn't interested in his relations with his neighbours. The second was his possessions: he just wanted to gloat over them. The third was his family life: he kept his wife out of this opportunity.

It is such things today which still keep people from God. 'Too busy; too far from home; too jealous to allow his wife to get involved with God, and so God is excluded from that family.'

WHAT THOSE MEN MISSED! God's great salvation.

Put to death therefore what is earthly in you: immorality, impurity, passion, evil desire, and covetousness, which is idolatry (Colossians 3:5).

In this third chapter of the letter to the Colossians, Paul is writing about normal Christianity. He begins the chapter by saying, 'If you are now risen with Christ, seek those things that are above' (verse 1).

But what does Paul mean here by his use of the word 'earthly'. Well, the next five words are his explanation: anything which draws us away from the heavenly, that is, from God.

Immorality is any lustful behaviour with the opposite sex. Impurity is immoral thinking or behaviour in yourself. Passion is the same as impurity. Evil desire is wanting something which it would be immoral for you to have. Covetousness is desire to have in your possession something which belongs to someone else, or which you know to be wrong. Why does Paul link up so many different immoral things with covetousness, as being the things that most specially draw us away from God?

I think the reason is that Satan knows what a strong power the sex instinct is in man and, therefore, he uses all his powers to defile sex and thereby defile man and drive an impassable wedge between man and God. Sex is a beautiful and lovely gift of God and, therefore, needs to be preserved and kept for its right, clean and proper use in a Christian marriage. Any passion which is outside of Christ can become an 'idol' - something we value more than our fellowship with Jesus Christ. But remember we are 'risen with Christ'.

The Lord disciplines him whom He loves, and chastises
every son whom He receives .... God is treating you as
sons .... He disciplines us for our good, that we may share
His holiness (Hebrews 12:6,7,10).

None of us likes to be disciplined, whether it be by use of the
cane (or other physical discipline), or by some other painful
process! 'Chastening' (*paideias*) in Classical Greek means
'education', but in Biblical Greek it means 'correction'.
When God sees faults in us, because He loves us He lovingly
applies reproof of discipline, so that we may be established in
the Faith.

So when trials come upon us, we need to remember that
this is part of our training in righteousness, and they are not
sent in anger, but in fatherly love.

The writer goes on to say: 'And if you are not disciplined,
you can't really be God's children ... It may not be pleasant at
the time, but later there is a harvest of righteousness, holiness,
and peace' (verse 11).

And he finishes by saying, 'So strengthen your arms, your
knees, and your feet.' Isn't that exactly what today's best
athletes are doing, undergoing painful exercises in order to
give them such vigorous health and strength that they can win
in the forthcoming Olympics?

That's what every Christian is meant to be, an Olympic
runner for Christ. So we should expect discipline from God,
even if we don't welcome it at the time. We should know that
God doesn't hate us; He loves us so much; He wants us to be
our very best for Him.

When He had said this, one of the officers standing by
struck Jesus with his hand, saying, 'Is that how you answer
the high priest?' Jesus answered him, 'If I have spoken
wrongly, bear witness to the wrong: but if I have spoken
rightly, why do you strike Me?' (John 18:22,23).

This is the preliminary to the trial of Jesus before the Crucifixion. It was before Annas, the ex-high priest. Annas had
asked Him about His teaching. Jesus simply said, 'I have
spoken openly. Ask those who charged Me. They must know
what I said.' 'That's not the way to speak to the high priest,'
they said, as they struck Him. But Annas wasn't the high
priest; he had been removed by the Roman Government, who
had allowed his son-in-law to succeed him. Jesus could have
reminded them of that. But He didn't. He was gentle with His
persecutors.

Annas then had Him rebound and sent to his son-in-law,
Caiaphas, the real High Priest. The secret plotting against
Jesus had been going on for weeks, and He knew it. He makes
clear that He never spoke in secret, His ministry was open for
all to hear.

In these days when persecution is rife in many parts of the
world, all Christian disciples need to watch their own behaviour; for we are being watched by more people than we shall
ever know. They tried hard to catch Jesus out, doing or saying
something unwise, but they could not fault Him.

When a known Christian commits a fault, it is often
published in the Press and comment is made that it is unbe-
coming in a Christian. In a non-Christian there might be no
notice taken.

Lord, guard my steps and my tongue today.

Now therefore fear the LORD, and serve Him in sincerity
and in faithfulness; put away the gods which your fathers
served beyond the River, and in Egypt, and serve the LORD.
And if you be unwilling to serve the LORD, choose this day
whom you will serve ... but as for me and my house, we
will serve the LORD (Joshua 24:14,15).

These are the last words of Joshua, that great and valiant man
who took over the leadership of the tribes of Israel from Moses
and led them into the Promised Land. He was issuing a final
challenge to them to make up their minds as to whom their
ultimate loyalty lay: to God or to the idols of the people of the
land into which God had led them.

Joshua gives his own testimony, very clearly: 'As for me
and my house, we will serve the Lord.' His children were
backing Dad, and so was his wife, and so were his servants;
all the family were in it together.

If and when you can make that commitment, not only for
yourself, but also for all your family, you are indeed a happy
and blest person. It's the high ideal, isn't it? But there's
nothing automatic about it - you can't commit your parents or
children, they have to make their own decision. But much may
depend on your personal testimony.

The upshot? Look at the epitaph on Joshua in Joshua
24:31: 'Israel served the Lord throughout the lifetime of
Joshua and of the elders who outlived him and who had
experienced everything the Lord had done for Israel.'

What a lovely thing to have said of you after you have
gone! May it be true for you and for me.

Lord, keep me close today.

Jesus said to the Jews who had believed in Him, 'If you continue in My Word, you are truly My disciples, and you will know the truth, and the truth will make you free' (John 8:31,32).

Jesus spoke these words at a point when public opinion had suddenly swung in His favour. It was becoming a popular thing to start following Jesus and listen to His words. It was a danger-point, because the real loyalty of the crowd had not yet being tested .

So Jesus is giving them a warning: 'If you're really going to be My disciples, you've got to keep on through thick and thin, right to the end of your days.'

Not so very many years ago, people in Britain used to say: 'Of course I'm a Christian. I'm British and Britain is a Christian country, so that's it.' But nobody today can say with truth that Britain is a Christian country. Yes, it contains many Christians and our laws by and large are based on Christian principles. But comparatively few of our people are church-goers, and churchgoing is a part of what it means to be a Christian, right from the very first days of the Faith.

As we read the Bible we find God's truth. Jesus said, 'I am the truth.' As we receive Him and walk in His truth, He sets us free from the slavery of sin. Becoming a Christian may be an instantaneous event, but living the Christian life is a daily and lifelong habit. There's always more to learn, however long we live.

Lord, help me to keep on keeping on.

Now when they heard this they were cut to the heart, and said to Peter and the rest of the apostles, 'Brethren, what shall we do?' And Peter said to them, 'Repent and be baptised every one of you in the Name of Jesus Christ for the forgiveness of your sins, and you shall receive the gift of the Holy Spirit' (Acts 2:37,38).

This took place on the Day of Pentecost, immediately after the Holy Spirit had come in power upon the apostles and other Christians. And it came out of Peter's sermon to the crowds of Jews who were wondering what it was all about.

What had Peter been preaching about? The Jews to whom he spoke all knew their Old Testament. They knew the prophecies about the hoped-for Messiah, so Peter quotes those hopes. Then he says, 'This Jesus is the longed-for Messiah. In Him, God took upon Himself human form and came and lived the perfect life among us. And you (we) crucified Him. But God has raised Him from the dead - death could not hold Him, the sinless Man, and He rose again. And now He is seated back at God's right hand.'

The preaching produced a conviction of sin. They could all recite the Ten Commandments with no emotion - but they could not now face Jesus Christ unmoved.

Peter spoke in the power of the Holy Spirit and his congregation were now touched by the Spirit. They knew they were sinners. 'What shall we do?' they cried. 'Repent - be baptised - receive the Holy Spirit - and your sins will be forgiven.' And 3,000 did just that, that very day. The original 120 grew rapidly. The Church had begun. And it's still here today.

Elijah came near to all the people, and said, 'How long will
you go limping with two different opinions? If the LORD is
God, follow Him; but if Baal, then follow him'
(1 Kings 18:21).

This tremendous showdown with the 400 prophets of Baal
took place at the foot of Mount Carmel. At the top of that
mountain today, you may see a carving of Elijah with his foot
on the neck of a Baal prophet, about to slay him!

The people of Israel had come to a point of decision in
their history. Were they going to adopt the heathen gods of the
people into whose land they had come, were they going just
to revert to paganism again? If so, God's calling of them out
to be His chosen people had come to an end.

There comes for all men a time when a vital decision has
to be taken. And we can so easily make a mistake, make the
wrong decision, and from then on our lives take a wrong
turning and it ends ultimately in disaster.

The people knew that a fateful decision had to be made -
they couldn't just leave it. But they said nothing to Elijah's
challenge. So Elijah put the issue to the test, and called upon
God to answer by fire. The Baal prophets tried first, with no
success. Then after Elijah prayed, God gave the answer. The
day was saved.

'Once to every man and nation,
Comes the moment to decide.'

The day of decision is God's choice - the outcome of
decision is man's choice. God asks us to choose.

Jesus came and said to them, 'All authority in heaven and on earth has been given to Me. Go therefore and make disciples of all nations ... teaching them to observe all that I have commanded you' (Matthew 28:18-20).

This verse has been, I suppose, one of the most influential in sending out men and women from every country to go and spread the gospel throughout the world. Who has to go? Just those who are called to be missionaries overseas? No, the call is to every single Christian.

If we are Christians, this is our chief job in life, to spread the gospel. We may be doctors, nurses, clergy, teachers, railwaymen, housewives, or almost any other job we can think of; but our main task is evangelism. The people with whom we start should be those nearest us - the people who are our friends, those we work with, our business acquaintances.

That doesn't mean we have to tackle everyone we meet. But we need to pray and ask God to guide us to whom we should speak, and when, and how. Our own testimony as to what Christ means to us personally is the biggest thing we can share. Often we can only do this as we begin to make friends, and people begin to trust us. Sometimes we have to wait for them to make the opening.

Our testimony will only ring true if we are keeping up to date in our own personal links with Jesus. What counts is what He means to us today, not what happened five years ago!

When a friend turns to Christ, what joy that brings to us. We can rejoice with them, and they in turn can begin to spread the Good News.

Good hunting!

My sheep hear My Voice, and I know them, and they
follow Me; and I give them Eternal Life, and they shall
never perish, and no one shall snatch them out of My Hand
(John 10:27,28).

Jesus has a lot to say about sheep and the Shepherd. Some
people say that Jesus never claimed to be God. But what is this
that He is saying here? 'My sheep ... I give them Eternal Life
... nobody shall grab them out of My Hand.' Who else could
ever say such things, but God? Only God could give Eternal
Life to anybody.

A wolf can come and steal a sheep - but not from this
Shepherd. People may fear that some day, as they get older
perhaps, they may drift away from God. But here Jesus says,
'Nobody can snatch us from Him'. We shall never perish if we
are His.

Have you ever watched the Sheep Dog trials on the TV?
I think they are fascinating. The dogs know exactly what their
master wants, whether he speaks or whistles to them, and they
obey. If you or I tried to control them, we should fail, because
they don't know our voices. If you have a dog of your own, he
will certainly know your voice - and he should know his own
name too.

It's like that between us and Jesus. When He speaks to us,
we know His Voice, we recognise His word to us. And we
follow Him. We don't take it from 'strangers'; we learn to
recognise the true shepherds amongst us, by their likeness to
the Good Shepherd.

That is the background to our ordinary everyday life; we
are in the perfect hands of the Good Shepherd. He is our
stabilising force.

Peace I leave with you; My Peace I give to you; not as the
world gives do I give you. Let not your hearts be troubled,
neither let them be afraid (John 14:27).

If you visit Israel, you will find that their normal greeting to
you is 'Shalom' which means 'Peace'. It's their equivalent of
our 'How-do-you-do?' And it means much the same thing.
When you greet someone for the first time, are you really
asking them if all is well with them? No, usually it's just a
formal greeting.

Jesus is telling us that the Peace He offers is not just a
worldly greeting. It is *his* Peace - the peace which is quite
incomprehensible, because it can be ours in the midst of war,
or in Hospital, or in unemployment, or in sorrow from
bereavement. It's the Peace which passes all understanding.

All of us have times of anxiety and stress, and we can get
'all het up' and worried. Things go wrong, people around us
are difficult, we are on edge, our friendships aren't working
out - all kinds of reasons why there is stress. And stress
undermines your general health, so it isn't good. When it
comes upon you, that is the moment you need to remember
that, in Christ, you have His Peace which passes all understanding. So you 'cast your care upon Him because He loves
you.'

The tangles which we see and are unable to disentangle
can be brought to Him, and left with Him. We don't know all
the answers and cannot solve all the problems, *but* we are in
touch with the Solver. When we remember that, we need no
longer fear.

A new commandment I give to you, that you love one
another; even as I have loved you, that you also love one
another. By this all men will know that you are My
disciples, if you have love for one another
(John 13:34, 35).

How can we ever love one another as Christ has loved us?
That is virtually impossible, isn't it? Yet, that's the aim that
Jesus asks of us, that our love for fellow-Christians should be
comparable to His love for us. It includes all or any other
Christian. Maybe we find some of our Christian brethren
rather difficult to get on with: awkward, difficult people who
rub us up the wrong way. Jesus says, 'Love them.'

Why should we? Because He does. Maybe they think we
are a bit funny ourselves, but they too should love us. Because
He does.

People used to say of the early Church, 'See how these
Christians love one another.' And they meant it. They still say
it sometimes of Christians today.

But it's true, it really is. In any church where that is a
characteristic of the congregation, there is very real love for
each other - outside people notice it and comment on it. I
suppose it is that reason, more than any other, why such
congregations tend to grow, because people know they'll get
a welcome there.

Watching the Games at Helsinki today, I saw three
American Negroes get into a little huddle just before the big
race. And one of them won it. Asked about it afterwards, he
said, 'Yes, we were praying that God would keep us close and
help us to live as true Christians.' I like that. What a witness
to the rest of the competitors.

A new heart I will give you, and a new spirit I will put
within you; and I will take out of your flesh the heart of
stone and give you a heart of flesh. And I will put My
Spirit within you, and cause you to walk in My Statutes
and be careful to observe My ordinances
(Ezekiel 36:26, 27).

The date at which Ezekiel was writing this prophecy was very
nearly 600 years before Christ. Ezekiel was looking forward
to an Israel which had been restored to its former glories, and
most of all to a spiritual renewal.

Our world of today is learning something about the
possibility of physical heart-transplants, giving a person a
new heart, transferred from another person who has died or
been killed by accident. We still don't know how long the
renewed person may continue to live after such an operation.

But, of course, Ezekiel's prophecy was eventually fulfilled nearly 600 years later, for the coming of Jesus into our
world ushered in the spiritual renewal that comes when
anybody has received Him as Saviour and Lord.

Bishop Taylor of St Albans has this to say on this verse:
'The terms heart and spirit are ... aspects of man's total
personality. The heart includes the mind and the will, as well
as the emotions ... The spirit is the impulse which drives the
man and regulates his desires, his thoughts and his conduct.
Both of these will be replaced and renewed ... by the Spirit of
God.'

This renewal of heart and spirit is to equip us so that we
truly can represent our Master in the world of today.

Whither shall I go from Thy Spirit? Or whither shall I flee
from Thy presence? .... If I take the wings of the morning
and dwell in the uttermost parts of the sea, even there Thy
Hand shall lead me, and Thy right hand shall hold me
(Psalm 139:7,9,10).

When you have a little time, it's worth while to sit down and
read right through this marvellous Psalm. It comes out of a
tremendous sense of God's Presence with the writer (David)
all through his life, from before he was born right up to the end
of his days. Whatever he does, he cannot escape from God.
Wherever he goes, God is there. Whatever he is thinking
about, somehow God is in it.

I once spoke from this verse when I was asked to lead the
funeral service of a woman missionary who had been killed in
a flying accident on the way back to her field of service. She
never got there - God took her on the way. But I think it turned
that service into a song of triumph rather than a disaster. Even
in the midst of that accident, in the depths of the sea, the Lord
was with her.

Do you remember how Jonah tried to escape from God?
He thought he could escape by ship, but he landed in the belly
of a fish! Later he hid under a juniper tree, but God met him
there too. Jonah was brought back to God.

If ever you are tempted to feel lonely or discarded,
remember 'even in the uttermost parts of the sea, Thy Hand
shall lead me.'

Lord, You will never let go of us, help us never to forget
that marvellous fact.

If the world hates you, know that it has hated Me before it hated you .... A servant is not greater that his master. If they persecuted Me, they will persecute you; if they kept My word, they will keep yours also (John 15:18, 20).

This may have been part of the teaching that Jesus was giving His disciples at the Last Supper, just before the Crucifixion. Certainly it was a part of His last words of encouragement to them, knowing that they were going to have to face suffering for His sake.

So He starts: 'If the world hates you, don't be surprised, it also hates Me.' And it hated Him first. Of course it does - because the world hates anybody and anything that doesn't follow exactly the way in which it behaves. You put your trust in Jesus Christ - the world doesn't. It says, 'Go your own way - please yourself - enjoy life - have a good time.' But Jesus says, 'If any man would come after Me, let him deny himself, and take up his cross daily, and follow Me.' The world wouldn't deny self, and it wants nothing to do with a cross. So it hates Jesus and thereby hates you too if you are following Him.

But be careful! Don't let the world hate you just because you are anti-social, or stand-offish, or selfish. You are in the world and can't help that. You are a part of it. But Jesus says you are there to give it a fresh flavour, a wholesome taste. You are to be like salt, to keep it clean. You are to be a light in a dark place. You are there to draw people to your Master. So you should be attractive and friendly. And some will follow you to Him.

August 29

For His sake I have suffered the loss of all things ... in
order that I may gain Christ and be found in Him, not
having a righteousness of my own, based on law, but that
which is through faith in Christ, the righteousness from
God that depends on faith (Philippians 3:8-9).

Paul had been a Pharisee before he became a Christian, so he
knew all about the 'righteousness based on law'. But now that
he has experienced what New Life in Christ is all about, he
sees his past 'legal righteousness' as base coin, not the real
thing at all.

Human nature likes to think that by superhuman struggle,
it is possible for man to do pretty well and to earn himself a
reasonably good right to stand well with God. Now certainly
human effort is part of the Christian race. But of itself it is not
sufficient, we can never reach perfection or blamelessness by
human effort.

No, the transformation in Paul's life did not come about
gradually, it came suddenly at the call of Christ and in
response to God's Grace offered to him on the Damascus
Road. So his struggle towards New Life was over in a
moment. New Life through Christ alone is his, and he will
never again rely on his own efforts.

But from now on, he sets his sights on knowing Christ
through love and obedience, in faith and trust only in Him. He
lets everything else go, to gain Christ. And that is the answer
for the Christian disciple today also. Jesus Christ is to be our
all in all. He is the ultimate winner and we can win only *in
Him*.

And Jesus came to Nazareth, where He had been brought up, and He went to the synagogue, as His custom was, on the Sabbath day. And He stood up to read; and there was given Him the book of the prophet Isaiah (Luke 4:16,17).

Jesus was at home here, his mother and family lived in Nazareth. So presumably the synagogue leaders knew Him well. They told Him what to read, the lesson for the day. He must often have been to that synagogue before, but perhaps this was the first time He had been invited to say a word on the reading for the day.

Don't you wonder if He enjoyed the synagogue services? I'm sure some of them must have been dull, but not if He was the preacher! Yet He regularly went to the service every Sabbath day, because even if the sermon was dull, the Scriptures were being read and He wouldn't want to miss that.

When the Christian Church first came into being, the Christians regularly met together for worship every Sabbath day, or on Sunday when that became the Christian worship day. And this is a considerable part of what it means to be a Christian - worshipping together.

If ever you find yourself in a dull service, do what I am sure Jesus did; pray for the leader and for all present that they may know that Jesus is, as He promised He would be, present there.

Thank God for the Christian Sunday and for freedom to worship in this country, which is denied in some other countries. Make Sunday worship also our 'custom'.

On the last day of the feast, the great day, Jesus stood up and proclaimed, 'If any man thirst, let him come to Me and drink. He who believes in Me, as the Scripture has said, Out of his heart shall flow rivers of living water.' This He said about the Spirit, which those who believed in Him were to receive (John 7:37-39).

Christian people often ask: 'How can anyone know when a person is filled with the Holy Spirit?' This is too big a question to answer fully here, but there are one or two guidelines.

1. Although Paul in Ephesians 5:18 says: 'Be filled with the Spirit', nowhere in Scripture do we find any apostle or disciple claiming 'I am filled with the Spirit', though frequently they write of others being filled. So, whilst we may see this in others and others may see it in us, it is doubtful if we should claim it for ourselves.

2. I once heard a minister speaking on this subject and he took with him into the pulpit a glass tumbler and a jug. He began to fill the tumbler. Near the top he asked, 'Is it full?' 'Not yet,' they replied. He added more till it reached the brim. 'Is it full?' 'Not yet,' they replied. He poured more till it overflowed all down the pulpit. 'Yes, now,' came the cry. How could they be sure? It overflowed. And that is what Jesus claimed for those filled with the Spirit. We shall overflow to others around us, and people will know.

If God fills us with His Spirit, it is not just for our enjoyment, but that we should be used to reach others for Him. We should overflow with His love.

Lord, fill me and use me.

September 1

Heaven and earth will pass away, but My words will not pass away (Matthew 24:35).

In this chapter and the next of Matthew, Jesus talked with His disciples about the future. They had asked Him, 'Tell us when these things will happen?' And He was very careful in what He told them. He spoke of His own forthcoming death - which they couldn't understand. He foretold the destruction of Jerusalem and its temple, which took place in AD 70. He saw beyond the Cross to His own resurrection. And He spoke very carefully about the end of the age without giving any dates, but indicating signs that would precede His eventual Return, such as wars and rumours of wars and earthquakes.

The first two parts of His prophecy have already been fulfilled - the Crucifixion and Resurrection, and the destruction of Jerusalem. His return in glory has yet to come, and some of the signs are with us.

But He also gave warnings. 'Let no man lead you astray,' He said. 'Some will come in My Name, saying, I am the Christ, and shall lead many astray.' He knew there would be plenty of false Christs, and much false teaching. 'When ye hear of wars and rumours of wars, don't be troubled, for the end is not yet.' Nobody would know when the end was to be; in verse 44, He said, 'Therefore you also must be ready: for the Son of Man is coming at an hour you do not expect.'

Jesus today quietly draws men and women to Himself. But He made it very clear that a day would ultimately come when He would return in Glory, and all over the world people would know immediately that He had come. When? That is in God's hands. We want Him to find us doing His will when that day comes.

Brothers, do not be children in your thinking: be babes in
evil, but in thinking, be mature (1 Corinthians 14:20).

In this chapter, Paul has been dealing with the vexed question
of speaking in tongues. He makes it clear that he can do so; but
he also says he doesn't think it is very helpful to do it in church
or publicly, because people won't understand. But he knows
that the Corinthians love things that are exciting and mysterious, so he gives a warning: 'If I pray in a tongue, my spirit
prays, but my mind is unfruitful. So what shall I do? I will pray
with my spirit, but I will also pray with my mind' (1 Corinthians 14:14,15).

In other words, don't lose your mind when you pray, know
what you are doing and don't let emotion carry you away,
which could happen if you are praying in tongues. So he says,
'Stop thinking like children. In regard to evil be infants, but in
your thinking, be adults.'

'The child prefers the amusing to the useful, the brilliant
to the solid' (Professor Tasker). Have the innocence of a child,
but the sense of a grown-up! And those are both very attractive
qualities, aren't they? But they must go together - either
without the other makes a stunted personality.

Lord, help me to grow, both in my behaviour and practice,
and in my thinking and sensibility, so that I may be a rounded
personality, and fit to take my full part in the life and witness
of Your Church.

But they were silent; for on the way they had discussed
with one another who was the greatest (Mark 9:34).

This was something that happened early on in Jesus' ministry.
He and His disciples had travelled to Capernaum, where they
entered a house that may have been Peter's. Jesus had heard
them having a heated discussion with each other on the road,
so He asked them, 'What were you arguing about on the way?'
Dead silence - they were ashamed to tell Him!

Whatever had caused that argument? Had they been
jealous of Peter and James and John who were specially close
to Jesus? Did they know about the mother of James and John
who asked Jesus if her sons could have the best seats in the
New Kingdom?

At the moment of the argument, Jesus had been speaking
of His Crucifixion that lay ahead. What a moment to be
arguing over who came first! Jesus told them, 'If any man
would be first, he shall be last of all, and servant of all.'
Remember that He Himself took the place of a servant when
He washed His disciples' feet.

Our real job, of course, is to help others to be their best, not
to be always striving to attract notice to ourselves. It was at
that point that Jesus took a child and, sitting him on His knee,
said: 'Whoever shall receive a little child like this in My
Name, receives Me; and whoever receives Me receives God.'

We don't think of a child as being the most important
person present in a discussion on greatness. Was Jesus
perhaps thinking of the child's potential, or was it his utter
simplicity?

Teach us, Good Lord, to serve Thee as Thou deservest.

No one who puts his hand to the plough and looks back is
fit for the Kingdom of God (Luke 9:62).

The words of Jesus Himself. In this chapter Luke records that
'Jesus set His face steadfastly to go to Jerusalem' (verse 51).
He didn't look back. And He knew what lay ahead.

Several in this chapter said they wanted to follow Him. To
the first Jesus said, 'Foxes have holes, and the birds of the air
have nests, but the Son of Man has nowhere to lay His head.'
Did the man follow? We are not told. The second said, 'Lord,
I will follow, *but* ...'. He couldn't leave his father. The third
said, ' Lord, I will follow You, but first let me say goodbye to
those at home.' It was to him Jesus spoke our word of today:
'No one who puts his hand to the plough and looks back is fit
for the Kingdom of God.' Had Jesus seen that his home folks
would urge him not to go, and that he would be drawn back to
them again?

I suppose at some time in our lives, most of us do look
back and wonder if it's going to be too hard to follow Jesus all
the way. Mark did so, and left Paul on his first missionary
journey. And Paul refused to take him on the second. But later,
Mark came back, and Paul welcomed him.

Thank God, there is forgiveness for those who look back,
if they turn again and come back to Christ.

And when Lydia was baptised ... she besought us saying,
'If you have judged me to be faithful to the Lord, come to
my house and stay.' And she prevailed upon us
(Acts 16:15).

We tackled this subject of hospitality to strangers once before
(on July 12). But this reference here today looks at it from
another angle, I think.

Paul, Silas, Luke and Timothy were on the middle of a
missionary journey and they had reached Philippi. They had
come into Europe. There they went down to preach at the
riverside, where a woman called Lydia, a dealer in cloth, was
converted, and she and all her family were baptised.

Immediately after the baptism, she invited the missioners
to come to her house to stay during their time in Philippi, and
they accepted.

This was a double benefit. It gave the missioners a
Christian base, and it also gave Lydia and her family an
opportunity to learn more about their new-found Christian
Faith. They could share together what was happening day by
day and pray about it. It also meant that this household could
be a focus of the believers there, the only 'church building'
they would have, for at least a time.

These days too, there is a return to this kind of method of
spreading the gospel, that is, getting focus-points in homes
where there are new believers, who are much more likely to
be close to non-believers than the seasoned Christians. When
people have just begun as Christians, their former friends are
intrigued at what has happened and come round to find out!

Pray about this, one such might start through you!

Faith comes from what is heard, and what is heard comes
by the preaching of Christ (Romans 10:17).

Paul is getting down to bedrock about how the gospel is
spread. It has to start somewhere, so where does it begin? He
takes it from the end and works backwards. So we may as well
start at the beginning and work forwards!

1. Some Christian person is 'sent'. By whom? Obviously,
first, by God who lays it on their heart that He wants to use
them to pass on the Good News of Jesus, either by preaching
or by personal witness to somebody else. The congregation to
which that Christian belongs should also be concerned, and
should encourage him.

2. They then start to go out to the place or person to whom
they have been directed and begin to find out how best they
can carry out their commission. If it's to a congregation, there
will be a nucleus of Christians there to welcome him or her in.
If it's to an individual, they may begin by finding out if there
are any other Christian friends there who can lend a hand. The
'preaching' may be by direct talking or by indirect friendliness towards the person concerned.

3. The person or people then begin to hear what it's all
about and what it means to become a Christian. This may be
a slow process, taking months rather than minutes!

4. The next stage is that the hearer begins to turn to Christ
and to pray to Him.

5. The final stage is their conversion, or believing in Him.

The 'preaching of Christ' is something that involves the
whole personality of the preacher - not just speaking, but
living Christ. And the 'preacher' should include every Christian believer.

It was I who taught Ephraim to walk. I took them up in my
arms; but they did not know that I healed them. I led them
with cords of compassion, with the bands of love
(Hosea 11:3,4).

The prophet Hosea was ministering to Israel in the darkest
period of their history, when they were going into captivity.
Hosea himself had a tragedy - his wife had left him, and gone
to the bad. Hosea found her sold into slavery, but he bought
her back and restored her as his beloved wife. This was a
picture of what was happening between God and Israel - the
nation had forsaken God, but God could not cast them off. He
loved them in spite of their turning away from Him.

By his own suffering, Hosea came to understand God's
suffering, when His chosen people rejected Him. Hosea
wouldn't give up his wife; in spite of her sin, he longed for her
to come back to him; and in the end, he bought her back from
slavery.

This is not only what God has done for Israel; it is also
what He has done for you, for me, for the whole human race.
Paul says, 'While we were yet sinners, Christ died for us.' We
get the echo of God's love all the way through Hosea's story.
It comes out again in verses 8, 9 of this chapter. God says,
'How can I give you up? ... How can I hand you over? ... How
can I destroy you? ... All my compassion is aroused.' And it
leads into 'God so loved the world, that He gave ...' (John
3:16).

In spite of our sin, God cannot let us go. He still loves us.

September 8

Daniel went to his house ... and he got down upon his knees three times a day and prayed and gave thanks before his God, as he had done previously (Daniel 6:10).

Obviously Daniel was a man of prayer; I suspect he prayed frequently, seeing that he was a captive in a foreign land. He and his friends were employed in the royal household and therefore were subject to a lot of supervision.

On the advice of his courtiers, the king proclaimed a decree that for the next month, no prayer should be offered except to the king. These courtiers were jealous of Daniel and knew that the only way they could get at him was through his loyalty to God. And they were right.

Daniel allowed nothing to interfere with his loyalty to and fellowship with God. I think the interesting thing is his insistence on a statutory prayer-time to be regularly kept three times a day, presumably morning and evening, and once at midday.

Today, most Christians keep a regular morning and evening prayer-time, but not so many a midday one. When I was a student at Cambridge, our Christian Union used to meet regularly for 20 minutes at midday. As many of us as possible met for prayer and we found it a huge help in our daily living. This would not be possible for many, but the thought of an extra time, even alone, for just a few minutes at some suitable time is worth thinking about.

Today's lions may be different from Daniel's - but just as tough to cope with! But Daniel's God is just the same for you and me. He never fails.

Now these Jews (the people of Berea) ... received the Word
with all eagerness, examining the Scriptures daily to see if
these things (as said by Paul) were true (Acts 17:11).

Paul had been preaching first in Thessalonica, and he had a
rough passage there with the Jews. Some believed, some
heard and reluctantly accepted what Paul said; but most
turned against Paul and his company. So Paul and his friends
left Thessalonica and went to the villages in Berea.

There he met with different treatment. In both places, Paul
had argued from the Old Testament Scriptures that the Messiah when He came was to be a suffering Messiah, that He
would be killed and rise again on the third day. Then, he told
them what actually happened and advised that they search the
Scriptures to see whether he had been faithful to what the Old
Testament said. Remember that the New Testament had not
yet been written. They had to listen to witnesses who had seen
and known Jesus.

In Berea, the people referred back to their Old Testament
Scriptures to check what Paul said against what the Scriptures
prophesied. The result was that many of the Jews and the
Greeks in Berea believed and put their trust in Christ.

It's just as true today, that the study of the Scriptures leads
to true belief and understanding of the gospel. As we study the
Old Testament, we find that the New Testament rings true.
And as we study the New, we see it being literally fulfilled in
many ways - though much is still in the future. Let us 'read,
mark, learn and inwardly digest' the Word of God. That is
how the Christian grows.

For Thou didst form my inward parts. Thou didst knit me together in my mother's womb. I praise Thee for Thou art fearful and wonderful. Wonderful are Thy works! Thou knowest me right well (Psalm 139:13,14).

This is one of the most marvellous of all the Psalms, and here in verses 13-18 the Psalmist deals with the mysterious creation of the human body. Today man knows more and more about the human body than ever before. Yet even so, no scientist can fathom all the mysteries of creation: many things are still unknown.

I once saw a film of the human body from its first inception, right up till the birth of the newborn baby. I could see its actual growth from the invisible cell through all the stages to birth. It's a marvellous picture, and when you see it, you realise the immense care that God has taken over each one of us, His creatures. And remember, God 'made man in His own image, in the image of God He created him, male and female He created them' (Genesis 1:27).

Since that is so, we must take the greatest care of that body which is yours and mine, because it is in God's likeness and made for His glory. It is to be exercised so as to grow to full perfection, it is to be nourished with wholesome food. It must not be starved nor over-indulged, it is 'in God's image'. Body, mind and spirit must be developed together, for we are redeemed by Christ, for His glory.

Wonderful are Thy works.

September 11

Let your light so shine before men, that they may see your good works and glorify your heavenly Father
(Matthew 5:16).

We sometimes hear this verse quoted by the minister just before the Church collection is taken up! I often wonder if the quote is right in that connection because your right hand is not supposed to know what your left hand is doing when you put something in the offering-plate! And certainly you don't flourish your gift before others.

But let's look seriously at this verse. Jesus is calling us to let our light shine. Does He mean the light we should be reflecting which comes from Him? I don't think so.

Just before, He said, 'A city set on a hill cannot be hid.' I remember at night looking up from the shores of the Lake of Galilee into the hills above. Away at the topmost hill there was a blaze of light from the city of Safed, glittering away to the valleys below and the shimmering lake. If it had been only one house there, I don't think we would have seen much. But every house was lit up, the whole city was full of light.

Isn't that a picture of what the Christian Church is meant to be like? Shining out into the darkness of the world, so that people take courage as they see the light and are drawn to visit the city, the Church? One individual can be a candle; but put thousands of candles together and what a difference we see! We talk about a lighthouse having a lamp which is 1,000 candle-power; it shines over the sea, so that ships will not be wrecked at night. When Jesus shines into our hearts, He lights the candle and we shine.

September 12

Do you not know that friendship with the world is enmity with God? Therefore whoever wishes to be a friend of the world makes himself an enemy of God (James 4:4).

Friends and enemies - what a choice to have to make! But the Christian has to make a choice, he can't go half-way in his relationship with God. It is all or nothing, that is, if he wants to be considered as one of God's friends.

The point is that much of the world is hostile to God, and much is quite indifferent to Him. We are all in the world, we cannot avoid contact with it. But where it is against God, we cannot go with it. Jesus tells us, 'The world hated Me before it hated you.' If we are truly on the side of Jesus, we shall incur the same hatred it metes out to Him.

Even after we become Christians we are still sinners, but we hate the sin we commit and we need constantly to seek God's forgiveness. We need to remind ourselves that though we are in the world, we are no longer of it. As St Paul wrote, 'Our citizenship is in heaven, from whence also we look for a Saviour, the Lord Jesus Christ' (Philippians 3:20).

When you find yourself alone in a group which does not acknowledge Jesus as Lord, you need to remind yourself 'whose you are and whom you serve' (Acts 27:23). This will give you courage to stand out from the others, with the hope that your standing may also encourage others who may be more timid to come and stand with you.

What greater title could be given us, than to be called 'The friend of God'?

He who believes in the Son has Eternal Life; he who does
not obey the Son shall not see life, but the wrath of God
rests upon him (John 3:36).

This word of Jesus needs to be examined carefully, so that we
don't mistake its meaning. Does it mean that if we refuse
Jesus, God condemns us out of hand? No, not that at all,
because God wants all men to be saved and to come to the
knowledge of the truth. But there are some who have heard the
Word of God about Jesus, who know it to be true and yet
refuse to put their trust in Him or to follow Him. Those who
follow Him have the 'light of life'. Those who don't, stay in
the dark.

I think Jesus explained it well when He was talking with
Nicodemus: 'This is the verdict: light has come into the world,
but men loved darkness instead of light, because their deeds
were evil' (John 3:19). In other words, the choice about our
destiny lies with us. If we deliberately choose to stay in the
dark, we won't see the Light, we won't see God. God has
provided us with a way to escape from the darkness of sin and
Satan. If we refuse that way out, we are condemning ourselves. As long as I am disobedient, the 'wrath of God rests
upon me'. The moment I turn to Him, I come into the Light,
I have Eternal Life, and I come out of the darkness.

It is not that God hates us; He loves us, He longs for us to
come to Him, but He won't force us to do so. He asks us to
choose; 'therefore choose Life' (Deuteronomy 30:19).

There is great gain in godliness with contentment; for we
brought nothing into the world, and we cannot take
anything out of the world; but if we have food and clothing, with these we shall be content (1 Timothy 6:6-8).

Paul is writing to his son in the faith, Timothy, on the subject
of money and possessions. In verse 10 of this chapter he says,
a grasping attitude will 'pierce us through with sorrows'.
Why? Well, there's a proverb which says, 'Great wealth is a
thing either to be guarded, or dispensed, or displayed, but
which cannot be used.' And I believe it's true. If you guard it,
other people are waiting to snatch it from you and you'll
develop an ulcer trying to hang on to it! If you display it, that
is obnoxious and vulgar! If you dispense it carefully and
wisely and lovingly, you can bring much help and comfort to
people in need and you will leave the world a happier place!

How many Christians have 'erred from the Faith' through
a wrong attitude to money.

In fact, any money we have is given us by God as a trust
to be wisely used. It can be used in all kinds of ways: for
ourselves in providing what we need by way of food, clothing,
books, household comforts and equipment; for others whom
we can help by bringing them some happiness which otherwise they could not afford; by using some of the money for the
spreading of the gospel at home or abroad.

Money is for use, not for hoarding. And not for wasting,
but for bringing joy into the world, and especially to others.

Thus says the LORD to you, 'Fear not, and be not dismayed
at this great multitude; for the battle is not yours but God's
.... You will not need to fight in this battle; take your
position, stand still, and see the victory of the LORD on your
behalf .... Fear not, and be not dismayed; tomorrow go out
against them, and the LORD will be with you
(2 Chronicles 20:15,17).

King Jehoshaphat of Judah had come under attack by a vast
army, and he was scared stiff. But he prayed, and if you have
a little time, it's worth reading his prayer which you find in 2
Chronicles 20:5-12. Especially note his closing word: 'We
have no power to face this vast army that is attacking us. We
do not know what to do, but our eyes are upon *You*.'

If we are Christians, and are under attack from evil forces
- temptations, persecutions, pressures, whatever - it is God's
responsibility to look after His property, for that's what we
are. Once we have placed ourselves under His care, we need
no longer fear, for He takes over. Yes, we go out against the
enemy, but Jesus is now in charge and we may stand still and
watch Him at work.

As a youngster, I once had to undergo a serious operation.
As I lay on the operating table I watched the surgeon laying
out his instruments, and I wondered! The nurse took one of my
hands, the matron took the other (both were Christians), and
they said, 'God is over you, we are beside you, have no fear.'
In twenty minutes, the job was done and I was through. God
was thanked! I was His concern.

And so are you!

And behold, the veil of the temple was torn in two, from
top to bottom (Matthew 27:51).

It was the day of the Crucifixion and Jesus had just died. And
this was the very next thing that happened. How? And why?
Matthew tells us that the veil was torn from the top down-
wards. What was this veil? It was the curtain in the temple that
shut men out of the Holy of Holies. Men were not allowed to
enter there. The veil of the Temple excluded men from God.

But when Jesus died, the veil was torn through and men
who had been shut out were now allowed in. The way into the
holiest was now possible through the Blood of Jesus.

Man didn't tear that veil open, God did. That is why, when
we pray today, we pray 'through Jesus Christ our Lord'. He is
the way into heaven, He is the way to God. Remember how
He said, 'No man cometh unto the Father, but by Me.'

Professor Tasker puts it this way: 'His death, as it were,
uncovered God so that man might have a vision of the glory
that shone upon His face.' You can find the full explanation
of it in Hebrews 10:19-22: 'Having therefore, brethren, bold-
ness to enter into the holiest by the blood of Jesus, by a new
and living way, which He has consecrated for us, through the
veil, that is to say, His flesh ... let us draw near ... in full
assurance of faith.'

So Scripture likens the veil to the 'flesh of Jesus'. His
body was torn for you and me, and that opens the way for us
into the kingdom of heaven. So the Christian believer now has
direct access to God, and we don't have to go through any
other priest, only through Jesus.

What blessings He gives us!

Godly grief produces a repentance that leads to salvation
and brings no regret, but worldly grief produces death
(2 Corinthians 7:10).

Paul had written an earlier letter to the Corinthian Christians,
which was not 1 Corinthians but almost certainly one written
between 1 and 2, which is now lost. He calls it his 'painful'
letter (verse 8), and he had taken them to task for some evil
behaviour in the Church there.

He knows the letter upset them, but he's glad he sent it,
because, although they were very sad about it, they had put
right the thing that was wrong. So it was 'a repentance which
brings no regrets'.

All of us have to bear rebuke when we have done wrong
- and we don't like having it, either. It may be hard to bear, but
it's very wholesome if it means we put right what has been
wrong.

When Peter denied that he even knew Jesus, Jesus just
looked at him - their eyes met. Jesus didn't have to say
anything - the grieved look did it. And Peter burst into tears.
He had let down His beloved Master - and he just couldn't
bear it. Yes, they were tears of sorrow and repentance, this
was something he would never do again. And it was eventually totally put right at that breakfast on the beach after the
Resurrection.

Worldly sorrow, says Paul, just leads to bitterness, cross
at being found out, shame at being exposed, self-pity and
depression - quite deadly. But godly sorrow cleanses and
restores.

The LORD was witness to the covenant between you and the wife of your youth .... And what does He desire? Godly offspring. So take heed to yourselves, and let none be faithless to the wife of his youth. For I hate divorce, says the LORD (Malachi 2:14-16).

The marriage relationship is one that has come under great strain today. It is estimated that one marriage in three comes to grief in this country at the present time. A godly marriage is one of the very greatest blessings of mankind. It is the closest human relationship there is, even closer than that between parent and child, because, as Genesis 2:24 reminds us, 'Therefore a man leaves his father and mother and cleaves to his wife, and they become one flesh.'

Do you ever fight against yourself? No, anyone who did so would be deemed mental. God says that in marriage two become one. So, quarrelling between husband and wife is virtually 'suicide'.

Every person should take great care when the possibility of marriage arises because, next to the step of becoming a Christian, this is the greatest personal relationship into which anyone can enter.

But a godly marriage is a marvellous experience. Each puts the other first (after God), and help one another to lead a godly life. Incidentally, they can also be a great help to other couples getting married, by showing them something of the immense joy of a truly Christian marriage.

Marriage does not come to everyone. Some men and women are called to the single life; and if God has called you to that, He will more than make up to you any thing you may feel you have lost.

This Gospel of the Kingdom will be preached throughout the whole world, as a testimony to all nations; and then the end will come (Matthew 24:14).

The Second Coming of Jesus, when He will come in Glory to this world of ours, to take up His power and reign, is something to which all Christians look forward. Only then will all wrongs be righted, only then will the New Age be ushered in, only then will Jesus take up His power and reign over all the world.

But notice what has to happen first: the 'Gospel must first be preached all over the world', so that every nation gets a chance of hearing it. It doesn't say every individual, but every nation. I suppose that, in one sense, this has already happened. Is there any nation still left that has never heard? I'm not sure. But remember this: every new generation of people starts life as a generation that has not yet heard. And that's true, even here in Britain.

So what? Surely, just this. Every single Christian should be taking their share of passing on this Good News to those who haven't yet heard. Parents to children, children to their fellows, all ages and all races sharing this Good News. You have to do it, so do I, so does every Christian. If we don't, we are to that extent delaying the Return of Jesus. If we do, we are bringing that Great Day nearer.

How we do it is between us and Jesus; for each one of us, the approach we make to others will depend on the kind of qualities with which God has equipped us. We must do it both individually and corporately with other Christians.

But we don't do it in our own strength or wisdom or alone. God is with us, and we are just 'His Ambassadors'.

But as for you ... from childhood you have been acquainted
with the sacred writings which are able to instruct you for
salvation through faith in Christ Jesus
(2 Timothy 3:14,15).

This verse is really a follow on from yesterday's, because if
you're really going to pass the gospel on to others, you need
to know what you are teaching. If a person is a history school
teacher, he will need to know his history well, and this
involves a lot of study. And the same is true of the gospel.

If ever you get a chance of hearing the gospel being
publicly proclaimed in the open, say in Hyde Park, go and
listen, and see how the speaker copes with questions from the
crowd! He (or she) has to be well versed in the Scriptures and
be able to quote chapter and verse, or they'll soon be defeated.

And the same is true in personal and private witness. It's
no good saying, 'Somewhere in the Bible it says ...'; we need
to be able to say word for word what it says and where it can
be found. Of course, all of us could be defeated at some time,
but a good knowledge of the Scriptures is very important.
Paul says that 'the Sword of the Spirit is the Word of God'
(Ephesians 6:17). You can't wield a sword until you have
learnt the art of swordmanship. This Word of God is our only
weapon of attack against our great enemy, Satan.

And Levi (Matthew) made Jesus a great feast in his house; and there was a large company of tax collectors and others sitting at the table with them (Luke 5:29)

Matthew was a tax-collector for the Roman Government. The custom was that Rome 'let out' the post for a sum of money, and then the person who had been appointed got his money back - and more - from the people from whom he collected the tax. Matthew was collecting from the fishermen by the lakeside when Jesus quietly spoke to him and said, 'Come and follow Me'. Instantly Matthew dropped everything and went with Jesus.

His fellow tax-collectors must have been surprised, so he invited them all to lunch to meet Jesus! And Jesus went. I'm sure Matthew knew Jesus liked to meet such people; His reputation was the 'friend of publicans and sinners'. He was anxious that his own friends and buddies should meet his new Master. Immediately the Pharisees said, 'Doesn't He realise that it just isn't done to eat with such people?'

But Jesus replied, 'I didn't come to call the righteous, but sinners to repentance.' Of course He was eating with them, how else could He call them? They wouldn't come to His preaching; but they came to lunch with Him.

What a marvellous opportunity He had that day, a lunch-party with people who would probably never come to a synagogue to worship; but He could chat with them over the table. That was Matthew's way of witness. What could ours be?

The Grace of the Lord Jesus Christ and the Love of God
and the Fellowship of the Holy Spirit be with you all
(2 Corinthians 13:14).

We looked at this Grace once before (April 18). But today
let's notice the order in which Paul places the Trinity. He puts
first the 'Grace of the Lord Jesus'. And in our thinking about
God, I think we do the same. Why? Because He is our
Redeemer and, without Him, we would not even know the
way to God. Our prayers are in His Name; our calendar dates
from His human birth; and most of our thinking about God
comes from His teaching and example.

Next comes the 'Love of God'. It was His Love for us that
sent His Son to be our Saviour. He loved us before we could
ever love Him back. He is the Father, welcoming back the lost
son. He made us in His image, to be like Him; and when we
think of Him, we remember that He is like Jesus, Jesus is like
Him. They two are one, and He wants us to be one with Him
too.

Thirdly in our thinking, but not least, is the 'Fellowship of
the Holy Spirit'. All who have accepted Jesus as their Saviour
come into that fellowship, a quality bestowed upon us all at
Pentecost, one which binds us to one another as Christians
and which breaks down all the barriers that tend to divide
mankind from one another today; a fellowship of forgiven
sinners, redeemed by the precious Blood of Christ.

No wonder that in our Services we sum up our prayers at
the end in the words of the Grace. It is God's blessing upon us
all, and a continual reminder of all that the Triune Love of God
means to all His children, all down the ages.

Blessed are the peacemakers, for they shall be called sons
of God (Matthew 5:9).

A word of Jesus from the Sermon on the Mount. Remember
that sermon was spoken, not to the crowds, but to the believers. When Jesus pronounces blessings like this one, it is a
blessing, not on what we do, but on what we are. Are you
merciful, are you pure in heart? Jesus says you are blessed. So
with the peacemakers. It is because we have the peace of God
in our hearts and show in our lives something of what God is
like, that we can help to bring peace to the hearts and minds
of people who are not at peace, either with God or with one
another.

I remember reading of a certain tennis player who had
become a Christian, the quality of the tennis had gone down
because of the loss of the 'killer instinct'. Does it mean then,
that if you are a Christian, you can't play any game in which
you seek to defeat your opponent? Surely not, but that the
game is but a game which both are meant to enjoy, and that
you show a high degree of sportsmanship and never lose your
temper in it.

In Northern Ireland today there are a number of little
bands of Protestant and Roman Catholic Christians who pray
regularly together for peace in their land, these surely are the
peacemakers. During the Mau Mau troubles in Kenya in the
1950's, a great many Christian Africans refused to join the
Home Guard because they said the other side could only be
won by love, not by hate and killings.

Proverbs has a wise word: 'When a man's ways please the
LORD, He makes even his enemies to be at peace with him'
(16:7).

Jesus said to His disciples, 'Truly I say to you, it will be
hard for a rich man to enter the kingdom of Heaven .... It is
easier for a camel to go through the eye of a needle, than
for a rich man to enter the Kingdom of God
(Matthew 19:23,24).

This tremendous statement of Jesus came directly out of the
visit of the rich young ruler. He had come to Jesus, wanting
truly to do what was right. When Jesus asked him about the
Ten Commandments, he said, 'As far as I know, I have kept
them all.' Then Jesus 'looked at him and loved him' (Mark
10:21). This was the kind of young man that Jesus would have
loved to have among His disciples. So Jesus put him to the
test: he was rich and Jesus saw how much that mattered to
him. Would he really be willing to put Jesus absolutely first
and to give away his money? If so, he would be wholehearted.

And we can see the young man, shaken badly, desperately
thinking, 'Does it really mean all that?' Sadly, he went away.
And sadly, Jesus looked after him as he went for He loved him
and wanted him.

How 'hard' is it for a rich man? Wealth means power, and
power is dangerous because it could lead to pride.

There is a story - perhaps only a story - that there was a
'Needle Gate' in Jerusalem. Was Jesus thinking of that? No
camel (it has been said) could squeeze through that gate
without first having all the load taken off its back. This man
had a load, his riches. Difficult? Yes. For all rich men?
Perhaps, but not impossible with God.

What would have happened if he had said yes? God would
have given him back 10,000% on it all, yes, and more. How
sad. He missed out on the greatest thing in the world.

Do not struggle to get rich; be wise enough to resist. Cast
but a glance at riches, and they are gone; for they will
surely sprout wings, and fly off to the sky like an eagle
(Proverbs 23:4,5).

This is a commentary on yesterday's reading, isn't it? I like
the thought of my pound notes suddenly flying up into the sky
and disappearing for good, don't you? You see, that is really
almost what happens to money. Suddenly, there's a financial
crash on Wall Street in America or in London, and overnight
money is valueless. And this really does happen.

Jesus never said it was wrong to be rich, but He did say it
was wrong and unwise to trust in riches, they can let you
down. Many think riches bring happiness, but when we read
about rich people in the newspaper, it isn't often they sound
very happy. So often they just heap it up and don't use it
properly. When they die, they can't take it with them, every
penny must be left behind.

If God ever allows you to have riches, as a Christian it will
be given you as a trust and you will need to pray as to how you
should use it: how much should be given directly back to God;
how much should be spent on your family; how much should
help to relieve the refugees and sick people; and how much
you need for your own reasonable expenses. Care will have to
be taken over your investments; you should not put money
into business that will lead people astray.

If you're still at school, you probably only have pocket-
money. But that's where your training in the right use of
money begins. Use it with care, and keep accounts!

God ... saved us and called us with a holy calling, not in
virtue of our works, but in virtue of His own purpose and
the grace which He gave us in Christ Jesus
(2 Timothy 1:8b,9).

Notice these words, 'Not because of anything we have done.'
When we talk with non-Christians, if we get far with them,
they will often say something like this: 'I'm not sure if I'll be
good enough to get into Heaven, but I hope I may.'

Have you ever felt like that? I know I have, and I try and
try, but I don't seem to get anywhere, because try as I will, I
cannot live a perfect life.

So, isn't it marvellous that it's not our Christian life that
saves us, but simply God's free Grace given us in Christ! We
can never earn our way to God. That was something that
Martin Luther discovered for himself some 500 years ago, at
the beginning of the Reformation. He had been striving to live
up to the Christian life and faith, but was in despair till
suddenly he discovered the truth. He wrote: 'God, out of grace
and mere mercy, makes us righteous through faith. When I
saw this, I felt immediately as if I was born anew, and had
found an open door into paradise itself.'

Timothy had been brought up in the Christian Faith. Both
his mother and his grandmother were Christians, and Paul had
helped to lead Timothy into personal salvation. Here Paul is
reminding him of what it means to be a real Christian. In
verses 13 and 14 he says to him: 'What you heard from me,
keep as the pattern of sound teaching, with faith and love in
Christ Jesus. Guard the good deposit that was entrusted to you
- guard it with the help of the Holy Spirit who lives in us.'

And we have to do the same.

By faith, Abraham obeyed when he was called to go out to
a place which he was to receive as an inheritance; and he
went out, not knowing where he was to go (Hebrews 11:8).

Abraham lived in a civilised place, Ur of the Chaldees. God
spoke to him and called him out of that civilisation to go out
to an unknown destination. And he went, taking his family,
and even his old father, Terah, with him. Terah got as far as
Haran where he died, but Abraham went on. When he arrived
in Canaan, he was a stranger, living in tents, always 'looking
for a city which hath firm foundations', the heavenly city
whose architect and designer is God. 'Strangers and pilgrims'
- that's what Abraham and his family were, and they were the
progenitors of the Christians who were yet to come.

We too 'look for a city', and we too are stranger and
pilgrims for we don't know where God may lead us. But there
is a perfect plan and destiny in God's mind for each of us and
our job is to pray that, bit by bit, He may show us His plan for
our lives and, like Abraham, we too may be led into His plan
for us.

Abraham obeyed, that was the secret of God's blessing
upon him. Later in the New Testament, we find Jesus speaking of Abraham, where He says in Luke 20:37, 38: 'God is the
God of Abraham ... but is not the God of the dead, but of the
living.' Some day in heaven, we may be privileged to meet
Abraham and hear how God led him out, how he obeyed and
became 'the Father of many nations.' Who knows what
anyone may become, if he obeys God?

'Can a man hide himself in secret places so that I cannot
see him? .... Do I not fill heaven and earth?' says the Lord
(Jeremiah 23:24).

Poor Jeremiah had a terrible time of it. He was a prophet in
Israel at one of the very worst periods of their history. Many
of them were away in captivity and exile, and the prophets
who remained in Judah were false prophets, trying to encourage the people that all was well, when in fact it was far from
well. The people had forsaken God, there was little real
worship of God left in the country. Jeremiah had been sent by
God to warn the people to give up their evil ways, for if they
didn't, God would forsake them.

Jeremiah was maltreated by king and people alike, because his message was not popular. They wanted him to say
nice things, but he couldn't; he could only say: 'Return to
God, or else ...'. And they called him a prophet of doom. The
false prophets thought God could not see them, that He didn't
know what they were doing. Jeremiah warned them to speak
the truth instead of telling lies to soothe the people.

How many people try to hide from God. Adam and Eve
did it in the Garden of Eden; they thought God wouldn't see
them hiding among the trees.

A small boy at a Christian Camp was asked one night at
Camp Prayers what he would do about sin, now that he knew
God could see him? He replied, 'I'd do it behind His back!'
God knows all about us, even our secret thoughts, we cannot
hide from Him.

What a privilege to carry
Everything to God in prayer.

The angel of the Lord encamps around those who fear
Him, and delivers them (Psalm 34:7).

Do angels exist? Most of us have never seen one We have our
Lord's own word for it that they do, and that they are
concerned for human beings too (Matthew 18:10). We can
only imagine what they are like, for no photograph of one has
ever been taken. Both Old and New Testaments mention them
in various connections.

I don't think we can talk to the angels, but God sends them
about His business, and sometimes we can sense when there
is some very special providence around.

The word 'angel' in Greek is *angelos*, meaning 'one who
has been sent'. Frequently they are spoken of as being
concerned for human safety. When God's servants are in
danger, either physical or spiritual, they often claim that God
will send His angel to protect them, and I am sure He does.

I travelled down by car from the Keswick Convention this
year and, as I left, one of the speakers wished me safe travel
saying, 'But don't forget, the angels leave you at 70 (mph)!'
In other words, don't expect God's protection if you are
breaking the law!

Yes, the Psalmist says it's those who 'fear Him' who can
claim His deliverance and care. Peter certainly knew this, for
he was in prison expecting speedy execution when suddenly,
'out of the blue', an angel stood beside him in the prison, took
him through all the locked gates, kept the eyes of his guards
shut, and freed him into the open street - and then left him. The
job was done, and Peter knew what to do next. 'Now I know
that God has sent His angel,' he said.

Thank God for the ministry of angels!

Be still, and know that I am God. I will be exalted among
the nations, I will be exalted in the earth! (Psalm 46:10).

Many of the Psalms were used in the Temple worship and
some, including this one, had musical accompaniment. Several are grouped together under a special title (this one, and
Psalms 42-49) are under the note of 'the sons of Korah'.
Presumably these were the authors of these Psalms.

It would be interesting if we could know the tune to which
this was set. It must have been written during a time of trouble.
See verse 6: 'Nations are in uproar, kingdoms fall. God lifts
His voice, the earth melts.'

And when trouble is upon us, we feel helpless. That is the
moment to sit back and watch quietly as God takes over. 'Be
still, and know that I am God.' When everything appears to be
going against us and against God, He is not inactive. He
knows what is going on, and ultimate results are in His hands.
So we needn't get in a ferment!

Our hospitals today are filled with folk who are having
nervous breakdowns; people who just cannot rest, cannot
trust to God, but feel frustrated and worried.

And God says to such, 'Be still! Take your hands off. Let
Me take over. Rest in ultimate trust in Me.' And so the
Psalmist writes in verse 7: 'The LORD of Hosts is with us; the
God of Jacob is our Refuge.' That ringing shout is brought in
again at the end of the Psalm. God knows what He is doing;
He is in control; I need not fear. Nations are again in uproar
today, and it's difficult to see how it will all end. What does
the Christian do in such a situation? He can alleviate a little of
the suffering. He can pray. He can encourage others. Above
all, he can trust.

The Lord is not slow about His promise, as some count slowness, but is forbearing towards you, not wishing that any should perish, but that all should reach repentance (2 Peter 3:9).

Peter wrote these two letters of his nearly 2,000 years ago, and he warned us in this very chapter that the day is coming when Jesus will return, and the world will be destroyed by fire - but that this is in preparation for 'a new heaven and a new earth' (verse 13). Peter says that people will mock, and say: 'Jesus promised to come back again. But He hasn't come, and we don't believe He ever will come.' Peter says, 'Their memories are too short.' God's time is not the same as man's time. And what God promised will surely come to pass.

But meanwhile, says Peter, God is giving people a chance to come to Him. He doesn't want the loss of any man. He wants all men to come to Him and find Him as their Saviour. So Peter is urging people to seize the opportunity, whilst there is still time. Look at verses 14 and 15: 'So then, dear friends, since you are looking forward to this, make every effort to be found spotless, blameless, and at peace with Him. Bear in mind that our Lord's patience means *salvation* ...'.

Peter knew that his own end was very near, and that soon he would be put to death for his faith (2 Peter 1:14). So he was anxious to get this urgent letter into the hands of those who didn't yet know Christ, before the day came when he could no longer speak to them. The time was short in his day. It is still shorter in ours. Don't let's fritter it, but use it faithfully.

When the younger son came to himself he said, 'How many of my father's hired servants have bread enough and to spare, but I perish here with hunger! I will arise and go to my father, and I will say to him, 'Father, I have sinned against heaven and before you; I am no longer worthy to be called your son (Luke 15:17-19).

This wonderful 15th chapter of Luke gives us three parables that Jesus told, each linked with the others: the Lost Sheep, the Lost Silver, and the Lost Son. The upshot of each story was *joy*. Joy when the shepherd got his missing sheep back; joy when the woman found her precious silver piece; joy for both father and son when the runaway came home again.

Not all stories have a happy ending, and if you watch television today, you will find that many of the stories unfolded seem to have no ending at all - they just leave you guessing!

But you will know without my telling you, that if ever you have lost something you value, and maybe you're not expecting ever to see it again, if and when you get it back, there's an immense sense of relief and thankfulness and joy and peace.

That is what Jesus was talking about in these three related stories. Straying away from God never breeds happiness for anyone, does it? That younger son wanted his freedom, and money to spend as he liked. And he got it. But it didn't last, and when it was gone, his friends faded away too - they were not real friends, they were only spongers. The emptiness was complete. So - back to Dad. Forgiveness, cleansing, and *joy*!

The secret. Keep coming back to Him.

October 3

So neither I nor ... the men of the guard who followed me,
none of us took off our clothes; each one kept his weapon
in his hand (or 'took his weapon to the water')
(Nehemiah 4:23).

What a terrific story this is of Nehemiah and his men, as they
sought to rebuild Jerusalem after its destruction, and their
enemies tried to stop them doing it! They were a small band,
working against great odds. But they took every precaution
not to be caught off their guard. Whether this means that they
actually went to bathe, carrying a spear in one hand is not
clear, but they were not going to be caught napping! Nehemiah knew that God had called him to this great task and, that
whatever happened, he couldn't afford to take any unnecessary risks - the enemy was both cunning and strong.

   The spiritual warfare that every Christian is engaged in is
a life and death battle, and our enemy, the devil, whilst he
knows he cannot win in the long run, hopes that he can do
something at least to cripple the soldiers of Christ and make
them ineffective. So he lays traps for us, offers us attractive
temptations, tries to deflect us from the main purpose, gets us
quarrelling with each other, suggests that there's plenty of
time; anything to stop us from witnessing for Christ or taking
our full share in the life and witness of the Church and the
building of Christ's Kingdom on earth.

   In this connection, one of my favourite verses is 1 Corinthians 16:13: 'Watch ye, stand fast in the Faith, quit you, like
men, be strong.'

October 4

When you pass through the waters, I will be with you; and through the rivers, they shall not overwhelm you; when you walk through fire, you shall not be burned, and the flame shall not consume you. For I am the LORD your God (Isaiah 43:2,3).

This is one of God's many and wonderful promises that His children can claim. If you are a Christian, you might expect that God would protect you against suffering, that you might not ever suffer the danger of drowning or the possibility of your house being burnt down with you in it! But no, God never promises that He will protect us from suffering. In fact, He expects that we shall have to suffer. He does not say 'if' you pass through fire or water, but 'when'.

So there will be at one time a flood of sorrow and at another a blaze of hatred that will come upon us, and it may well be more than once. When these things come, we may well feel that they are more than we can bear. And that's where God's Promise comes in - we shall not have to bear them alone. He will be with us at that very moment. Do you remember how, when Shadrach, Meshech and Abednego had been thrown into the blazing fiery furnace, there was seen to be a fourth figure in the fire with them; and King Nebuchadnezzar said, 'The form of the fourth is like the Son of God' (Daniel 3:25). He was right - it was the Son of God. Yes, they had to go through the fire, but not alone, and the fire did not burn them. Water cleanses, fire purifies, and Jesus wants us clean to serve Him. So, no fear when troubles come for He is there too.

I have been crucified with Christ, and yet I live; but it is
not I but Christ who lives in me. And the life I now live in
the body, I live by faith in the Son of God, who loved me,
and gave Himself for me (Galatians 2:20).

Paul had argued with Peter about whether a Gentile must first
become subject to Jewish laws and customs before he can
become a Christian. And he ends his argument by saying that
the only thing for anybody - Jew or Gentile - is to remember
that he is saved by God's Grace, not by any kind of law
observance. As he looks at his own life, he can now see that
the man he used to be was now dead, crucified upon the Cross
with Christ. And yet, Paul is alive - ah! - but it's now no longer
the old Paul, but the new Paul, and the new power within him
is not Paul, but none other that Jesus Christ Himself.

'Jesus,' says Paul, 'has done for me what I could never
have done for myself. He has come to live permanently in my
body, so now I am His. I no longer run my own show. I live
by faith in Jesus who died for me, lives in me, and loves me.'

There is a hymn that has been written upon that theme: you
may know it.

Not I, but Christ, my every need supplying
Not I, but Christ, my strength and health to be;
Christ, only Christ, for spirit, soul and body,
Christ, only Christ, live then Thy life in me.

My personality is still there, but it is being transformed
daily to become more and more like that of my Master, Christ.

Two are better than one ... for if they fall, one will lift up
his fellow; but woe to him who is alone when he falls, and
has not another to lift him up (Ecclesiastes 4:9,10).

The writer of this book was Solomon, once described as 'the
wisest man that ever lived'. Certainly Solomon wrote much
that was wise, but he didn't always live up to the best of his
own sayings. In this particular saying he has given us a bit of
real wisdom. Man is a being who needs fellowship, and to try
and live without fellowship is disastrous.

You'll have noticed that when a baby is learning to walk,
he usually has a hand or a finger to hold him, or which he can
hold, till he has learnt to walk without a tumble. As we grow
older, we tend to enjoy showing our independence but, sooner
or later, we learn that to have a wise friend alongside us can
often help us avoid complete disaster.

Obviously this is particularly true of marriage, when
husband and wife need each other to maintain a true balance
and equilibrium in life. Larger or smaller tumbles will take
place and to have a loving partner beside you can make all the
difference. So, take care where a life partnership is involved,
you need a reliable 'other half' who can help you pick up the
bits and make a fresh start.

But, married or single, a real friend whom you can trust is
quite invaluable. You can share hopes and fears, take rebukes
and counselling, and as Christians work together for Christ.
You will remember that Jesus sent His disciples out evange-
lising two by two, not singly.

'The perfect friend is one who knows the worst about you,
and loves you just the same.'

October 7

Now the serpent was more subtle than any other wild
creature that the LORD God had made. He said to the
woman, 'Did God say, "You shall not eat of any tree of the
garden"?'.... and he said to the woman, 'You will not die'
(Genesis 3:1-4).

This is where we read of how sin and sorrow first came into
the world. As you read it, and the conversations that took
place between Satan and Eve and Adam, you realise that just
the same kind of things are said by men and women today. So
it rings true to human nature!

'Did God say?' The suggestion that Satan makes here is
that if God really loves you, He wouldn't deprive you of
something that looks like good food. So, surely, God couldn't
have meant you to take Him literally? This is making God out
to be less kind and good than He really is.

'You will not die.' A deliberate contradiction now of what
God had told Adam and Eve. 'You try it, you won't die.' But
they did; they died spiritually then and there, and physically
later on. One of Satan's lies.

When questioned by God, Adam made excuses. 'The
woman You gave me, she gave me to eat.' That's right! put the
blame on someone else. 'All her fault, not mine.' Or was he
blaming God for having given him a dud partner? Hiding
behind trees - or behind his wife?! Satan scored a victory that
day, but - thank God - it wasn't the end of the story. To Satan
God said, 'Her seed (the woman's) shall bruise thy head, and
thou shalt bruise his heel.' The first promise of the coming
redemption by Jesus Christ.

What then is Apollos? What is Paul? Servants through
whom you believed .... I planted, Apollos watered, but God
gave the growth (1 Corinthians 3:5,6).

The Corinthian Christians had been getting into cliques, and
some had said, 'Paul is a better preacher than Apollos.' Others
said, 'Apollos is a better one than Paul'. So they followed two
separate leaders. Here, Paul is calling them to order. He says,
'Who are they?' Both are just 'waiters at table', people who
are there to serve you, ordinary people who are not there to be
leaders, but to show you how you should follow the true
Leader, Jesus.'

But Paul is also careful to point out that both he and
Apollos have a duty to perform. One first planted the seed of
the gospel among them, the other came in and helped them to
grow as Christians.

That's a bit of guidance to us as we seek to win other
people for Christ. All sorts of people may be needed to build
up real Christians, so we shouldn't expect that one man or
woman can be used by God to do it all for them. Each is just
a servant of Jesus, each has a part to play, so we need to work
together with each other and not to have any rivalry.

Ultimately, nothing will happen apart from God's Holy
Spirit. We can't turn other people into Christians. Only God
can do that. Think for a moment about all the people you know
who have influenced you for Christ. I'm sure there has been
more than one in it; there may have been many.

Planting, watering, growing; we are workers together
with each other, and with the Lord.

This whole chapter is one of the very loveliest in the whole Bible. It's worth reading aloud, so that you get the marvellous build-up in it, rising to the crescendo, 'Love never faileth'. Every other quality may have its weaknesses, but not true love.

I wonder what makes jealousy of someone else? Is it fear that people may not notice *us* enough, is it the constant urge to come top of everything, is it a desire to have the better quality that we see in some people but not in ourselves?

Jealousy is a terrible gnawing gangrene that eats into our very soul and ultimately destroys us, unless we can get it out and destroy it.

Its opposite number - love - is the quality that makes us want to build the other person up so that they become their very best. And love is not displeased when others succeed. I think sometimes we need to remind ourselves that God has no favourites, He doesn't love one person better than another, He loves us all equally.

We find sometimes in a friendship that one of the friends wants the other to be his or her exclusive friend, so that they have no other friends, and that one has to give all his attention to the other alone. This is another facet of jealousy, which has to be avoided; keep out of an exclusive friendship, it's destructive.

Love binds together, it doesn't separate people from each other, it's a positive quality that draws us to each other and to Christ.

On that day there shall be a fountain opened for the house of David and the inhabitants of Jerusalem to cleanse them from sin and uncleanness (Zechariah 13:1).

Zechariah was a wonderful prophet during the time of the exile of the people of Israel under Darius. He prophesied that God would bring His people back to Jerusalem once more. He also prophesied the coming of the Lord Jesus, an event which was still 500 years away. And he described what Jerusalem would be like once the people were back there: 'Boys and girls playing in the streets' (8:5). But the people must first be prepared, they must be clean.

'The fountain opened for cleansing' was of course, to be the precious Blood of Christ, shed for us all upon Calvary's tree. Zechariah also prophesied the Second Coming of Christ, in which he portrays Jesus as standing on the Mount of Olives to take over the Kingship of all the world (14:4).

Zechariah knows that the Jews will again be scattered, but that one day they will return and the Gentile world will be judged according to how they treat the Jews. In chapter 2:8, he describes God as saying, 'This is what the Lord Almighty says, "After He has honoured me and has sent me against the nations that have plundered you - for whoever touches you touches the apple of His eye - I will surely raise my hand against them so that their slaves will plunder them." Then you will know that the Lord Almighty has sent me.' Again, in chapter 8:7, 'I will save my people from the countries of the East and West. I will bring them back to live in Jerusalem; they will be my people.'

All Christians need that daily cleansing at the fountain, if we are to serve Christ faithfully.

Always be prepared to give an answer to everyone who asks you to give the reason for the hope that you have, but do it with gentleness and respect (1 Peter 3:15).

Anybody at any time may suddenly ask us to explain why it is that we believe in the Lord Jesus Christ. And we need to be ready with just the right answer, one that truly comes from the heart. I doubt if this will happen very often, but to most of us it does come sometimes. The occasion can be a very important one because the questioner may be very much influenced by the reply that we give.

Certainly we must not be always preaching at people, but Peter is here concerned with the other person making the opening. Peter himself knew what he was talking about, for he hadn't forgotten his own reaction when he was suddenly asked by a maid if he was a disciple. He missed his chance then, and denied Christ. How easy this is if we are not ready. But Peter also says that when we give an answer, it must be a gentle and respectful one, because the way in which we answer will govern the reaction of the enquirer. Peter had answered the maid with a curse! I'm quite sure he never did that again, for he truly loved the Lord.

Lord, keep us ever on the watch so that when such a moment arrives, we may be ready, and faithful, and gentle. For Jesus Christ's sake. AMEN.

How beautiful upon the mountains are the feet of him who
brings good tidings, who publishes peace, who brings good
tidings of good, who publishes Salvation, who says to
Zion, 'Your God Reigns' (Isaiah 52:7).

Isaiah is expanding upon the return of the Jewish exiles from
Babylon, when 1,700 of them were released and allowed to go
back home to rebuild their shattered, but beloved, Jerusalem.
The story is told in the book of Ezra, and it has taken the exiles
four months tramping over the mountains to get back home.
But as they go they sing for joy, because God is with them, and
I'm sure they sang some of the Psalms as they went.

Isaiah expands on the beauty of their feet! Why does he
think them beautiful. Surely it is because they are the means
by which the bearers of Good News reach their destination,
and the people can hear that Jerusalem is now at last to be
rebuilt. When Nehemiah saw the heaps of rubbish where the
temple had been, he burst into tears. But the promise was
there, and Zion was told by trumpet and voice, 'Your God
Reigns'.

People today sometimes sing a hymn with that refrain, and
this is where it comes from. But the News only reaches its
destination, when people stir their stumps and get moving.
The Good News of Jesus is just the same. How is the world to
hear that News? Every Christian must answer that query with
a clear conscience; we are on a job for Jesus Christ, to spread
the News of His Salvation to the uttermost parts of the earth,
and we have to get up and go. Where? Wherever God calls us
- and we have to ask Him where that should be. One thing is
certain, we can't do it in a sitting position; feet have to move
us!

And they were on the road going up to Jerusalem, and
Jesus was walking ahead of them; and they were amazed,
and those who followed were afraid (Mark 10:32).

Jesus told His disciples what was going to happen in Jerusalem, His arrest, torment, and death - and Resurrection. And He
had set His face deliberately to go to His death. No wonder
they were amazed. And the listening crowds were scared stiff.
Does this follow on yesterday's reading? I think it does. Jesus
could only get there on foot. He was to proclaim the gospel
again in Jerusalem. Although He would be rejected, He went
on.

Who knows what it may cost to fully follow Jesus? No
wonder there is fear. But notice this: it is Jesus who goes first,
He sets the pace, so we never go alone.

Many a missionary has gone out into the Moslem world
and to other hostile parts to carry the Good News of Jesus, and
often there has been little if any apparent fruit. But remember
this: Stephen proclaimed the Good News to the Jews, and the
upshot was that they stoned him. Paul took part in that stoning;
yet ultimately Paul was to become probably the greatest
missionary the world has yet seen. Stephen was not to know
that till after his death. But it happened, and I'm sure that now
they will have talked it all over together in Heaven, with tears
of joy on both sides!

'Jesus leads the Way.' If He didn't, none of us could go on.
But with Him ahead, fear can go out by the back door.

Jesus not only leads the Way, He is the Way.

October 14
I am the Bread of Life
(John 6:35).

These words of Jesus were spoken to the Jews very soon after the feeding of the 5,000. The people followed Him, and He said to them, 'You followed Me, not because you saw miraculous signs, but because you were given a feed of bread.' And He went on to say, 'I am the Bread of Life.'

They wanted material bread - for nothing - so as to give them lasting satisfaction. And Jesus in effect said that material things will never give the kind of peace and joy that nobody can ever take away. That is a spiritual thing, not a physical. And He Himself was, and is, the embodiment of that satisfaction.

How often have you striven to get something you really want, and then when you've got it, found that it doesn't give you what you wanted from it? Jesus offered the woman at the well Living Water, and she said, 'Give me that water, so that I never again come to the well to draw.' Material water was what she wanted.

In the same way today, people strive to amass a lot of money, hoping it will give them lasting satisfaction. But it cannot. Some people have everything that money can buy, yet are dissatisfied.

But when you are absolutely right with God, and your relationship with Jesus is unimpaired, you know in your heart of hearts that you are totally satisfied.

The Prodigal Son left home because he wanted Life - and he lost it. He came back and he found it was always under his father's roof. And that is true with our Heavenly Father too. In Christ, all our needs are met, forever.

*Onesiphorus ... often refreshed me; he was not ashamed of
my chains, but when he arrived in Rome he searched for
me eagerly and found me ... and you well know all the
service he rendered me at Ephesus (2 Timothy 1:16).*

This is Paul's last letter before his martyrdom, and only in this
letter do we hear anything of Onesiphorus. Paul mentions him
again in 4:19 where he speaks of 'the house of Onesiphorus',
so he was evidently a family man. So he helped and encouraged Paul, both in Ephesus and in Rome.

When Paul came to Rome, Onesiphorus hunted for him,
and when he'd found him, Paul gave him a great welcome.
How lovely to find a welcoming friend when you come to a
strange place. It always warms your heart, doesn't it?

Of course we have to be constantly looking out to see how
we can win others for Christ. But we must never forget the
needs of our Christian friends either.

I have just been to visit a town I was brought up in, but had
left over 60 years ago. It was wonderful to find a few old
friends still there - and a great many new ones - ready to give
me a warm welcome back, and make me feel at home still!

When we think of old friends, it's worth sitting down and
asking yourself, 'Is there anything specially nice I can do with
or for them, to encourage them and make them feel they're
loved?' Paul was obviously delighted at the special care that
his friend gave him when he knew his own martyrdom was
very near. Paul was in prison at that time, and Onesiphorus
must have chatted with him and prayed with him just as
though they were free to go anywhere, so Paul forgot all about
his chains for the time.

Who can you bring a gleam of sunshine to today?

You search the Scriptures, because you think that in them
you have Eternal Life; and it is they that bear witness to
Me; yet you refuse to come to Me that you may have life
(John 5:39,40).

Jesus had healed the paralysed man at the Pool of Bethesda,
and at once He came into controversy with the Jewish
religious leaders, because He had healed the man on the
Sabbath Day. He had 'broken' the Sabbath, and more - He
called God His Father, so making Himself equal with God. So
Jesus took them right back to Moses, whose Scriptures they
read, and said: 'If you really believed Moses, you would
believe Me, because Moses in fact wrote about Me.' Their
study of Moses was a superficial one, they didn't go deep
enough into what Moses said.

In other words, Jesus was saying, 'Yes, the Scripture can
certainly show you how to find Eternal Life. But you can read
the Scriptures for years (with head knowledge) and get
nowhere. The Scripture points you to Me, and only in Me can
you find Eternal Life.'

The Scriptures are the written Word of God; Jesus is the
Living Word of God. Life doesn't come from the Scriptures,
but through the Scriptures to Jesus. So when we read the
Scriptures it is like studying a road map. But don't think when
you've studied the map that you've reached your destination.
No, you have to get up and go. Jesus said, 'I am the Way.' So
He is both the Way and the Destination.

And once you have got the Guide beside you, as long as
you keep with Him the destination is certain, because He said,
'Lo, I am with you always, even unto the end of the world'
(Matthew 28:20).

Why do the wicked live, reach old age,
and grow mighty in power? (Job 21:7).

Why? Why? Why? Poor Job, he had a very difficult time of
it with his 'comforters' in his troubles. They told him that his
troubles could only have come upon him because of his evil
ways, that God never lets disaster overtake godly people.
How can he refute that? And he does so here by saying: 'Just
watch the wicked people. Lots of them seem to flourish. They
grow rich, they are popular, they have big families, and yet
they are thorough scamps, and they don't care what God
thinks - they reckon He can't touch them. So they die, and
when they do, they have great gravestones erected in their
memory. But the day is surely coming when they will appear
before God's judgment seat, and then they will be condemned.'

All the way along, Job put himself time and time again
back into God's hands. He knew that the ultimate of everything was with God; that the righteous would be justified and
the unrepentant sinners would be condemned. Job saw very
close to the New Testament. As he looked at his own troubles
he said, 'But He knoweth the way that I take: when He hath
tried me, I shall come forth as gold' (23:10). And when he
looked at God he said, 'I know that my Redeemer liveth, and
that He shall stand at the latter day upon the earth ... yet in my
flesh shall I see God' (Job 19:25,26). Looking forward to the
Coming of Christ, and his own future resurrection!

How little he had! Yet how close to God he lived! And he
was rewarded, even in this life. His trust was not in vain. Nor
will ours be.

Luke, the beloved physician ... greets you
(Colossians 4:14).

Who was Luke? We don't know a great deal about him, but he first appears on the scene in the middle of the Acts, when he joins Paul on his second missionary journey in Acts 16:10. He suddenly appears for instead of writing about 'them', he changes to 'we'. From then on, he was partner with Paul, right up to the end of his life. And Paul calls him, 'the beloved Physician', so he was a doctor.

He wrote the Gospel according to Luke, also the Acts of the Apostles, and these two books, addressed to Theophilus, were written to instruct him in the Christian faith.

Traditionally he was a Jew of Antioch, as Paul was of Tarsus, so they may well have met up soon after Paul's conversion. In the Gospel, he related all that 'Jesus began to do and to teach'; and in the Acts he tells of all that the Holy Spirit continued to do through the disciples, and in a sense, the Acts has never finished, for God is still working by His Holy Spirit in the hearts and lives of His followers today, continuing to bring the gospel to bear upon all who don't yet know Christ.

In Paul's last letter before his death (2 Timothy), he says that he is now almost alone; Demas had forsaken the gospel, Crescens had been sent elsewhere, and so had Titus; and Paul says, 'Luke only is with me.'

He must have been glad to have his 'beloved physician' with him in his old age, caring both for his physical and his spiritual needs. What a marvellous thing is Christian friendship! We need one another.

In Him ... you have heard the word of truth, the gospel of
your Salvation, and having believed in Him, were sealed
with the promised Holy Spirit (Ephesians 1:13).

We looked at this verse away back on July 30, when we saw
that the Holy Spirit was the 'earnest' of our inheritance. In
other words, He is a foretaste of all that is yet to come from
God to us.

But today I want to examine this word *sealed*. Important
letters, even today but much more in days gone by, were not
only licked up by the flap, but the flap made more secure by
the use of a stick of sealing wax, which was burnt so that it
dripped on to the back of the envelope where it joined up, and
then had impressed upon it a 'seal', which bore the family
crest of the writer on it. When one saw it, they knew that it was
genuine. It was also a guarantee that what was in the envelope
had not been interfered with for the letter was intact.

To the Jews, circumcision was the seal that marked them
(Romans 4:11). The Holy Spirit is the Christian's seal. God's
image is impressed upon us, and we belong to Him; it is His
mark of ownership. If we are genuinely His, it will be noticed
by other people, both believers and non-believers. And He is
there within us to keep us intact until we see Jesus face to face.
This is our safe-guard.

The Holy Spirit dwells within all who put their trust in
Jesus, and He enters the moment when we believe. And the
Promise is surely the promise of what is yet to come.

God's guarantee for us!

And this is the confidence that we have in Him, that if we
ask anything according to His will He hears us. And if we
know that He hears us in whatever we ask, we know that
we have received the requests made of Him
(1 John 5:14,15).

So often people ask, can I be sure that God will answer my
prayer? Well, there are conditions, and John gives us some of
those conditions in these verses. He says first of all that for
what we pray must be 'according to His will'. Can we always
be sure that for what we pray is? No, we can't. So we say to
God, 'If it is according to Your will.' Do we know that He
hears us? Yes, if we are His children, He does. If we ask it 'in
His Name', we are asking that what we want may be to His
glory. If it's just something we would like to have, that may
not be glorifying to Him. If it is for the conversion of our
friend, that would certainly be according to His will; it would
certainly be in His Name; it would be to His glory.

It may be a long-term thing, and we may have to wait and
to keep on praying. It may be something we can commit to
God once and then leave it and forget it, because we are
trusting Him to do what is right.

And then we can thank Him for doing what He knows to
be right, even if as far as we know, it hasn't yet happened.
'Before they call, I will answer; while they are yet speaking,
I will hear' (Isaiah 65:24).

It's quite a good thing to keep a list of prayers, with the
answer on the other side of the page, when it comes. Then we
will remember to say 'thank you'.

The Lord is faithful; He will strengthen you and protect
you from the Evil One (2 Thessalonians 3:3).

In the previous chapter, Paul had been writing about the
attacks of the Evil One, Satan, against God's people. So that
is what he is referring to here, that God will not allow Satan
to get the advantage of us. If it is a matter of our own will, it
is a promise that God will strengthen our will. If it is Satanic
power, then he won't be allowed to harm us.

Paul finishes this letter by asking that God's peace may be
upon all His people. It's a lovely thing to know that, even
when there is turmoil all round us, the peace of God is there
to shield our hearts and lives. 'The Lord be with you' (3:16),
he says (a phrase which is picked up in the Prayer Book and
to which we reply, 'And also with you', so that it becomes a
kind of Christian greeting).

When we know He is with us, it certainly quietens our
hearts, because we know that inner peace that nothing can
disturb.

Have you noticed that there are some people who seem to
be always serene and gentle, however much there is hurry and
bustle around them? They are never hurried, but they are
quietly efficient, and you feel you can trust them and confide
in them.

Other folk may be always on the run, and they can't stop
a moment, they are so busy; in fact they seem to think it is a
virtue to have no time to do anything! The Christian should be
ready to stop when there is need, and to give time when friends
need help. And God's protection is extended to cover them
too.

Then Amos answered Amaziah, 'I am no prophet, nor a
prophet's son; but I am a herdsman, and a dresser of
sycamore trees. and the LORD took me from following the
flock, and the LORD said to me, 'Go prophesy to my people
Israel' (Amos 7:14,15).

So many people when they are faced with God's call to them
say, 'But I just can't do this. I'm not educated to do this kind
of work for God. I don't think I have the brains, the capacity,
the ability to do what God seems to be asking.'

This was what Amos, the cowman said of himself! 'I'm
not a prophet, I just herd cows in the field. I can't become
suddenly a preacher.' The job was a very difficult one; it was
to predict coming disaster to an Israel which seemed to be
very prosperous, because the people had turned away from
God. He was not likely to be popular if he had this kind of
message. But he accepted, in spite of all his misgivings,
because he knew God had called him.

Every Christian has been called by God, and to each of us
God assigns the kind of task He wants us to do for Him. But
He never sets us a task which is impossible. He does for us
what He did for Amos, He gives us the ability to carry out the
job. We may be scared stiff of it because it requires superhuman powers. But it is that very power that is available to us -
God's Power.

In our own strength we can accomplish nothing. It was
Paul who was later to say, 'I can do all things through Christ
who strengtheneth me' (Philippians 4:13).

He chose you before you were born, to serve Him!

October 23

Remind them ... to speak evil of no one,
to avoid quarrelling, to be gentle,
and to show perfect courtesy toward all men
(Titus 3:1,2).

Whoever was Titus? Well, you have to hunt for him a bit, but if you look up 2 Corinthians 7 and 8, you will find him mentioned quite a bit, and also in Galatians 2:1. He was a Greek disciple who had gone with Paul on several of his missionary journeys, and was sent by him to Dalmatia. Eventually Paul left him in Crete to look after a rather renegade type of church and try and bring it to some sort of order. Titus 1:12 tells us, 'Cretans are always liars, evil beasts, slow bellies', so Paul tells Titus, 'Rebuke them sharply, that they may be sound in the Faith'. But he begins by saying, 'be gentle, be courteous'.

Not an easy task for a young man to do! How to be gentle, yet sharp. In other words, Titus had to be tactful, so as not to drive them away, yet absolutely firm so as to make them see he meant business. I think Titus might have felt a bit like Amos in yesterday's reading, he was hardly the man for such a difficult task. But God had just as surely called him as he had Amos, and the needed powers would be there for him too.

And that same power is available for us, the gentle, persuasive appeal of the Lord Jesus who said, 'Come unto Me, all ye that labour and are heavy-laden, and I will give you rest' (Matthew 11:28).

I think I would like to have sat under the ministry of Titus, to see how he coped with the disreputable folk of the church in Crete!

October 24

This was why the Jews sought all the more to kill Him,
because He ... called God His Father, making Himself
equal with God (John 5:18).

You may know that the Jehovah's Witnesses do not believe
that Jesus is God, and perhaps you have had some of them
trying to persuade you. Well, here is one of the many proofs
of His Godhead. The Jews said He was claiming to be God,
so they later brought that accusation against Him at His trial.
If it was true that Jesus is not God, then He had only to say so
and avoid the charge. But He never did this. Instead, He used
the next nine verses of this chapter to assert His relationship
with the Father. 'What the Father does, the Son does.' 'The
Father raised the dead ... so does the Son.' 'Judgment is left to
the Son, so that all may honour the Son just as they honour the
Father.' 'The dead will hear the voice of the Son of God and
will live.' And elsewhere He says, 'I and the Father are One'
(John 10:30).

Anybody who denies that Jesus claimed to be God is just
twisting the Scriptures to make them agree with his own ideas,
for the Word of God is quite plain.

This is the difference between the 'sects' and the 'churches'. None of the sects are clear about the Godhead of Jesus -
most the churches are. The apostle John later on in his first
Epistle makes this clear when he says, 'God has given us
Eternal Life, and this Life, is in His Son. He who has the Son
has Life; he who does not have the Son of God has not Life'
(1 John 5:11,12).

Never let go of that fact, your Life depends on it!

October 25

*Flesh and blood cannot inherit the Kingdom of God ....
This perishable nature must put on the imperishable, and
this mortal nature must put on immortality*
(1 Corinthians 15:50,53).

Paul is writing about what lies ahead for us after this life. Christian people whom he knew had been wondering what heaven was to be like, and he is trying to explain.

But certain things are clear. There will be no more sin in heaven, no more sickness of the body, no kind of decay through old age. Our life here is short, the one to come is eternal. So, the body in which I live is a kind of house in which the real me lives; so going to heaven is like moving house, into a larger sphere where I shall be much freer than at present.

After His resurrection, during the forty days Jesus was here on earth, I think we get a glimpse of what our own future life may be like. He was not tied by space or time. Yet He still had a body, though it was changed from the body He had before His death. The disciples thought He was a ghost when they saw Him, but He said, 'A ghost does not have flesh and bones, as you see I have. Give me something to eat.'

It was that body that went back into Heaven when the time for the Ascension came, and the disciples saw Him go away into a cloud. And the angel said He would come back again in due course. So it is that Day to which we look forward, when 'we, too, shall all be changed'.

Meanwhile, our present life here on earth is gradually changing us in preparation for what is yet to come, as we get to know our Lord Jesus better and better day by day. There is plenty yet to do for Him now. So keep it up!

October 26

Our beloved Barnabas and Paul, men who have risked their
lives for the sake of our Lord Jesus Christ
(Acts 15:25,26).

It was, under God, these two men who prevented the Faith of
Christ from just becoming a little 'off-sect' of Judaism. The
crisis was in the early days of the Christian Faith, when most
of the converts were Jews. But it was beginning to spread to
Gentiles, and there was a feeling in Jerusalem that the new
converts ought first to become Jews by the rite of circumcision before they could become Christians. Paul and Barnabas,
who had been sent out as virtually the first missionaries of the
Christian Church, made it very clear that the gospel was for
the world, not just for Israel, so that those who came in must
be joining the world-wide Church of Christ. Certainly there
had to be rules, but they must not be peculiarly Jewish rules.

When the Church had agreed this, they sent Paul and
Barnabas together with Jude and Silas, to explain their decision to the Gentile converts. This was, virtually, the opening
of the door to the Gentiles, and so eventually the gospel came
across to Europe, and has since spread all over the world.

And that, too, is our job today as their successors in the
Christian Faith. We have still to spread the Good News
wherever we can, to all who don't know Christ. And we have
a whole life in which to do so, sharing all that we know of
Jesus with anyone who doesn't yet know Him.

But you are a chosen race, a royal priesthood, a holy
nation, God's own people, that you may declare the
wonderful deeds of Him who called you out of darkness
into His marvellous Light (1 Peter 2:9).

Specially picked out by God! Does that mean that we are
God's favourites? Not a bit - it means that we have a job to do
for Him! But I like the phrase 'a royal priesthood'. The
Queen's Chaplains wear a scarlet cassock to show that they
are in her service. Christians don't wear anything to show who
or what they are, but they must never forget that they are on
the King's Staff, His ambassadors. They are 'a holy nation',
that is, they are consecrated to God. They are 'a peculiar
people' and it doesn't mean strange folk, as in our modern
sense, but a people for God's personal possession. We are
here, not to show how wonderful we are, but how wonderful
our Master, Jesus, is.

'Out of darkness into light' describes the amazing transformation that takes place in us through the impact of the
gospel upon our hearts and lives. By our life and behaviour,
we are to show that this is what happens when Jesus Christ
takes hold of a person.

There's a verse I love to couple with this one, and it is
Colossians 4:5: 'Redeeming the time'. We haven't got long,
so let's make the most of it, buying up the opportunity while
we still have it.

Joint-heirs of the Grace of Life (1 Peter 3:7).

Peter is talking about the relationship of husbands and wives, when both are Christians. All over the world today, the marriage relationship is breaking down, partly because they have a wrong view of what it's all about and partly because both are determined to get what they want for themselves out of it. 'My wife doesn't satisfy me'; 'my husband doesn't understand me'.

When you are unmarried, and perhaps looking forward to the day when you will have a life-partner, if you are a Christian, the first thing to make sure of is that your partner is also a Christian and that together you will learn to live out the Christian life. Better far to remain single, than to make a marriage with a non-Christian partner.

But often, the Christian Faith will come to one partner of an existing marriage, and when that happens, the responsibility rests on the Christian partner to try and win the other to Jesus Christ. And that's not easy, partly because when you married, neither was a Christian, and now one has changed. The need is to go very gently with the non-Christian partner, and to show by behaviour towards him or her that love is stronger than before, and that the Christian is now a nicer person than before because Jesus has become Lord.

The joy of a Christian marriage is something that far outweighs any other kind of union, because both are living for Christ and both want to please each other. When children come, the parents share the responsibility of seeking day by day to lead their children to know God too, so that the whole family may be growing up together in Christian life and service.

October 29

Now to Him who is able to keep you from falling, and to present you without blemish before the presence of His glory with rejoicing, to the only God, our Saviour through Jesus Christ our Lord, be glory, majesty, dominion, and authority, before all time and now and for ever. Amen (Jude 24,25).

The blessing is one which we often use at the end of a Sunday morning or evening service, the committal of God's people to His infinite grace and mercy.

What I think Jude is really reminding us is that, both for all time that is ahead and for all time that is past, the Lord Jesus as Saviour can protect us, keep us, and cleanse us. So that when we finally stand before God at the last day, He will see us as without sin any more, since all our sins have been forgiven and we stand spotless before Him. But this is not of our doing, it is the Lord who has washed us white in His Blood. So at this moment, in anticipation, we give Him all the glory for what He has done, is doing, and will do.

Nobody and nothing will be allowed to separate us from the Love of God. We believe in Jesus now; one day we shall see Him face to face, and it will be both for us and for Him exceeding joy! Where there is no sin, there will also be no sorrow; where it is perfect holiness, there will also be perfect joy. Knowing all this we want to praise the Lord with all our heart and soul and mind, and our voice, now!

Which of you, desiring to build a tower, does not first sit
down and count the cost, whether he has enough to
complete it? Otherwise, when he has laid a foundation, and
is not able to finish, all who see it begin to mock him,
saying, 'This man began to build,
and was not able to finish (Luke 14:28-30).

The danger of a sudden and perhaps emotional decision to
become a Christian! Before we undertake such a step, we
need to try and see something of what it means. It costs
nothing to take the step of deciding for Christ, but afterwards
it costs us the whole of life, because we are handing it over
unconditionally to *Him*.

You'll remember the rich young ruler who wanted to
follow Christ. Jesus loved him, wanted him, and hoped he
would take that step. But first he warned him of at least a part
of the cost. The young ruler's heart was deeply set upon his
riches and Jesus knew that the ruler would have a divided
loyalty unless he was prepared to let his wealth go. The ruler
could not face this.

Afterwards the disciples told Jesus they had given up
everything for Him. Jesus told them they would never lose by
doing so, they would gain far more than they lost, both in this
life and in the next. God is no man's debtor!

Do we drift back? Sadly, most of us do sometimes. But the
pull of His love is greater, and we come back. He will not let
us go.

'Counting the cost'. None of us really knows all that it
may cost. We can only pray that when the test comes, the Lord
may take a firm hold of us. Without Him, we can do nothing.

And God is able to provide you with every blessing in
abundance, so that you may always have enough of
everything and may provide in abundance for every good
work (2 Corinthians 9:8).

Do you know what a portmanteau is? I don't think they are
very much used these days, because they would be much too
heavy to carry. They are large oblong bags for carrying
clothing and all you need when you go away on a journey.
They open like a book, with hinges in the middle of the back;
but they hold everything you can possibly need! Well, this
verse used to be described as 'The Christian's Portmanteau'!
And you can see why. There is nothing we shall lack when we
are God's servants. He will meet our every need.

No, it does not mean we shall get all we want, but we shall
get all we need. I think sometimes we think we need more than
God sees we need, but He knows better than we do. The
purpose is that we shall be fully equipped to do the job God
has set before us. He certainly does not tell us we shall have
no hardships; Paul had plenty. He was beaten, stoned, imprisoned, shipwrecked, mocked, and finally martyred.

Shall we be treated like that? Who can tell? But there are
men and women, today, in prison for Christ, and many of them
have been and are still being tortured for Christ. Yet they are
standing firm. How can they bear it? I think the same way Paul
did. God said to him, 'My grace is sufficient for you' (2
Corinthians 12:9). That was more than enough. You cannot
face this kind of thing in advance. But when the moment
comes, the Lord is there with you. And that is what matters,
isn't it?

November 1

We would not have you ignorant ... concerning those who are asleep, that you may not grieve as others do who have no hope (1 Thessalonians 4:13).

Paul is here writing to people who were expecting Jesus Christ to return again during their lifetime. They were worried because people were dying daily, and they were afraid they would miss His Coming. So Paul has to make it very clear that, for Christians, the death of the present body is purely a transformation, which is described as 'sleep'. Death for a Christian is very often in the Bible described as sleep, though if you turn to Revelation 7:15, you find that in fact the dead are active in heaven; the sleep refers to the condition of their old bodies.

The old body has served its purpose, it is worn out. So when the Resurrection comes, we shall have new and imperishable bodies, with none of the aches and pains which so often trouble us now. Of course we are sad when our friends and loved ones are taken from us. We miss them, but at the same time we rejoice for them because, as Paul says elsewhere, their condition is 'far better'.

'Others have no hope' - that is the saddest thing of all. Christians should be as active as possible, pointing out to non-Christians what they will miss, both in this life and in that which is to come, if they don't turn to Christ.

If there is no resurrection, why on earth should Christ have died? He could have escaped death on a cross, as He told Pilate (John 19:11) and those who arrested Him (Matthew 26:53). But He knew that His death would mean our Life and Resurrection. Praise Him for that - and for our certainty.

O Lord, Thou hast searched me and known me! Thou
knowest when I sit down and when I rise up; Thou
discernest my thoughts from afar. Thou searchest out my
path and my lying down, and art acquainted with all my
ways. Even before a word is on my tongue, lo, O Lord,
Thou knowest it altogether .... Such knowledge is too
wonderful for me; it is high, I cannot attain it
(Psalm 139:1-4,6).

If it were anybody other than God, I think I would be scared
stiff! None of us would like to have all our secret thoughts laid
bare. But with God it's different. He knows everything about
me, both good and evil. I can't hide from Him, and I don't want
to. Nor can I make excuses to Him when I've done wrong; I
can only repent and ask His cleansing and forgiveness. Other
people might despise me if they knew all about me, but not
God.

Sometimes when I want to talk to Him, I have no words to
say. But He knows even before I attempt to speak, and I can
just meditate upon Him. Sometimes when we are with a
friend, neither of us talk. Just being with each other is enough
- and that is amazingly true of God.

Are there things you cannot talk to anybody else about?
Take them to God, He understands. And if there's a problem,
He is on the solving end of that problem.

'Come unto Me all ye that labour and are heavy-laden, and
I will give you rest,' said Jesus. Rest and peace of heart are
with Him, and tensions can be relaxed, thank God.

One thing I know, that though I was blind, now I see
(John 9:25).

This is one of the most wonderful stories of healing by Jesus in the Bible. The man concerned was born blind, he had never seen anything at all; so how could he even imagine what things were like? The disciples assumed that this was the result of sin, either his or his parents. They asked Jesus about it, and got the answer, 'Neither.' Of course, all three were sinners but that was not the cause of his blindness.

But Jesus was to heal him. He sent him off to wash, and he came back seeing. By then Jesus was gone. But the man attracted immediate attention. People began to argue. 'It's not the same man - someone like him - no, it is him.' The man settled it, 'I am he.' Arguments at once. 'Healing on the Sabbath?' 'That is forbidden.' 'Who did it?' The man answered, 'He is a prophet.' The rulers called his parents, 'What do you say?' 'Yes, he is our son, but let him speak for himself.' They were afraid to answer for him.

They turned to the man, 'Give glory to God: we know that this man is a sinner.' He replied, 'Whether He's a sinner or not, I don't know. One thing I know; I was blind, now I see.' More arguments, till he gets tired of answering. 'Do you also want to become His disciples?' I like that word, 'also'. He had begun to realise a little who Jesus really was. From then on, the Pharisees wouldn't let him enter the Temple any more, they chucked him out. But there, Jesus picked him up! And when Jesus explained who He was, the man answered, 'Lord, I believe.' And he worshipped Jesus.

For though by this time you ought to be teachers, you need someone to teach you again the first principles of God's Word. You need milk, not solid food; for everyone who lives on milk is unskilled in the word of righteousness, for he is a child (Hebrews 5:12,13).

No Christian can remain static, we either go forwards or we go backwards. We either grow in our knowledge of God, or we get lazy and slack, and drift away. The original people who first read this letter were going back. They should have been teaching others, but they had forgotten what little they had learnt, and had to start again from scratch!

We give milk to babies, not to grown-ups, they can take meat. Feed a grown-up on nothing but milk and they soon become flabby. As we get older, we need to spend more time really studying God's Word for ourselves, and seeing its application to the whole of our life. We cannot do much about teaching other people the gospel, if we are still in the kindergarten.

In the Church of England, the second Sunday in Advent is usually called 'Bible Sunday', and the Prayer for that day reads: 'Blessed Lord, who hast caused all Holy Scriptures to be written for our learning; Grant that we may in such wise hear them, read, mark, learn, and inwardly digest them, that by patience and comfort of Thy Holy Word, we may embrace and ever hold fast the blessed hope of Everlasting life, which Thou has given us in our Saviour Jesus Christ. Amen.'

Do not be deceived; God is not mocked, for whatever a
man sows, that he will also reap (Galatians 6:7).

Here Paul is very clear. He is stating a fact, and it's a fact that
we must reckon with. We cannot expect to live a life of sin and
get away with it. We cannot count on God's forgiveness
removing all the consequences of sin. If we break somebody's
heart, the scars will remain, even if we are later forgiven.
William Barclay puts it this way: 'If a man allows the lower
side of his nature to dominate him, in the end he can expect
nothing but a harvest of trouble.'

Conversely, if we always walk in God's way and serve
Him all our life, even if nobody else notices it, God won't
forget. Does that mean that any of us can get through life with
no scars? I don't think so. I'm sure Paul never forgot that he
had assisted at the murder of Stephen, though Stephen would
have been the first to forgive him. Perhaps it was because of
this that Paul once called himself 'the chief of sinners'.

But it would be a very sad thing if at the end of our days,
we had to offer God a forgiven soul, but a useless life,
wouldn't it? We want to be able to offer Him a life that has
been lived to His glory, and perhaps one day to hear His 'Well
done, good and faithful servant. Enter into the Joy of thy
Lord.'

When does that kind of living begin? It begins at once, as
soon as we have made a start with Jesus, and it never ceases
until we stand face to face with Him at the end of our days.

Walk with Him today.

If they sin against Thee - for there is no man who does not sin - and Thou art angry with them ... yet if they lay it to heart ... and ... if they repent with all their mind and with all their heart ... then hear Thou in heaven Thy dwelling-place their prayer ... and forgive Thy people who have sinned against Thee (1 Kings 8:46-50).

This is part of Solomon's great prayer at the dedication of the newly-built Temple in Jerusalem. The whole nation had taken part in the building, and the whole nation was now gathered to dedicate it and themselves to God's service. It was a long prayer, and a wonderful one. If only the nation, and Solomon himself, had lived up to that prayer!

You may commit yourself and your family wholly to God. But in fact you cannot answer for the family, for every one has to make their own decision. All you can do is pray for all those in your family that God may bless and keep them, and that they may always want to put Him first. And if that happens, you are greatly blest.

Many Christians keep a prayer-list, putting on it all for whom they have a special concern, making both a daily and a weekly list, for you cannot dwell on all of them every day, especially when there will be others outside your immediate family for whom you want to pray. Try to visualise each as you name them, remembering what their special needs may be.

Solomon ended his prayer like this: 'May the Lord our God be with us as He was with our fathers; may He never leave or forsake us. May He turn our hearts to Him' (1 Kings 8:57,58).

Train yourself in godliness; for while bodily training is of
some value, godliness is of value in every way, as it holds
promise for the present life, and also for the life to come
(1 Timothy 4:7,8).

I don't know whether young Timothy was an athletic type, but
he would probably have watched the Olympic Games of those
days. He would see how necessary it was for any athlete, who
wanted to excel, to keep himself fit by a daily training
programme.

Sometimes I look out of my window at breakfast time, and
I see youngsters in running shorts and shirts going side by side
for a run to keep themselves fit. That's a healthy way of life.

Paul knew that an athlete for God must also keep his body,
as well as his spirit in proper trim. But here he's concentrating
on the life of the spirit. That too needs discipline and training,
so that our inner man is strengthened by God. We shall often
be faced with loneliness and have to stand in a godless
company, but yet stick to true Christian standards which other
people know nothing about.

We have to be able to persevere in times of failure, and not
to compromise in times of success. All that needs backbone
and determination of heart and mind. The secret of that
power? The daily meeting with Jesus Christ, as we put
ourselves afresh into His hands, and study our handbook, the
Bible, for a healthy spiritual life.

All this is from God, who through Christ reconciled us to
Himself and gave us the ministry of reconciliation; that is,
God was in Christ reconciling the world to Himself ... and
entrusting to us the message of reconciliation. So we are
ambassadors for Christ. God making His appeal through us.
We beseech you on behalf of Christ, be reconciled to God
(2 Corinthians 5:18-20).

This is another of Paul's quite tremendous passages concerning all that it means to become a Christian. What a long word
is this word 'reconciliation'. What exactly does it mean?

It means 'putting straight all the disagreement that has
taken place between God and me'. Now, this is not something
that I can do for myself. As Professor Tasker says in his
commentary, 'I cannot say I will be a friend of God and no
longer regard Him as my enemy, because, as a sinner, I was
God's enemy, and so was banished from His Presence.'

No, the gospel is that God in His love has brought about
this reunion. So, whenever this word of reconciliation is
proclaimed by God's ambassadors and some individual sinner accepts it as God's gift, then peace is made between that
person and God. God no longer counts that person's sins
against him or her.

Who are the ambassadors? Every forgiven Christian is
one. You are. I am. We are therefore important persons; but
only important because we are Christ's messengers. We
speak with authority, not our own, but His. So here Paul is
calling on all people in Corinth who hear this message, to
accept this reconciliation. 'We pray you in Christ's stead,' he
says. So we must be very tactful and courteous - we are
speaking for Him, in love. What a wonderful privilege is ours!

November 9

So we do not lose heart. Though our outer nature is wasting away, our inner nature is being renewed every day. For this slight momentary affliction is preparing for us an eternal weight of glory beyond all comparison, because we look not to the things that are seen but to the things that are unseen; for the things that are seen are transient, but the things that are unseen are eternal (2 Corinthians 4:16-18).

How old are you? At what age do you think you begin to get old, and to go down hill physically? A tennis player is considered to be past his prime by the age of 35; after that he's on the way out. People begin to forget things once they are over 25 (some perhaps a good deal earlier than that!). I remember hearing with a shock a young agricultural recruit speaking of his boss as 'a man with one leg in the grave' - and his boss was then 40. I was 45.

The fact is, of course, that you begin to perish as soon as you are born, though you may not feel the effects until you are 80. So you start bright and shining, but you gradually get weaker. But here, Paul is reminding us that spiritually the very opposite is true.

When you first come to Christ, you have begun, but very tentatively. And you grow stronger day by day, as you feed upon Christ. Each day, therefore, it is most important that you have your 'daily bread', your food for the day, as otherwise you are weaker that day and may give way to some sin which attacks you. Your food comes from your study of God's Word and from fellowship with other Christians and through your prayers. Bit by bit you grow stronger. As Paul says, 'our inner nature is being renewed every day'. So that as our physical body weakens, the spiritual grows.

Beloved, do not imitate evil but imitate good. He who does
good is of God; he who does evil has not seen God
(3 John 11).

Have you ever studied the art of handwriting? So many people
produce all their letters nowadays on a word processor, that
the art of handwriting is dying out. But a handwritten letter is
so much more interesting than a typed one, because the
character of the writer comes out in a written letter.

I well remember the handwriting of a former London
Rector; it was so beautiful that all his curates tried to copy it!
And they copied his mannerism in preaching too; so that you
knew where they came from when you heard them preach!

And we copy people's speech. I was once on the staff of
the Alliance High School in Kenya, and you could tell which
Mission each boy came from by his pronunciation of English
- American or English! 'Do not imitate evil,' said John,
writing this tiny letter to his beloved Gaius; and he said 'I had
many things to write, but I will not write with pen and ink,
because I hope to see you soon.' But his tiny 'pen and ink'
letter was just a wee encouragement to a young Christian from
the aged apostle.

Paul sometimes wrote a PS to his letters, saying, 'I've
written this bit with my own hand', so that they would know
it was genuine. They would recognise the writing. I wish we
could see a bit of his own hand; what a precious piece of
writing it would be!

'Imitate God,' said John. I suppose a real Christian is in
some sense a copyplate of God, a recognisable part of the Lord
Jesus Christ.

Do not yield your members to sin as instruments of
wickedness, but yield yourselves to God as men who have
been brought from death to life, and your members to God
as instruments of righteousness (Romans 6:13).

'Men who have been brought from death to life'; that is what
a Christian has become, and it's a marvellous experience.
Before, in God's sight, we were like dead people, with no
spiritual life. Then, something happened, and we became
alive in Christ. But that is just the start.

We move on from that first coming to Christ, we have a
job to do. What is an 'instrument'? I turned it up in my
dictionary which said: 'A thing used in performing an action,
or a person so made use of.' So an instrument can be used in
two ways: either in doing evil and destructive actions or in
doing good and constructive things. Paul says: 'When you
have become a Christian, you have a number of delicate
instruments. Be careful how you use them. You have a brain,
a mouth, legs and arms and feet; you have a face and a body.
All of these are instruments that enable you to do things.
Without them, you would be useless. With them, you can do
a lot. Then give them to God, and use them for Him.'

Being a Christian is not just receiving Christ, saying your
prayers, reading the Scriptures; it means making use of every
instrument you have to do God's work. God usually does not
work without people. If He wants a word spoken, He gets a
person to do it. If He wants to bring joy to a sad person, He
sends someone to bring it. He has no hands to use, but our
hands; no feet to go, but our feet. So, have a fresh look at your
'instruments' today. They need to be daily exercised if they
are not to decay. Put them to work for Jesus Christ.

And the government will be upon His shoulder, and His Name will be called Wonderful Counsellor, Mighty God, Everlasting Father, Prince of Peace. Of the increase of His government and of peace there will be no end
(Isaiah 9:6,7).

Isaiah's prophecy was written some 700 years before Christ came. So it's very interesting to see how he foreshadowed the coming of Jesus. The first part of this verse runs: 'Unto us a child is born, unto us a Son is given.' It hadn't happened yet, but that was what the people of Israel had to look forward to.

And as Isaiah sees Jesus coming, he gives Him four qualities which describe what this Messiah would be like.

A Wonderful Counsellor. Wonderful, because He will be both God and Man. *Counsellor,* because He has been in God's counsel for all Eternity, and who better could describe God to man?

Mighty God. He and the Father are one, so in fact, it will be God Himself come down to us. *Mighty,* because He would be 'able to save to the uttermost those who come to God by Him' (Hebrews 7:25).

The Everlasting Father. He was to be the author of Everlasting Life to all who come to God, the guarantor of Eternity to man.

The Prince of Peace. It was the angels who announced at His birth, 'Glory to God in the highest, and on earth peace, good will towards men' (Luke 2:14).

And of the everlasting nature of His gospel, we can bear witness, for after nearly 2000 years, His Kingdom has greatly increased, and all nations have had his gospel proclaimed to them.

And Peter said, 'Now I am sure that the Lord has sent His angel and rescued me from the hand of Herod and from all that the Jewish people were expecting' (Acts 12:11).

King Herod now had arrested Peter, after earlier arresting James, the brother of John, and putting him to death. His intention was to put Peter also to death, and indeed Peter himself was expecting it.

But, and so often there is a 'but' which seems to make all the difference, the whole Church in Jerusalem was praying for Peter, and asking God to deliver him. Didn't they also pray for James? I'm sure they must have done. Then why didn't God also set James free? James must have discovered the answer to that question immediately after the flashing sword took off his head! Perhaps we shall know the answer one day. But just as surely, God knew what He was doing with James.

The Church prayed. But did they believe that God would answer their prayer? It doesn't sound like it, when you read what happened as soon as Peter was released and came to the door of the praying Church! They kept him outside, they just couldn't believe.

But Peter knew. It must have seemed like a dream to him at first, as the angel appeared in his cell, struck off the chains, walked through the opened doors, took Peter down the street; and then just as suddenly disappeared.

The ministry of angels is still with us, though we don't see them. 'The angel of the Lord encampeth round about them that fear Him' (Psalm 34:7). It's true for you today, and every day.

Thus says the Lord God: 'Come from the four winds, O
breath, and breathe upon these slain, that they may live'
(Ezekiel 37:9).

This was a marvellous vision that the prophet, Ezekiel, had
when his people of Israel were in captivity in Babylon. Their
position looked hopeless, but Ezekiel reminds them that God
can change things.

In his vision he saw the whole great valley filled with
hundreds of dead men's bones - a gruesome, grisly sight. God
told him, 'This is what the children of Israel are now like; but
the waste cities shall be filled with live people. I will do it.'
And God told Ezekiel to prophesy over the bones, so that life
should come into them.

Ezekiel did so. 'And behold, there was a shaking, and the
bones came together, bone to his bone, skin came over them,
but no breath in them.' Then God said, 'Call the wind and say,
"Come from the four winds, O breath, and breathe upon these
slain, that they may live".' Ezekiel did just that, 'and they
lived, and stood upon their feet, an exceeding great army.'
What a sight! And God said, 'I shall put my Spirit in you, and
you will live again.'

What a wonderful foreshadowing of what was to come
when the Holy Spirit came upon the Church in Jerusalem.
And He has been with us ever since, in the hearts and minds
of all who receive Jesus as their Saviour and Lord. He gives
us power where there is no power. He sends us out into our
world of today, to witness to Jesus in the Holy Spirit's power.
When God has hold of you, there is no knowing what He can
do with you. Trust Him with your Life.

If you confess with your lips that Jesus is Lord, and believe in your heart that God raised Him from the dead, you will be saved. For man believes with the heart and so is justified, and he confesses with his lips, and so is saved (Romans 10:9,10).

These two verses might well have been one of the earliest forms of a Christian creed. Certainly they have the basis of it; they are a truly important statement of belief.

In this chapter, Paul is trying to win over the Jews. The Jews held that a man was justified by the law, and that Gentiles were excluded from God's covenant unless they became Jewish proselytes. But of course the statement applies equally to all, the Good News is for everybody.

Note the sequence of statement.

1. 'Jesus is Lord.' If you say Jesus is Lord, you really mean that He is God. The Greek word *kurios* (Lord) is the Greek translation of the Hebrew word *Jehovah*.

2. 'He is risen from the dead.' This was absolutely essential in Christian belief. If Christ be not risen, your faith is vain. You are still in your sins' (1 Corinthians 15:17). He is alive today, and we know Him.

3. 'Confess with your lips.' Secret belief isn't enough. Certainty comes with confession before men. We have to let our fellow-men know that we are Christians. How often? Whenever the challenge is there. And then the certainty rings true in your own heart. You have 'burnt your boats behind you'; there is no turning back. It's a challenge, but acceptance of it brings inexpressible joy.

And the King will answer them, 'Truly, I say to you, as
you did it to one of the least of these My brethren, you did
it to Me (Matthew 25:40).

'And the King will say ...'. Jesus is describing His Second
Coming, and how He will deal with the people who come
before Him then. As He looks forward, He sees something of
the suffering and hunger there will be in the world, among
both Christians and non-Christians. But it is the disciples to
whom He is talking (Matthew 24:3).

Is He then speaking about how we treat our fellow-
Christians? Certainly that is included. But I think it is also a
general look at men's needs everywhere. We get constant
appeals made to relieve the starvation in the world, and the
needs of the homeless. Obviously we cannot cover all those
needs. But we can do something.

Governments can also do something. And most of us, as
well as most governments, could do a lot more than we do. If
Jesus were here in the flesh, and hungry, and we met Him,
would we offer Him a meal? Of course we would! It would be
an enormous privilege to have Him to lunch! So Jesus says,
'When you help someone in need, in My Name, it is just the
same as if you were helping Me. And you will have My
thanks.' And conversely, 'If you close your heart against
them, do you expect Me to welcome you?' That puts it in
perspective doesn't it?

Where on earth do you begin? Just where you are, just
when the need is pressing, just when you know you can help.

God be with you.

At that time Jesus declared, 'I thank Thee, Father, Lord of Heaven and earth, that Thou hast hidden these things from the wise and understanding and revealed them to babes ....

No one knows the Father except the Son, and any one to whom the Son chooses to reveal Him (Matthew 11:25,27).

When Jesus was here upon the earth He met many people, including the leaders of the Jews, both political and religious. Most of the leaders rejected Him because He was not their idea of what the Messiah was to be like. Indeed the Sanhedrin, the ruling religious body of which Nicodemus was a member, once sent soldiers out to arrest Jesus. When they returned empty-handed, they were asked, 'Why haven't you brought Him?' When the soldiers answered, 'Never man spoke like this man', the leaders retorted, 'Are you also deceived? Have any of the rulers or Pharisees believed on Him? But this people who don't know the law are accursed' (John 7:45-52).

In other words they were saying, 'Only ignorant people follow Him. Wise men wouldn't dream of it.' They thought they knew everything but Jesus said, 'No; small children can understand and accept the truth. Very often the wise and intelligent folk, who think they are clever, haven't begun to grasp the Word of God.' Why? Because spiritual truth comes by revelation from God, not from human intelligence.

The only way to the Father is through the Son, which is why Jesus was to say next, 'Come unto Me.' Talk with a person who has come out of atheism into trust in Christ, and ask him if it was his intelligence that brought him to faith and usually he will say, 'No, it was a blinding flash in my heart and mind that came from God, not just my cleverness.'

A double-minded man is unstable in all his ways
(James 1:8).

At the very beginning of his letter, James is writing about prayer and he says, 'When you pray, you must believe and not doubt, because if you doubt, your mind is not made up. You are not sure about God, nor about your prayer; you are not a person who trusts.'

But of course, this whole question of single-mindedness goes much deeper than just the matter of prayer. If you're going to be a Christian, your whole mind and purpose must be committed to Jesus Christ, or you really cannot expect God to bless you. In your prayer, don't expect God to answer you, unless you truly believe that He can, and that you are putting your faith in Him wholly.

Prayer involves the turning of the whole of one's mind to God at that moment. A half-hearted Christian is a half-baked one. Do you remember, when Peter saw Jesus walking on the Lake of Galilee, he said, 'Lord, if it really is You, tell me to come to You.' Jesus just said, 'Come.' Peter went. But after a few steps he began to hesitate. He wasn't sure of Jesus, of himself, of anything except that he was doing the impossible. And he became frightened, and down he went! He was doubting and it nearly sank him. But he cried out, 'Lord, save me.' At once, Jesus grabbed him back. Those three words had put him back into Jesus' keeping, and he was safe.

He wants the whole of us to be given to the whole of Him.

Watch, therefore, for you do not know when the Master of the house will come, in the evening, or at midnight, or at cockcrow, or in the morning - lest He come suddenly and find you asleep (Mark 13:35,36).

Matthew, Mark and Luke all report this saying of Jesus, and all report it as having taken place in the last week before Jesus was crucified.

Was Jesus trying to warn His disciples about His coming death, or was it a reminder that death was not the end and that they would see Him again?

He was looking away beyond the resurrection, which was near; away beyond the destruction of Jerusalem and the temple, which was 40 years away; He was gazing on into space to the very end of the age, when His Coming again in power and great glory would take place. Notice the four times of the day that He mentions - early morning, midday, evening and midnight. In fact, of course, when He does come, it will be all of those times, depending on what part of the globe people are living in.

So we are to *watch*! To be ready for Him when He does come, because it will be sudden. Will there be signs? Yes. There will be continual conflict and war; there will be earthquakes; there will be famine; there will be false prophets; there will be disturbances in the stars and planets. But we will not know the day in advance.

Watching does not mean gazing up into space. No, watching is working and praying and being alive to every opportunity of serving Him; so that when He comes, He may find us active and faithful, and ready.

'Even so, come Lord Jesus' (Revelation 22:20).

You have been born anew, not of perishable seed, but of
imperishable, through the living and enduring Word of God
(1 Peter 1:23).

Peter wrote two little letters, and our verse is from his first one.
His scribe was Silas, and Mark was with him as he wrote. It
was sent to 'the scattered Christians all over Asia Minor' to
encourage them in their faith and to remind them that God's
Word does not fade away. It still continues to speak to men
with as strong authority as it ever had.

'You have been born anew,' he says, 'through the Word
of God which is living and powerful, and true for all time.'

Many of his readers were far away in distant parts, and
may have wondered if God's Word still applied to them; no
longer in the warm company of the original believers in
Jerusalem, but in lonely places where there were perhaps only
a few Christians around. 'Yes,' says Peter, 'whatever you
may be, the Living Lord Jesus is with you just as closely as the
day when you first became believers. You may find that some
of you die, indeed we shall all do so in time, but God's Word
never dies, never loses its power. And it's the same Word that
first brought you to Christ.'

No wonder, then, that as the Word is preached in many
parts of the world today, and sometimes to people who cannot
even read or write, it is still the 'living and vitalising Word of
God to all men in every land'. As they come to Christ, they
join with us in the great company of His friends and disciples,
'all one in Christ Jesus' (Galatians 3:28).

By faith Noah, being warned by God concerning events as yet unseen, took heed and constructed an ark for the saving of his household (Hebrews 11:7).

What a man Noah was! Told to build an ark which would float, miles from any navigable water, anyone seeing him do it would think he was crazy! 'What are you building it for, Noah?' 'God has told me he is going to save our lives.' 'The man must be mad!' But Noah went steadily on and on, till the job was done. How long he took over it, the Bible doesn't tell us. But when the rains finally came, it was twelve months before they could get out of that ark on to dry ground.

And the comment of Hebrews is: 'By which he condemned the world, and became heir of the righteousness which is by faith.' When God calls a person to action, even if the action appears contrary to common sense, the man of faith will do what God is asking of him. But you need to be sure that it really is God's call, and not just your own whim of fancy.

How then can we be sure? There are certain guides. It will not be contrary to Scripture: it will not be damaging to your neighbour: it will foster the growth of God's kingdom in the world. You may need to consult your Christian friends, and if they all think it wrong, you should hesitate before going ahead with it.

Keep us, O Lord, in the way of righteousness.

November 22

One who in every respect has been tempted as we are, yet
without sinning (Hebrews 4:15).

Lots of people, even Christians, have thought that because
Jesus was God and did not sin, therefore, He knows nothing
of the sort of temptations that beset us frail human beings. It
is here that the writer of this letter to the Hebrews corrects this
impression.

He tells us that 'Jesus was in every way tempted with just
the same kind of temptations that come to us.' When He took
on human nature, He was subject also to the usual limitations
and trials that come to us. He knew what it was to be tired. He
wept over other people's sorrows. But although He was often
tempted, He did not yield to sin.

It is just because He was tempted, that He can understand
the temptations that beset us, and can come to our rescue when
we are weak and unable to stand.

He certainly knew what it was to suffer pain, and He bore
it without complaint. You will remember that on the Cross He
cried out, 'I thirst.' Yet He asked His Father to forgive those
who crucified Him.

'We do not have a High Priest who is unable to sympathise
with our weaknesses,' says the writer. No, He's been through
it all, short of actually sinning. And when we sin, we come to
our Master in sorrow and penitence, knowing that He not only
understands, but that He also forgives us. He suffers when we
suffer and I'm sure He also rejoices with us when our hearts
are full of Joy.

So you also must consider yourselves dead to sin, and alive
to God in Christ Jesus (Romans 6:11).

In the first eleven verses of this chapter, Paul is wrestling with
the problem of sin in the Christian. If you have become a
Christian, why do you go on sinning? How can you stop it?
And it's a problem that you and I and every other Christian has
to face.

Paul reminds us that two different things have happened
to us. When we became Christians, we died, as far as Satan is
concerned. Offer a dead man a thousand pounds, and there is
no response. He is dead, he can't move, he doesn't even hear
you. So Paul says, when Satan comes along with a nice juicy
temptation, we need to remember that we are dead. And we
must stay dead till the temptation has gone.

But the second thing that happened at our conversion was
that we became alive, for the first time, to God. So when God
comes to us with a proposal, we must remember that we are
alive. Dead to sin, yes, but alive to God. We have become new
people, God's people. What has happened to us should make
all the difference in the world. We are now united with Christ.
We are in Him, and He is in us, and our whole way of life is
different from what it was, before we came to Christ.

Our love for Jesus has to be translated into action, and
there is plenty of action before us. God wants to use our hands,
feet, tongues and hearts to encourage and strengthen other
Christians, and bring good news to non-Christians. No time
for sin, only time for God.

Do not be mismated with unbelievers. For what partnership
have righteousness and iniquity? Or what fellowship has
light with darkness? ... Or what has a believer in common
with an unbeliever? (2 Corinthians 6:14,15).

Marriage between a Christian and an unbeliever is almost
always disastrous. The whole attitude to life is quite different.
One is serving God, the other is pleasing self. This was a very
real problem for the new Corinthian Christians, because most
of their city was given over to idolatry, and all that went with
it.

But it's just as true today, since the world in which we live
can in no sense be called a Christian world. Most people are
non-Christians. Christians have been called 'out of darkness,
and are now light in the Lord' (Ephesians 5:7). So, to link up
in the closest possible human relationship - marriage - with a
partner who is still (spiritually) in 'the dark', would lead to all
sorts of problems. Would they go to Church together, say their
prayers together, bring up their children for Christ together,
say grace at meals? No - all these things, and many others, the
Christian partner would have to do alone.

It's quite different if the marriage took place before either
was a Christian. When one is converted later, then he or she
has the task of trying to lead the partner in the same way; and
that needs grace and tact and wisdom and gentleness, and
much prayer (1 Corinthians 7:12-14).

The temptation is there, for a Christian who is looking
forward to marriage one day, especially if there is not a likely
Christian partner. But better far the single life, than union with
an unbeliever. God will always honour Christian steadfast-
ness in this matter. A godly union is worth waiting for.

He has fixed a day on which He will judge the world in righteousness by a Man whom He has appointed, and of this He has given assurance to all men by raising Him from the dead (Acts 17:31).

Paul was preaching from Mars Hill in Athens, from which the philosopher, Socrates, had discoursed some 400 years earlier. The people before him there were the Stoics and Epicureans who loved to hear philosophical arguments. The place was covered with hundreds of idols and Paul had told them, 'I discovered one altar erected to the Unknown God. I know Him and have come to tell you about Him.' They said of him, 'He seems to be a setter forth of strange gods.'

The whole city of Athens was a city living in the dead past, but Paul had to come to show them the living present - in Christ. It was not so very different from our world, for how many people today truly believe that there is a God in heaven who loves and cares for His people?

The philosophers of Paul's day looked on him with mild amusement, a slightly interesting person with a new idea. But not one whose whole purpose was to bring people to their knees before Jesus Christ! But Paul says to them, and to us, 'In Him we live, and move, and have our being.' But when they heard of the Resurrection, they mocked Paul.

Today, many people (like the Athenians) believe vaguely that somewhere there is a god, but don't think He has anything to do with them. Of course, they would have to repent, and believe, and put their trust in the Living Christ. The door is open, but not for ever. Judgment will come one day. But 'Now is the accepted time, now is the Day of Salvation (2 Corinthians 6:2).

Where two or three are gathered in My Name, there am I in
the midst of them (Matthew 18:20).

When a Christian wants to pray, where should he go? To a
church, to his or her bedroom, out into the garden, up the
hillside, or where? In fact, anywhere.

But our verse for today suggests that it's a good thing to
pray with other people - not always, of course, but sometimes.
The lovely thing is that Jesus promised that if there are just
two or three praying together, He Himself is there.

Prisoners can do it in their cells, and He will be there. At
the bedside of a sick person, in a den of lions (as Daniel did),
in the belly of a whale (as Jonah did), on a Cross of wood (as
Jesus did). I'm sure you can think of many other places even
stranger, there is no place in the world where you cannot meet
with God in prayer. And, of course, at any time of the day or
night. But always, always, in the Name of Jesus.

Thank you, Lord, for that wonderful promise of Yours,
always to be there with us where we are, as we turn to You in
prayer, turning the occasion into a little corner of heaven as we
meet You.

November 27

He who goes about as a tale-bearer reveals secrets, but he
who is trustworthy in spirit keeps a thing hidden
(Proverbs 11:13).

What a temptation it is, when you hear a bit of really spicy
news about someone else, to run off at once and tell a friend
about it, especially if it is something not very much to the
credit of the person concerned. And don't the newspapers
love to get hold of something like that; they will even pay a lot
of money for it!

When we hear something of that nature, before we pass it
on, we should ask ourselves a few questions.

1. Is it true?
2. Will it help or hinder if I spread it?
3. Can I help the person involved, in any way?
4. Is it kind to reveal it?

Our job, as Christians, is to try and make the world better,
not worse.

A faithful friend is a treasure worth having. If you have
slipped up in some way, it's marvellous to have a wise friend
alongside you to counsel and help you to get straight again. If
you believe that, then be that kind of person yourself; you
never know when you may be yourself in that kind of need.

This does not mean, of course, that criminal acts should be
allowed to go undetected, but that petty weaknesses should be
dealt with in love to the person concerned (when that is
possible). And remembering always that we ourselves are by
no means faultless. We need God's Grace as much as anyone
else.

When Jesus was baptised ... behold the heavens were opened and He saw the Spirit of God descending like a dove, and alighting on Him; and lo, a voice from heaven, saying, 'This is My Beloved Son, with whom I am well pleased' (Matthew 3:16,17).

If ever you need a reference to the Trinity, here is the very first one in the New Testament! Father, Son, and Holy Ghost, all three mentioned in the same verse.

Here is the King at the age of thirty, at the very start of His ministry. What had happened to Him since we last heard of Him, when at the age of twelve, He was taken by Mary and Joseph up to Jerusalem? Eighteen years of silence, His time of preparation for His three years of public ministry. I expect He worked in the carpenter's shop, assisting Joseph in his work.

In Psalm 2:6-8, there is a promise given to Jesus by the Father: 'I have set my King upon my holy hill of Zion. I will declare the decree; the Lord hath said unto Me, "Thou art My Son; this day have I begotten Thee." Ask of Me, and I shall give Thee the heathen for thine inheritance, and the uttermost parts of the earth for Thy possession.'

Here was the beginning of the fulfilment of that prophecy: Jesus coming into His possession, with His Father's guarantee behind Him and the Spirit's seal upon Him. What a wonderful unity of purpose that was!

> Man of sorrows! What a name
> For the Son of God, who came
> Ruined sinners to reclaim!
> Hallelujah! What a Saviour!

If one suffers as a Christian, let him not be ashamed, but
under that name let him glorify God (1 Peter 4:16).

In this letter Peter is warning Christians that, just because they
are Christians, other people will be watching to see if they can
catch them in behaviour which is not in accord with their
profession as disciples of Jesus.

But he goes on to say, 'But if you get persecuted just
because you are a Christian, this is something to be happy
about, because it is the way Jesus Himself was treated. So you
are sharing in His suffering, and when this happens, 'the Spirit
of glory and of God rests on you' (verse 14).

In fact, if you don't ever get ill-treated because you are a
Christian, it is a little doubtful if you are really showing signs
of belonging to Christ. But of course you are not to seek for
persecution, nor to be self-conscious about being a Christian,
but to live naturally on friendly terms with everyone as far as
you are able.

In other words, a Christian should try to be an attractive
person; happy in relationships with others, and seizing the
opportunity to speak for Christ when an opening occurs
naturally to do so, and quietly giving their own testimony of
what Christ means to them. Quite often the most determined
opponents of the Christian Faith can be touched by the
friendliness of believers.

Don't be afraid to speak, for Jesus is with you!

One of His disciples, Andrew, Simon Peter's brother, said to Him, 'There is a lad here who has five barley loaves and two fish; but what are they among so many?' Jesus said, 'Make the people sit down' (John 6:8-10).

Crowds had come to hear Jesus. Now, at the end of the day, Jesus turns to Philip and asks where they could buy bread? Philip totted up and reckoned it would cost 200 pence of bread, but even that wouldn't cover. Andrew then volunteered that there was a little food: 'a lad who has five buns and two sardines!' Was he perhaps amused at his own ridiculous suggestion?

Nobody asked Jesus to deal with it. But Jesus takes Andrew at his word, and says, 'Make the people sit down.' And down they sat, expecting what? A snack? Nobody knew. The boy is brought to Jesus, and Jesus takes his tiny lunch and breaks it up after saying grace, and the disciples take it round. Everyone had a hearty meal, and at the end, the bits left over would have been worth more than Philip's 200 pence

What did the crowds then do? They tried to take Him by force, to make Him a king! Their stomachs might have been full, but their hearts were untouched.

Next day the crowds found Jesus again, and He said to them, 'You only want Me for the food, not for Myself.'

Three things to note: (1) the initiative of Andrew; (2) the trust of the small boy; (3) the misunderstanding of the crowd. Not many people understood Jesus in those days. How much do we truly perceive Him today?

December 1

Take care, brethren, lest there be in any of you an evil, unbelieving heart, leading you to fall away from the living God. But exhort one another every day ... that none of you may be hardened by the deceitfulness of sin
(Hebrews 3:12,13).

The writer of this epistle is talking very plainly to Christian people. Is it possible that anyone, who has once truly accepted Christ as Saviour and Lord, could ever drift back into denying Him? Sadly, it does happen. Why? Is it perhaps that commitment has never been truly complete? Is it some particular sin into which they have fallen, and are now trying to justify themselves by saying they no longer believe? Or is it a recognition that the Christian life is harder than they thought, and that sadly they feel it is not for them?

So many things may cause backsliding. What is the safeguard? Well, he says, 'Exhort one another daily.' And that means that friends should encourage one another constantly. If there's a difficulty, or a particular temptation, share it with a friend. If you see a friend of yours drifting, get alongside him or her and speak an encouraging word. That is one of the ways by which faith is warmed and strengthened. None of us is always on top; and a friend to help out can be a very great blessing. We can so easily be blinded by the attractiveness of sin.

Lord, help me today to stand firm, and to encourage my friends to do the same.

If we live by the Spirit, let us also walk by the Spirit. Let us
have no self-conceit, no provoking of one another, no envy
of one another (Galatians 5:25,26).

'In other words,' Paul says, 'Be consistent. You have been
redeemed by Christ, and the Holy Spirit is in you. Then
behave as one who is in tune with the Spirit.'

Dr Barclay puts it like this: 'Keep step with the Spirit.' If
you were in the army, you would have to learn how to march
in proper order. And one of the first things you would learn is
how to keep in step. Otherwise the march would look ragged
and untidy.

It is just as true in the Army of the King of Kings.
Christians need to be seen to be Christians by their behaviour.

Here Paul says, 'No self-conceit', that is 'no swanking'.
If you've done something well, it's very tempting to say so,
isn't it? But Paul says, 'No.' Leave it to other people, and if
they say, 'Well done,' give the glory to God.

And 'no envy'!' No wishing you had someone else's gifts.
God has given you your own, use them and be thankful. It is
when people see Christians living and working happily together, that they begin to want that kind of fellowship for
themselves.

There are always people around who will want to humil-
iate you, make you feel small, put you down. What do you do
about that? Hate them? No, because verse 22 of this chapter
says 'the fruit of the Spirit is *love*.' So you will always want
to seek their highest good! Does that seem hard? Yes, of
course it does. But it's the way by which enemies of the gospel
are won to Christ.

'Keep in step.'

Abide in Him, so that when He appears we may have
confidence and not shrink from Him in shame
at His Coming (1 John 2:28).

We thought about the Second Coming of Jesus on November
19, when we quoted his own words in Mark. Here is John on
the same subject, where John makes it clear that Jesus'
Coming should be a spur to us to be ready for Him, and to be
found faithful and working for Him when the moment flashes
upon the world.

Then there will be no further 'time for amendment of life'
- for time will be past and gone. If there are things to be put
right, now is the time to do so, whilst we still have the chance.
Then when He comes, we shall rejoice to see Him, and not be
afraid at His coming.

It's a sobering thought, isn't it, that the only time that
belongs to us is *today*? All our yesterdays have gone, and we
cannot alter what has happened. None of our tomorrows have
come, and we cannot predict in advance what tomorrow will
bring. Certainly our yesterdays can be forgiven. For all of us,
much of yesterday will need forgiveness. Thank God for the
cleansing that Jesus brings us as we come to Him and ask for
pardon. And thank Him too for the power He provides us with,
so that we can be victorious in the fight.

Lord, help us to abide in You every moment of the day,
and use us to the utmost in Your Service, through Jesus Christ
our Lord. AMEN.

But if anyone has the world's goods and sees his brother in need, yet closes his heart against him, how does God's love abide in him? Little children, let us not love in word or speech, but in deed and in truth (1 John 3:17,18).

I think John intends us to apply these two verses to our relationships with our fellow-Christians. The Christian fellowship is a worldwide society, in which all the members are to care for one another's needs. And that obviously affects our relationship to the many missionaries who are serving God in many different situations overseas. They should be in our prayers; more, they should be in our giving too.

'Deed and truth' are what John emphasises here. I remember hearing of a doctor who decided he ought to help a brother doctor who was serving Christ in an overseas hospital. So he set about it this way: whenever he bought a new medical book for himself, he bought a duplicate for his overseas partner in Christ. 'Deed and truth.'

And this also affects family relationships, doesn't it? So often we find some lonely member of a family neglected and ignored, because they are difficult to get on with, where the whole situation might be changed by a caring member of the family who was prepared to receive a snub and cope with it, for the sake of the 'family'.

Sometimes the needs are financial, but as often they are just for friendship and warmth, and when that is given, often the response is immediate and overwhelming. Can you think of any such need today?

December 5

This is how one should regard us, as servants of Christ and
stewards of the mysteries of God. Moreover it is required
of stewards that they be found trustworthy
(1 Corinthians 4:1,2).

'Servants of Christ.' The word Paul uses for a servant here
means a slave who rows in the lower rank of a ship; in other
words, a sort of 'underdog', doing the rough work! Such a
slave would have to do exactly what his master ordered, and
not ask questions!

'Steward' was a much higher position. Although still a
slave, he was a supervisor of the other slaves; in other words,
he had a responsibility for others, not just for himself. So it
was essential that he be a trustworthy person.

Every Christian is, of course, called to be a steward of
God's mysteries. The 'mysteries' are the things of God that
are hidden from non-believers, but are revealed to those who
are true Christians. Sometimes, if we read a novel which may
describe what the writer thinks to be a Christian belief, we
realise at once that he hasn't any idea of what Christians really
believe, it's just his imagination. It is 'hidden' from him.

To bring an unbeliever to the point where they begin to
trust, and then to see a glimpse of the real truth, is an immense
privilege with which God has entrusted us.

And the steward is responsible for his behaviour, to his
Master, Jesus Christ.

'Lord, keep us faithful.'

When you received the Word of God which you heard from us, you accepted it - not as the word of men - but as what it really is, the Word of God (1 Thessalonians 2:13).

'The Word of God.' This is what the Bible is, God's Word not man's. Yes, it was given by God to man, and written down by men to men, who knew full well that it was not their own record, but a Word which they had received from God.

It is authenticated by its action upon men. In Romans 1:16, Paul says: 'the gospel ... is the power of God for salvation to every one who has faith.'

Jesus often spoke of the Old Testament teaching as being God's Word. When the New Testament came to be written, the Church had to decide what of the many writings should be included in 'The Word of God'. Some they refused as being unworthy, but eventually the complete canon of Scripture was made up and accepted.

Article 6 of the Church of England puts it like this: 'Holy Scripture contains all things necessary to Salvation; so that what is not read in it, nor may be proved by it, is not to be required of any man that it should be believed as an Article of Faith, nor be thought necessary to Salvation.'

There is a warning in Revelation 22:18,19 which says, 'If any man adds to the words of the prophecy of this book, God will add to him the plagues described in this book. And if anyone takes words away from this book of prophecy, God will take away from him his share in the tree of life.'

So, let us beware of adding to what Scripture says is necessary to Salvation, or taking away any part of the received teachings of Scripture and saying it is irrelevant to us today. God's Word is as true now as when it was first written.

December 7

To this end we always pray from you, that our God may make you worthy of His Call, and may fulfil every good resolve and work of faith by His power, so that the Name of our Lord Jesus may be glorified in you, and you in Him (2 Thessalonians 1:11,12).

So often when we pray for someone else we tend to be a bit vague in our prayers, perhaps just asking God to bless them, without saying what we really mean.

Here Paul is giving us, I think, an example of what it means really to pray for someone else. In 1 Thessalonians 3:12 he had prayed for them that God would help their love to one another to increase. In 2 Thessalonians 1:3 he is able to thank God for the answer to that prayer, because their faith is growing, and their love to each other increasing.

So now, he's praying something else for them. He wants to be sure that, at the last day, they will be shown to have been worthy of God's Calling; in other words, that they may live to the glory of Jesus every day, and then share in the Glory of God when the time came.

He wouldn't, of course, live to see the answer to his prayer. But when he himself was in heaven, he would see them coming in, one by one, covered in the great Glory of Jesus Christ. That's when he would see the answer!

Whenever we can, we should be specific in our prayers for others; and sometimes it's possible to know exactly what their particular need is.

Do our prayers make any difference? Indeed they do. So often a Christian friend, who has been in special need, will afterwards say, 'I was tremendously conscious that someone was praying for me.'

December 8

When Joseph's brothers saw that their father loved him
more than all his brothers, they hated him, and could not
speak peaceably to him (Genesis 37:4).

Hatred within a family! I suppose nothing is more destructive
of a family than this. Usually it tends more to the destruction
of the hater than the hated. This was certainly so in the case
of Joseph. Who do you blame for this hatred? I think one
person more to be blamed than most was Jacob, Joseph's
father. No parent should ever show favouritism amongst the
children, for it immediately divides the family. Yet so often
you hear a friend say, 'Which is your favourite son or
daughter?'

It is good when the family determine to stand together,
keeping the family as a strong unit. But it has to be constantly
guarded. I wonder why?

I think partly because each member has a self-preserva-
tion instinct, nobody wants to be of less value than another in
the family. You have your rights, why should anyone else
threaten them? In God's sight, each is of equal value, each has
a contribution to make; none can opt out without doing harm
to the whole family.

This is also true of the wider family of God's children all
over the world. We should have a special care for those who
are under-privileged, sick, homeless, lacking love.

Jesus told us to love our enemies and those who hate us.
That's very difficult, isn't it? But He did it, and turned many
of them into friends. And it is possible for us, under God's
grace, to do the same.

The righteous will never be moved .... He is not afraid of
evil tidings; his heart is firm, trusting in the LORD. His heart
is steady, he will not be afraid (Psalm 112:6-8).

With half the world disintegrating around us today, it's a
wonderful encouragement to get a word like this out of the
Psalms, isn't it? What is the secret of this calmness and
confidence? It's central to this verse - just look at it: 'Trusting
in the Lord'. That is the steadying factor.

When we know that ultimately God has the whole of His
world in control, we can lessen the heartbeats, no need to
despair: 'He's got the whole world in His Hands'! Yes, the big
disappointments will still come, the sicknesses and bereave-
ments will still be with us, evil men will still seem to get away
with it. But we need not fear, we can have a steady heart. The
Lord has hold of us, and of the problem we face.

Have you a problem, a need, an anxiety today? What are
you doing with it? Put it straight into His Hands, and let the
Peace of Christ rule in your heart and life at this moment. It
doesn't mean you may not have to tackle the issue. But you are
only an assistant-surgeon as it were; the Master-Surgeon is in
control, and the ultimate issue is His.

And don't forget, 'Your life is hid - with Christ - in God'
(Colossians 3:3).

God, the Lord, is my strength; He makes my feet like
hinds' feet (Habakkuk 3:19).

Habakkuk wrote in the later years of Josiah. The prophet had
hoped for good things, but God told him there was to be a
Chaldean invasion - so his hopes were dashed. There are only
three chapters to his book, and the third is a prayer to God - for
Habakkuk was very afraid. He foresaw destruction and desolation, and sorrow in every place.

But he finishes his prayer with a note of hope and joy. In
spite of all the trouble, God has never left his people, and
freedom and rejoicing are coming back.

'He makes my feet like hinds' feet.' Have you ever
watched a fast-running deer in full flight? We used often to see
them in Kenya, great herds together, when suddenly something would set them off, and they would race away, flying
through the air just as though they were on wings, and some
of their leaps would be anything up to thirty feet.

So can you imagine Habakkuk the prophet suddenly
jumping for sheer joy: 'The Lord God is my strength!' And for
that to happen when desolation and ruin is all around would
certainly cause comment among the people: 'Why has he
gone suddenly mad with joy? Whatever is there to rejoice
about?' They didn't know. But he was a man of faith, and I'm
sure his joy was infectious and spread to others.

We too are in a difficult world today, with much trouble,
sorrow, famine, perplexity all round. But our strength is Jesus
our Saviour. Let our joy be seen!

There are six things which the LORD hates, seven which are an abomination unto Him: haughty eyes, a lying tongue and hands that shed blood, a heart that devises wicked plans, feet that make haste to run to evil, a false witness who breathes out lies, and a man who sows discord among brothers (Proverbs 6:16-19).

Seven steps in evil which a Christian must avoid, and every one of them to do with his or her relationship with other people. These are the sort of things that destroy fellowship, because they at once put a hostile barrier between people.

1. 'Haughty eyes.' How do you look at other people? Scornfully sometimes, so people say: 'If looks could kill'. Or with freshness and welcome, and without fear?

2. 'A lying tongue.' Mostly people lie through fear to protect themselves. But almost always the truth comes out, and it's terrible to be known as a liar.

3. 'Hands that shed blood.' That is murder, but often people damage one another physically or morally. Quarrelling can lead to this. It builds up, until at last it boils over.

4. 'A wicked heart.' Nursing a grievance can ultimately mean deliberate plans to cause sorrow and hatred in return; it's purely destructive.

5. 'Feet that run to evil.' What your heart plans, your feet carry out.

6. 'A false witness.' Twisting the truth when speaking of other people, instead of building up their characters. Ultimately, it destroys your own projection and image.

7. 'Setting people against each other.' That is what causes wars. What a terrible category of evil. For us it must be, love, joy, peace, instead.

December 12

According to His Promise we wait for new heavens and a
new earth in which righteousness dwells (2 Peter 3:13).

'His Promise' - where does it come from? It's in Isaiah 65:17
and Peter picks it up and tells us that this is what we shall
experience when Jesus comes again. The righteous life is the
result of salvation by Christ, and this, of course, we begin to
experience here and now. So I think that this is one of those
prophecies which have a double fulfilment. The ultimate rule
of righteousness will only come about at the Second Coming
of Jesus. But as soon as you became a Christian, you began to
live in a 'new heaven and a new earth.'

There is a well-known hymn describing this aspect: *Loved
with Everlasting Love*. And its second verse begins like this:

> Heaven above is softer blue,
> Earth around is sweeter green;
> Something lives in every hue
> Christless eyes have never seen.

And it ends:

> Since I know, as now I know
> I am His, and He is mine.

When you became a Christian, you moved into a new element
of life, all under Christ. You are different, you have a new
Master. Your attitude to life is changed, you are now serving
Him. You even take a fresh look at the natural world and see
it as it truly is, part of God's wonderful Creation. In fact what
you are experiencing is a tiny microcosm of what things will
be like ONE DAY.

Thou preparest a table before me in the presence of my enemies: Thou anointest my head with oil, my cup overflows (Psalm 23:5).

We looked at verse 4 of this most famous Psalm on April 12. It's so good that we could easily have a session on each verse of this Psalm. People use it for weddings and funerals and many other occasions too. Look at this verse.

When we have got enemies all round us, God is laying on a special menu for us, whilst they watch - hungrily - do you think? We would think it was the moment to be most afraid, scared as to what our enemies would do with us. Well, let them watch.

'You anoint my head with oil'; this is only done to special people, to make them happy and joyful. Others may not see the oil, but they should see the resultant joy.

'My cup overflows.' When I have tea on my lawn in summer, my friend the robin usually comes round to see if there are any crumbs for him - he usually gets some too. If our cup overflows, there'll be someone around who would love a taste of what we have got; let them have a sip of our heavenly peace and joy.

Yes, our enemies may be there, but don't worry about them. Just behave naturally (if we can); who knows if it may turn some of them from enemies into friends? When Stephen was being stoned to death, they saw his face like the face of an angel. Saul saw that face, and I'm sure he never, never forgot it. I'm quite sure it was a factor in his conversion.

What a lovely Psalm to live with, and what a marvellous Saviour we have!

December 14

I saw ... the Son of Man ... and His voice was like the sound of many waters; in His right hand He held seven stars, from His mouth issued a sharp two edged sword, and His face was like the sun shining in full strength. When I saw Him, I fell at His feet as though dead. But He laid His right hand upon me, saying, 'Fear not ...'
(Revelation 1:15-17).

Who made the stars? How are they controlled? Scientists can tell, almost to the minute how any one of them is going to behave. How do they know? Because the stars all work to a pattern, and they don't deviate. And why don't they? Because God who made them is holding them in His Hand.

We would think, to be controlling seven of them at once must be like an enormous juggling trick, because they mustn't slip or disaster might follow. Of course He doesn't only control seven, He controls the whole Universe.

But John noticed something else that Jesus was doing with that right Hand of His: he says, 'He laid His right Hand upon *me*.' What? God who controls the whole universe still has time to be concerned for me and my welfare. Yes, that's true, just as true as that He holds seven stars in that right Hand of His - His Hand is on *me*.

The stars obey Him; they are inanimate objects, they have to. But I am different; I could refuse to obey Him. How could I dare to do so? If I did, disaster could come on me and mine. But He's prepared a table for me - we saw that yesterday - and I'd be a fool to refuse Him.

Lord, pour out Your joy, in and through me, and help me to shine for You.

Then Moses said ... 'Kill the Passover lamb ... and touch
the lintel and the two doorposts with the blood ... For the
Lord will pass over the door, and will not allow the
destroyer to enter' (Exodus 12:21-23).

What a tremendous story this is, the story of the ultimate
rescue of the Israelites from the slavery of Egypt following the
last of the plagues to be imposed upon the aggressors. On the
night before, the Israelites had to slay the Passover lamb and
sprinkle its blood on the exterior of each house, so that when
the destroying angel arrived, he could see the shed blood and
spare the inhabitants.

And that story was to be the foreshadowing of the rescue
that God brought, not just to Israel, but to the whole of
mankind. When the Lord Jesus shed His Blood upon the
Cross, it was for our Salvation, and as His Blood is applied
figuratively to our Lives, His Salvation for time and for
Eternity becomes our God-given inheritance. Our sins are
forgiven, they are laid upon His shoulders; as Peter has it:
'Who his own self bare our sins in His own body on the tree,
that we, being dead to sins, should live unto righteousness: by
whose stripes ye were healed' (1 Peter 2:24).

But there's nothing automatic about it. Just as the Israelites had to act and to sprinkle the blood, we too need to act, in
accepting the Blood of Christ, and asking His forgiveness of
all our sins; and then committing our lives to Him and His
service. So Paul has it: 'There is, therefore, now no condemnation to them that are in Christ Jesus' (Romans 8:1).

Safety, Certainty and Enjoyment.

December 16

And if I have the gift of prophecy, and understand all mysteries and all knowledge ... but have not love, I am nothing (1 Corinthians 13:2).

On October 9, we looked at the fourth verse of this great chapter, and its comment on jealousy, the enemy of love. In verse 2, Paul is touching on some of the gifts people have, one of which is the gift of prophecy. Now a prophet is a man who proclaims the Word of God; mostly today we would call him a preacher.

There are some great preachers in the world, as there were in Paul's day. And people are often thrilled by the way in which a preacher proclaims God's Word.

But if in his home life he is rough and hard with his wife or his family, or in his talks with people rarely does so with Christian love for them, Paul says 'he's nothing.' A man may be an extremely clever and well-educated person, may write learned books, but all that without love misses the chance to reach deep into people's hearts.

I think people know when someone really loves them for themselves; not even just to win them to Christ but more, to want to give himself to them, and to enter into their fellowship, to give time to them. Real love will persist, even when the person loved spurns that love.

Of course, it all springs out of God's love for us. 'We love, because He first loved us' (1 John 4:19).

Elijah pleads with God ... 'Lord, they have killed Thy prophets, they have demolished Thy altars, and I alone am left, and they seek my life.' But what is God's reply to him? 'I have kept for Myself seven thousand men who have not bowed the knee to Baal' (Romans 11:2-4).

This is Paul re-telling the story from the Old Testament. So often, truly godly people like Elijah go through a period of deep depression and despair, and begin to wonder whether God really does care, or whether He has deserted them.

And this is just as true of Christian people today; even they can get into the same kind of feeling that they just can't go on; it's no good, they've tried to keep true to God, but they're left absolutely alone, everybody else has left the practice of the Christian Faith and they just can't cope by themselves

Elijah had to learn that, even if there is only a tiny number left who are truly being faithful to God, they can't die out. There'll always be some, and usually far more than we suspect. Certainly he couldn't expect that the whole nation would be converted, but there would always be some. Always a Remnant would be left, who would be absolutely true.

But more than that: God would never leave us without help. The world will not be saved as a whole, but individual people will be called out one by one, and together they will form God's Church. Time and time again, in both Old and New Testaments, we read the account of how God has comforted His people, and told them not to be afraid. He is always with them.

Hang on to that certainty if ever you feel lonely. God says, 'I am with you always.'

But God, who is rich in mercy, out of the great love with which He loved us, even when we were dead through our trespasses, made us alive together with Christ (by grace you have been saved) (Ephesians 2:4,5).

In this chapter, Paul begins by describing what we were like before we were saved by Christ. He says we were 'dead', 'disobedient', playing with 'sin'. And then he says, *But God*. He broke into our evil ways, and His love brought us to Christ.

God's Grace was what made the difference. He loved us in spite of our evil ways; He longed to see us joyful in His way of truth, and His freedom from sin. Yes, we were 'dead in sins', but His great love reached down and touched us, and He brought us to life. And not just life on our own, trying to find our own way again, but life with Christ, so that our Guide is always with us, and indeed in us. From now on we are 'together with Christ'.

This 'togetherness' doesn't just mean we are alone with Christ, but we are also together with every other Christian person wherever in any part of the world we meet them. People of every nation under the sun, suddenly find themselves at one with people of every other nation. Even if our respective governments are at war with each other, the love of Jesus crosses the barriers of war, language, colour, class, age or sex to make us at one with each other, just because we are 'all one in Christ Jesus' (Galatians 3:28).

Lead us not into temptation (Luke 11:4).

This is a petition from the pattern prayer that Jesus gave His disciples when they asked Him, 'Lord, teach us to pray'. He knew that, once they had become Christians, they would suddenly discover the power of evil and the strength of temptation. Often and often I have it said to me by a person who has just come into the light and joy of life in Christ, 'Why is it that since I became a Christian, temptation is almost ten times as great as it was before?'

I think the answer is along these lines. Before, when temptation came, even though they may have known it was sin, it didn't bother them overmuch, because they frequently gave way to it. But now, they know that they belong to Christ; they no longer want to be in bondage to sin, because they know it will grieve Him. So they resist - but it's hard, and often they will fall.

I think the second reason is because Satan now knows he has lost them to Christ. He is angry, but he can't get them back in his power, so he tries to do what, in his view, is the next best thing. He tries to get them back into sinful ways, so as to dishearten them. He wants to make them useless instead of useful in Christ's service. And if he can destroy their Christian witness, he is limiting the effectiveness of Christ's power in them.

And so, they pray, 'Lead us not into temptation, but deliver us from the evil one'.

If you have asked God to do this, you mustn't walk back into temptation. Turn your eyes upon Jesus. Turn away from the evil thought. 'Whatsoever things are lovely, think upon these things.'

For from Him, and through Him, and to Him, are all things.
To Him be glory for ever. Amen (Romans 11:36).

I think when three of the disciples of Jesus were privileged to stand on the Mount of Transfiguration and see Him in His heavenly Glory, they must have been almost breathless with excitement. They will have remembered His lowly behaviour amongst them, His compassion on the multitudes, His concern for the sick and the bereaved, and His wonderful teaching for His disciples. Then suddenly to be confronted with the first glimpse of the majesty and glory from which He came, must have made them realise what a marvellous privilege it was to be His humble servants.

So Paul speaks of Him with awe and wonder: 'Our Lord, Jesus Christ ... in Him all things were created in heaven and earth ... He upholds the universe by His word of power ... He is before all things, and in Him all things hold together' (Colossians 1:15-17; see also Hebrews 1:3).

When you begin to realise who He truly is, you can do nothing but praise Him from the very bottom of your heart.

> Praise Him, praise Him, Jesus our blessed Redeemer.
> Heavenly portals, loud with hosannas ring!
> Jesus, Saviour, reigneth for ever and ever,
> Crown Him, crown Him! Prophet and Priest and King!

However much we may know about Him, it is only a fraction of what there is to be known, and a life spent in His service will constantly reveal more and more of His amazing love and peace and joy.

In church today, as prayers were being said, I heard a three-year old baby saying 'Amen' after each one. She was just beginning to know Him!

Thomas ... was not with them when Jesus came ... He said
to them, 'Unless I see ... I will not believe' ... Eight days
later ... Jesus came ... and said to Thomas ... 'Have you
believed because you have seen Me? Blessed are those
who have not seen, and yet believe' (John 20:24-29).

Have you ever wondered why Thomas was not present on that
first Sunday night when all the disciples were in the Upper
Room together? A little earlier he had said to his friends, 'Let
us go up to Jerusalem that we may die with Him.' Was he now
just sitting miserably at home, thinking: 'This is the end. He's
dead?' And when they told him after that first Sunday that
they'd seen Him alive, He just couldn't believe it. 'Unless I
can see ... and touch ... I will not believe.'

The unseen Jesus - unseen, yet ever-present - must have
heard those words. On the second Sunday, Thomas was back
with them. Jesus Himself also came back that second Sunday,
specially to meet Thomas. The door, as usual, was locked. But
suddenly, Jesus was in the midst of them.

Thomas had insisted on evidence; and Jesus offered him
that evidence, 'Put out your hand and put it into My side.' But
He went on, 'And be not faithless, but believing.'

Thomas looked at the wounds, looked at Jesus, and fell
down on his face, crying out, 'My Lord and my God!' He
believed that Jesus was God, because he had seen Him. But
Jesus gave another Blessing that night: 'Blessed are they who
have not seen, and yet have believed.' Who were they? Not
the Apostles, they had seen, but you and me. We have not seen
but we believe. We are blessed!

Behold I stand at the door and knock; if any man hear My voice, and open the door, I will come in to him, and will sup with him, and he with Me (Revelation 3:20).

I suppose this is one of the greatest passages in the Bible which has helped people to come into New Life in Christ. A great painter of the past, Holman Hunt, has painted a picture of this, and it hangs in St. Paul's Cathedral in London.

Notice that the Promise is to anyone. Whoever you are, however good, however bad, you are invited to hear the voice of Jesus. He is saying, 'Come to Me.' What then do we have to do? To 'open the door.' The door of your house, or of your heart, can only be opened from the inside. A friend once told Holman Hunt, 'You've made a mistake, there's no door-handle.' 'No mistake,' said he. 'It must be opened from within.' God doesn't compel you, He invites you.

The original invitation was made to the church of Laodicea. So it comes also to nominal Christians. You may be baptised, confirmed, and a churchgoer, and yet never have really opened your heart to Christ. So it means first repentance, then a turning from sin and asking God's forgiveness.

Jesus promises to 'Come in' to the opened heart. When does He come? At once, as soon as the door is open. How long does He stay? For keeps, for always.

And He says, 'I will sup with you.' When do you have supper? In the evening, and if you have a friend to supper, after supper you do friendly things together, you enjoy each other's company.

Lastly, how do you 'open' the door? In your own way, asking Jesus to come in, either on your own, or with a friend. And when you have done so, tell a Christian friend. It helps.

Joshua fought with Amalek; and Moses, Aaron and Hur
went up to the top of the hill. Whenever Moses held up his
hand, Israel prevailed, and whenever he lowered his hand,
Amalek prevailed. But Moses' hands grew weary; so ...
Aaron and Hur held up his hands ... so his hands were
steady until the going down of the sun (Exodus 17:8-12).

This story is there to help us to see the great value of sustained
prayer. I suppose every Christian finds that prayer is one of the
most difficult exercises of the Faith. We know that prayer is
essential for a fresh and lively expression of what a Christian
life is meant to be, but, like ordinary conversation, it has to be
learnt bit by bit if it is to be sustained.

When you are talking with a friend, what do you talk
about? If it is a perpetual grumble on your part about life in
general, you won't get very far, will you? It has to be
interesting, informative, intelligent, to both the teller and the
hearer. Each of you should be concerned for the satisfaction
of the other.

Your prayer-life with God needs to be similar. As God is
interested in your needs, you must also care for His. The
fellowship is mutual. Look at this story of Moses and the
Amalekites: Moses, the leader, looks to defeat the enemy, so
he prays to God. After a time, his hands grow heavy, he is
tired. He stops praying. But the battle is not yet won. It turns
against Israel - till Moses starts again. He can't manage on his
own, so Aaron and Hur come to the rescue. They pray
together, holding each other up.

Prayer to God in company with others is a great strength
to all. Find a friend to pray with, if you are beginning to flag.
And together, the victory comes.

They gave according to their means, as I can testify, and
beyond their means, of their own free will
(2 Corinthians 8: 3).

Paul gives two chapters of this letter to the question of
Christian giving, so obviously it is something very important.
Here in this part of the letter, Paul tells the Corinthians how
well the Macedonian Christians had been giving to the Lord's
work. They were poor people, and they'd been badly persecuted. But in spite of their sufferings (or was it *because* of their
sufferings?) they gave freely, and with great joy.

It is this kind of giving that is being exhibited today
amongst Christians in Uganda, where, in spite of persecution
and loss and violence against them, their giving is *most*
generous (this is still true in 1994).

Some churches in the world make a practice of fixing a
statutory amount which each Christian is expected to give, but
this is unfair because some are rich, some are poor. So Paul
says: 'According to their means'; and that was also the
principle of Jesus. Do you remember how He and the disciples
stood at the Temple gate and watched people throwing their
gifts into the Treasury? One woman threw in two half-
farthings, the smallest copper coins and Jesus commented:
'She has given more than all of them, for she gave all she has.'

The more conscious we are of God's love to us, the more
we shall want to give Him. And the more we give, the greater
the joy that is ours.

For to us a Child is born, to us a Son is given; and the Government will be upon His Shoulder, and His Name will be called 'Wonderful Counsellor, Mighty God, Everlasting Father, Prince of Peace' (Isaiah 9:6).

This is the Central Day of the world: the day that divides BC from AD: the Day from which we count our calendar: the Day that has made the whole difference between life and death: the marvellous Day when God Himself, in the Person of His Son, Jesus, came down into our world to be one of us, and to raise us up to be one with Him: the Day when we could begin to know God personally as our Saviour and Lord.

Luke tells us, in chapter 2 of his Gospel, that the Emperor of the whole world, great Caesar Augustus, had decreed that 'the whole world must be taxed and enrolled'. So two, rather insignificant people in the far-flung Province of Judea went to Bethlehem to be taxed, Joseph and his bride, Mary. Most people today wouldn't even know the name of that Emperor (Octavius Caesar); but millions know the name of that young couple, and still more, the Name of the baby Son who was born to Mary in a stable that night.

'She wrapped Him in swaddling clothes, and laid Him in a manger, because there was no room for them in the inn'. In the outhouse - no bed - no chair even - just a feeding-trough for cattle, there she 'brought forth her Firstborn Son' (Luke 2:7). Turn to Colossians 1:15, where we read, 'He is the Image of the Invisible God, the Firstborn of all Creation'. Go on a step further, to verse 18, where Paul tells us, 'He is the Head of the Body, the Church: He is the beginning, the Firstborn from the dead'.

GOOD TIDINGS OF GREAT JOY!

And gazing at him, all who sat in the Council saw that his
face was like the face of an angel (Acts 6: 15).

Don't you sometimes wonder what the face of an angel really
looks like? Is it something inhuman or superhuman? Is it a sort
of reflection of the face of Jesus? That is certainly a wonderful
sight and a great privilege to see. I have sometimes seen it, and
I think it looks as though the person concerned has some sort
of inner light which really shines out of his or her whole face,
and transforms them. How does it happen?

I think it happens this way: the person lives daily in close
touch with Jesus. They have served Him faithfully for years,
and in doing so have begun bit by bit to grow so like Him that
it reflects out into their whole life and witness.

This was true of Stephen. He has been given the job of
being a deacon, 'serving tables', that is, looking after the
needs of the elderly and poor widows. Not a great preacher but
ready to preach if occasion came his way.

And the chance came. The Sanhedrin, the ruling council
of the Jews, had arrested him on a charge of 'blasphemy
against Moses and against God'. Yes, he had said that the
Temple would be destroyed, as Jesus had prophesied. But this
gave him the chance to proclaim Jesus as the Messiah.

And it was because he was in such close touch with Jesus
that when the test came, the truth of his inner life began to
show in his face. As they began to stone him, he cried out: 'I
see the heavens opened, and the Son of Man standing at the
right hand of God' (Acts 7:56). Nobody else saw that sight,
but Stephen certainly did. Jesus was standing there to welcome His faithful servant. Stephen heard His 'Well done!'

The Revelation of Jesus Christ, which God gave Him to show to His servants what must soon take place; and He made it known by sending His angel to His servant John, who bore witness to the Word of God, and to the testimony of Jesus Christ, even to all that he saw (Revelation 1: 1,2).

Do you think that Jesus had favourites, and that John was the one He loved best of all? I don't think so, but perhaps John was closer than the others to the whole purpose that Jesus had for the world. If not - then why did He entrust His Mother to John as He lay dying on the Cross? Jesus once said (Luke 12: 48b): 'To whom much is given, of him much shall be required.' I think He saw that John could be trusted more than most, and so He gave him a special commitment.

John's writings are most meaningful. The Gospel, three Epistles and the Revelation between them cover an immense amount of the teaching of Jesus. It may well be that if he hadn't been sent into exile on Patmos, we would never have had the Revelation - which would be greatly to our loss.

And surely, this is just as true today. There are some Christians upon whom Jesus has heaped very great responsibilities, because He knows that they are capable of carrying them out. We should regularly pray for such people when we know them, because Satan will always try his hardest to nullify their witness and destroy their influence.

But each Christian carries a lot of responsibility and as Jesus finds us faithful, He may give us more. But I am sure His love for us all is an equal love.

Blessed be His glorious Name for ever: may His Glory fill
the whole earth (Psalm 72:19).

The Psalmist only knew God's Name as Jehovah or Elohim,
because Jesus had not yet been born into our world, as was to
happen at Bethlehem hundreds of years later. The Psalms are
divided into five sections, of which Psalm 72 is the end of
Section 2, and note that at the end of this Psalm it says, 'The
prayers of David, the son of Jesse, are ended', a kind of
doxology. Each of the other sections end with a similar
doxology or gloria (cf. Psalm 41:13; Psalm 89:52; Psalm
106:48 and Psalm 150:6).

And isn't this a lovely thing to do, as we come to the end
of another year, to celebrate it by thanking the Lord Jesus for
all His goodness to us, and to praise His Name for all that He
is and all that He does? When we sing Psalms in church, we
always end with this note of praise in the Gloria, and many of
our hymns end the same way. The Name of Jesus is, of course,
the most wonderful Name in all the world, and we shall want
to spread the news of Him in and by all that we are and do, day
by day.

Can you think of some of the special things for which you
want to thank Jesus for in this past year? He loves to hear our
voices in thanksgiving and praise. Make a note of what you
have to thank Him for, and then thank Him!

Christ Jesus, who, though He was in the form of God, did
not count equality with God a thing to be grasped, but
emptied Himself, taking the form of a servant, being born
in the likeness of men (Philippians 2: 5-7).

This is a tremendous saying of Paul's. He is saying that,
before Jesus became Man, He was on an equality with God in
Heaven, but now that He had come to earth and become one
of us, He didn't want to take an unfair advantage of us, by
having Divine privileges which were denied to us. So He set
aside some of His heavenly qualities such as having 'all
knowledge' (which as God He had), and when His disciples
asked Him about the future, He could only say, 'Of these
things knoweth no man, but the Father'.

He was born into poverty, lived the life of a carpenter's
son, did not become an earthly ruler, and so shared our human
nature with all its frailties, except that He was without sin.
Could He have sinned? As a real man, surely, for if not, what
was the meaning of His temptations? We read, 'He was in all
points tempted like as we are, yet without sin.' He could but
He did not.

He went all the way with us, 'even unto death', and that
death a death on the cross - the lowest form of death. He took
our sins upon Himself on that Cross, so that we might find
forgiveness and liberty and Eternal Life through Him. This
was the only way that He could bring us back to God.

'Hallelujah! What a Saviour!'

When Christ had offered for all time a single sacrifice for
sins, He sat down at the right hand of God, then to wait
until His enemies should be made a stool for His feet
(Hebrews 10: 12,13).

This verse is a very clear description of what happened on the
Cross, as Jesus died. In His death, He made 'one sacrifice for
sins forever', in contrast to the old Jewish priests who stood
daily offering their sacrifices which could not take away sins.
They stood, because their task was not finished, but Jesus sits,
because His Sacrifice is a once-for-all, and it was finished for
all time on the Cross.

Where does He sit? 'At the right hand of God'. Yes, His
enemies are still active, as we know to our cost. But they are
a defeated foe, and the ultimate signal of their defeat will be
when Christ comes back to our world to take up His throne and
reign. Meanwhile, we are at war, and we are called upon to
wage that war with all our might, until the final victory has
taken place. Nobody knows when that will be.

The enemy? Satan and all his minions, and here is their
description: 'Our struggle is not against flesh and blood, but
against the rulers, against the authorities, against the powers
of the dark world and against the spiritual forces of evil in the
heavenly realms. Therefore put on the whole armour of God
...' (Ephesians 6:12, 13). And listen: 'But thanks be to God!
He gives us the victory through our Lord Jesus Christ!' (1
Corinthians 15:57).

If you find the battle hard - and you will - remember that
your Captain is always with you, and the ultimate victory is
certain.

December 31

Moses my servant is dead; now therefore arise, go over this
Jordan .... No man shall be able to stand before you all the
days of your life; as I was with Moses, so I will be with
you; I will not fail you or forsake you. Be strong and of
good courage ... for the LORD your God is with you
wherever you go (Joshua 1:2,5,6,9).

If you began these readings on January 1st, we have been
reading together for a whole year. The preparing of them has
been an encouragement to me, and I hope the study and
meditation of them has been a blessing to you.

We have come to the end of another year, with all its joys,
its sorrows, its defeats and its victories. Don't look back too
far, or you may be discouraged. And don't look on in fear of
what next year may bring, but take courage from what God
said to young Joshua as he took over the leadership of the
sorely tried people of Israel from the great stalwart, Moses.
'As I *was* ... so I *will be,*' that was God's word to him.

The very same word is equally true for you, as you face
what lies ahead. The same Lord Jesus, who empowered Peter
and James and John to 'fight the good fight', is there beside
you, and within you, and He will never fail you. Yes, you may
fail Him, but if you do, come back quickly in true repentance,
and His forgiveness and fresh strength is yours.

Learn from Paul: 'One thing I do, forgetting what lies
behind and straining forward to what lies ahead, I press
towards the goal for the prize of the upward call of God in
Christ Jesus' (Philippians 3:13,14).

Every Blessing of Christ as you go into next year with
Him.

From Carol To You

Dear Reader,

These notes were written for me week by week for a year. My grandfather wrote them when I was seriously ill in hospital with anorexia, aged 14, and he continued through the following year. They enabled me to keep a faith in God that held me through many a struggle and helped me want to live and fight through to a full and enjoyable life.

Now twelve years on, I find that these notes continue to challenge me and give me a vision of what I could be, how God would like me to be and of His amazing love for me despite my ups, downs and difficulties in life.

My grandfather had a deep faith in God that was related to those around him in kindness, wisdom, love and friendship. This comes across in these notes for he does not give the tough and challenging side of following Jesus, without backing it up with encouragement and reassurance of God's love, faithfulness and continued forgiveness.

When reading these notes it is important to have an open mind, allowing God to speak through them, and then be ready to change. They face up to the practical issues in all of our lives - Do we open up our homes to welcome people we don't know? Are we loving? Do we always tell the truth and never say bad things about people?

These notes encourage me to always look forward, asking to see what God would have me do. They cause me to look at myself, to see where I could be more like Jesus and how I need to change. They then show me where to look for the strength to do this.

Up until the end of his life - in January 1993 - my Grandfather had a strong faith. He became muddled about many things but held onto his faith in a loving God. I hope that these notes will help all who use them to aim for such a faith

- a faith that is real, comes from what the Bible says, is shown in practical ways, and lasts until the day we meet our loving God in heaven.

May God bless and be close to each one of you.

Carol Bewes.